A STAR IS BORN

A STAR IS BORN

THE MOMENT AN ACTRESS BECOMES AN ICON   **GEORGE TIFFIN**

HEAD
of ZEUS

10   INTRODUCTION

18   MARY PICKFORD   *Hearts Adrift* (1914)

22   LILLIAN GISH   *The Birth of a Nation* (1915)

26   CLARA BOW   *It* (1927)

32   GLORIA SWANSON   *Sadie Thompson* (1928)

38   BARBARA STANWYCK   *Ladies of Leisure* (1930)

44   JEAN HARLOW   *Hell's Angels* (1930)

50   MARLENE DIETRICH   *Morocco* (1930)

56   GRETA GARBO   *Mata Hari* (1931)

62   HEDY LAMARR   *Ecstasy* (1933)

68   GINGER ROGERS   *Flying Down to Rio* (1933)

72   MAE WEST   *I'm No Angel* (1933)

78   BETTE DAVIS   *Of Human Bondage* (1934)

84   CLAUDETTE COLBERT   *It Happened One Night* (1934)

90   CAROLE LOMBARD   *Twentieth Century* (1934)

94   VIVIEN LEIGH   *Gone with the Wind* (1939)

100   INGRID BERGMAN   *Intermezzo: A Love Story* (1939)

106   RITA HAYWORTH   *Only Angels Have Wings* (1939)

114   KATHARINE HEPBURN   *The Philadelphia Story* (1940)

CONTENTS

120   JANE RUSSELL   *The Outlaw* (1943)

124   LAUREN BACALL   *To Have and Have Not* (1944)

128   TALLULAH BANKHEAD   *Lifeboat* (1944)

134   JOAN CRAWFORD   *Mildred Pierce* (1945)

140   AVA GARDNER   *The Killers* (1946)

144   LANA TURNER   *The Postman Always Rings Twice* (1946)

148   DEBORAH KERR   *Black Narcissus* (1947)

152   ELIZABETH TAYLOR   *A Place in the Sun* (1951)

156   GRACE KELLY   *High Noon* (1952)

162   AUDREY HEPBURN   *Roman Holiday* (1953)

166   JUDY GARLAND   *A Star is Born* (1954)

172   KIM NOVAK   *Picnic* (1955)

178   BRIGITTE BARDOT   *And God Created Woman* (1956)

184   JEANNE MOREAU   *The Lovers* (1958)

188   MARILYN MONROE   *Some Like it Hot* (1959)

194   ANITA EKBERG   *La Dolce Vita* (1960)

200   SOPHIA LOREN   *Two Women* (1960)

204   URSULA ANDRESS   *Dr. No* (1962)

210   JULIE CHRISTIE   *Billy Liar* (1963)

214   JULIE ANDREWS   *Mary Poppins* (1964)

218 CATHERINE DENEUVE *The Umbrellas of Cherbourg* (1964)

222 ANOUK AIMÉE *A Man and a Woman* (1966)

226 LIV ULLMANN *Persona* (1966)

230 VANESSA REDGRAVE *Morgan: A Suitable Case for Treatment* (1966)

234 FAYE DUNAWAY *Bonnie and Clyde* (1967)

240 BARBRA STREISAND *Funny Girl* (1968)

246 LIZA MINNELLI *The Sterile Cuckoo* (1969)

252 JANE FONDA *Klute* (1971)

258 CHARLOTTE RAMPLING *The Night Porter* (1974)

262 SISSY SPACEK *Carrie* (1976)

266 DIANE KEATON *Looking for Mr. Goodbar* (1977)

272 HELEN MIRREN *The Long Good Friday* (1980)

278 MERYL STREEP *Sophie's Choice* (1982)

282 MICHELLE PFEIFFER *Scarface* (1983)

286 DEMI MOORE *About Last Night. . .* (1986)

290 UMA THURMAN *Dangerous Liaisons* (1988)

296 JULIETTE BINOCHE *The Unbearable Lightness of Being* (1988)

300 NICOLE KIDMAN *Dead Calm* (1989)

306 JULIA ROBERTS *Pretty Woman* (1990)

312 JODIE FOSTER *The Silence of the Lambs* (1991)

CONTENTS

318   PENÉLOPE CRUZ   *Jamón Jamón* (1992)

324   EMMA THOMPSON   *Howards End* (1992)

328   TILDA SWINTON   *Orlando* (1992)

332   SANDRA BULLOCK   *Speed* (1994)

336   JULIANNE MOORE   *Boogie Nights* (1997)

342   KATE WINSLET   *Titanic* (1997)

346   CATE BLANCHETT   *Elizabeth* (1998)

350   GWYNETH PALTROW   *Shakespeare in Love* (1998)

354   ANGELINA JOLIE   *Girl, Interrupted* (1999)

360   CATHERINE ZETA-JONES   *Traffic* (2000)

364   JENNIFER CONNELLY   *Requiem for a Dream* (2000)

368   SCARLETT JOHANSSON   *Lost in Translation* (2003)

374   NATALIE PORTMAN   *Closer* (2004)

378   AMY ADAMS   *Junebug* (2005)

382   KEIRA KNIGHTLEY   *Pride & Prejudice* (2005)

386   MARION COTILLARD   *La Vie en rose* (2007)

390   JENNIFER LAWRENCE   *Winter's Bone* (2010)

394   NOTABLE FILMS

404   INDEX

407   CREDITS

INTRODUCTION

THIS BOOK IS NOT ABOUT MERE MOVIE CELEBRITIES, for they are shooting stars – meteors, flashing in the heavens before burning up as they fall to earth. Here, we encounter true stars – permanent celestial bodies who radiate their own light, and who form constellations by which we navigate the history of cinema itself.

A genuine star is ageless, unchangeable and fixed, even as the world turns beneath her. Some court that fame, like Gloria Swanson:

> *I've gone through enough of being a nobody. I have decided that when I am a star, I will be every inch and every moment the star!*

Others shun it, as Ava Gardner did:

> *What I'd really like to say about stardom is that it gave me everything I never wanted.*

Even so, everyone applauds when a star is born. This book charts the history – and, most especially, the very first appearance – of seventy-five actresses who have not only established themselves as beacons in our culture, but who have shaped the way we experience the movies we flock to see.

Cinema – compared to poetry, drama and fiction – is a young art, which is why all of these portraits seem so fresh. We know next to nothing about those who kept the Homeric tradition of oral poetry alive, little of the troubadours, and we have only portraits and gossip about Shakespeare's Thomas Burbage or King Charles II's favourite player, Nell Gwynn. But we live in an era where the entire world can see the same movie, and each outstanding performance becomes a celluloid Rosetta Stone – a permanent record of both a moment and an age.

The first picture to be released in a form we would recognise as a feature film was *The Story of the Kelly Gang*, depicting the infamous outlaw and bushranger Ned Kelly, directed by the Australian Charles Tait in 1906. It ran for sixty minutes. Barely five generations have passed since that milestone production, yet visual story-telling is pervasive and influential to a degree no other medium has ever enjoyed; and because we are human, with the timeless desires and emotions that condition dictates, we seek faces just as much as we seek stories. The photographs of the icons in this book are distinct but instant signifiers of character – which remains unchangingly intriguing – as well as of beauty, whose qualities shift in mysterious ways as fashions ebb and flow.

Each brief biography here is a sketch of a unique career, but read as a whole, the book reveals that the gifts required to move us share remarkable similarities. Whether it comes about through perseverance, luck, the blessings of circumstance or raw talent, every breakthrough role confirms that those who inspire and elevate us draw us ineluctably into their orbit – and that when they do, we never forget them.

The choice of subjects may seem to some comprehensive, to others controversial; to rank any artist against their peers is invidious, but the public acclaim and enduring fondness for every one of these idols is indubitable. Many faces will be familiar, others less so to a younger generation – fans of Angelina Jolie may be delighted to learn about Bette Davis, and vice versa – but I hope each essay shows that the presence of each actress included in this book is wholly deserved. Most importantly, the particular movie I have chosen to focus on will not necessarily be the subject's best known, but the one that established them as a star in the fullest sense of the word. Other films will be mentioned, if only to confirm the magic unleashed in those first scenes; for each star, a listing of notable pictures spanning their entire career will be found at the back of the book.

For simplicity, dates cited are of the public release of the film. This will often differ from the year in which the film was shot, and from the year in which awards ceremonies took place. Key accolades, such as Oscars, are useful guides to success as well as acclaim, but are by no means the only justification for inclusion here: for every Meryl Streep with nineteen nominations and three wins, there is a Lauren Bacall with none. And yet who would deny the Bacall of *To Have and Have Not* her place in the pantheon? Earnings and production budgets, too, are purely of anecdotal interest. Where appropriate, figures are shown with their inflation-adjusted modern equivalents [in square brackets].

Above all, this is a book about stories – of the movies that created the stars, and of the stars who made those movies eternally memorable.

Let there be light...

For Titan, Hero and Mercy

George Tiffin, May 2015

FROM
SILENT TO
SOUND

MARY PICKFORD

LILLIAN GISH

CLARA BOW

GLORIA SWANSON

BARBARA STANWYCK

JEAN HARLOW

MARLENE DIETRICH

GRETA GARBO

HEDY LAMARR

GINGER ROGERS

MAE WEST

BETTE DAVIS

CLAUDETTE COLBERT

CAROLE LOMBARD

VIVIEN LEIGH

INGRID BERGMAN

RITA HAYWORTH

*I saw Hollywood
born and I've seen
it die*

MARY
PICKFORD

Gladys Louise Smith
8 April 1892–29 May 1979

We were pioneers in a brand-new medium. Everything's fun when you're young.

I was forced to live far beyond my years when just a child; now I have reversed the order and I intend to remain young indefinitely.

It would have been more logical if silent pictures had grown out of the talkie instead of the other way around. The refined simplicity should develop out of the complex.

Make them laugh, make them cry, and back to laughter. What do people go to the theater for? An emotional exercise. And no preachment.

I am a servant of the people. I have never forgotten that.

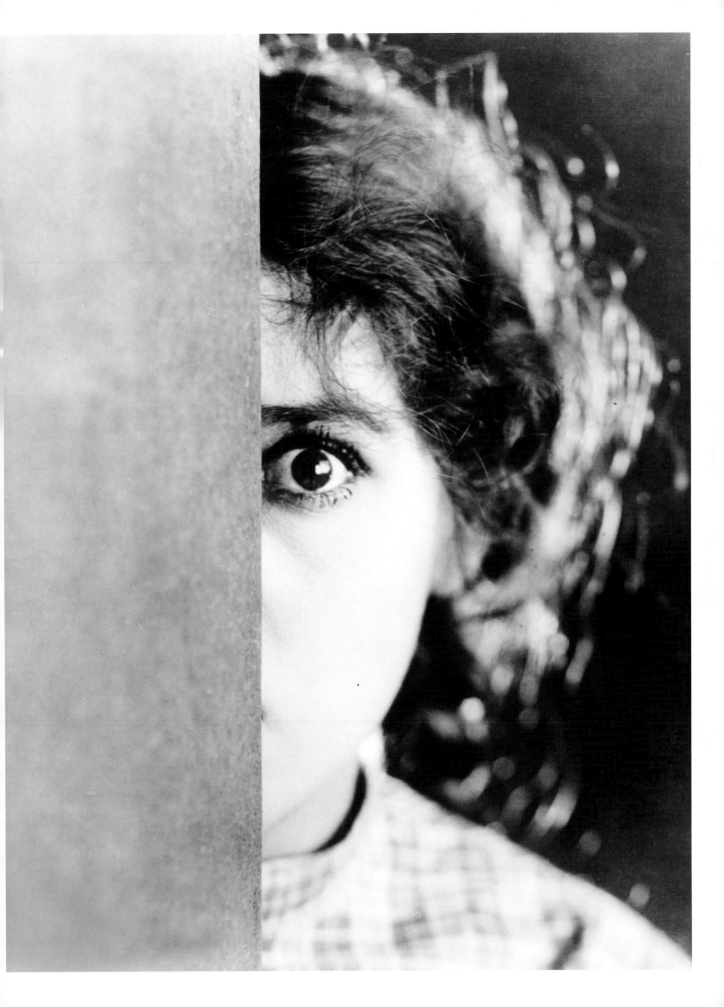

Mary Pickford, cinema's earliest superstar, appeared in eighty-five films between 1909 and 1911 without receiving a single credit under her own name. Audiences simply knew her as 'The Girl with the Golden Curls', 'Blondilocks', 'The Biograph Girl' or 'America's Sweetheart'; not until *Their First Misunderstanding* (1911) did the title card admit her true identity.

Pickford's mother, inspired by a theatrical manager who had stayed at her boarding-house, encouraged her three young daughters to form a troupe of travelling players and they had moved to New York in 1907 to try a shot at Broadway when director D. W. Griffith signed Mary, aged fifteen, to his Biograph company. Pickford seized her chance:

> *I played scrubwomen and secretaries and women of all nationalities. . . I decided that if I could get into as many pictures as possible, I'd become known, and there would be a demand for my work.*

And demand there was: as early as 1912 theatres in America were selling thirty million tickets a year. By the time Adolph Zukor's Famous Players Film Company released *Hearts Adrift* (1914), producers had realized that cinema-goers were paying to see their idols, not just to watch a story on screen. Setting a precedent that remains the *sine qua non* of fame and power to this day, Zukor displayed Pickford's name above the title of the picture itself, and the breathless blurb in the press advertisements ran:

> *Mary Pickford portrays the role of Nina, the little castaway, with a dramatic power and emotional expression which, even fully calculating her talent, is nothing less than a revelation! She endows the character of Nina, the little Spanish girl, with a combined savagery and gentleness that will automatically amaze and charm.*

The film proved so popular that Pickford felt emboldened to ask for a pay rise. However bitterly Zukor must have chafed at her demand, his surrender was to prove wise. After the smash hit of her follow-up picture *Tess of the Storm Country* (1914), one reviewer declared Pickford to be 'the best known woman who has ever lived, the woman who was known to more people and loved by more people than any other woman that has been in all history'.

This may not be an exaggeration. The staggering popularity and startling growth of cinema as a visual medium changed the nature of fame and public recognition utterly, and Pickford was quick to capitalize on its attendant power. In 1919 she joined forces with Griffith, Charlie Chaplin and Douglas Fairbanks (whom she married in 1920) to found United Artists, a studio system through which they could keep a far greater degree of artistic freedom – and a far greater share of distribution revenue. Pickford's *Pollyanna* (1920), *Little Lord Fauntleroy* (1921) and *Rosita* (1923) all took over $1m [$11m] at the box office, with *Photoplay* magazine praising her 'luminous tenderness in a steel band of gutter ferocity'.

> *We maniacs had fun and made good pictures and a lot of money.*
> *In the early years, United Artists was a private golf club for the*
> *four of us.*

Her personal life continued to compel her fans: when she and Fairbanks spent their honeymoon in Europe, their appearance caused riots in both London and Paris. Their return home was no less momentous, and before long they found themselves entertaining at their home in Beverly Hills – named Pickfair – such luminaries as Albert Einstein, George Bernard Shaw, H. G. Wells, F. Scott Fitzgerald, Amelia Earhart and Noël Coward. Even at the grandest parties in Hollywood, other guests would stand up as they entered the room. Nothing, it seemed, could tarnish their brilliance – until the advent of audio recording. Pickford likened this technical innovation to 'putting lipstick on the Venus de Milo', but the very public who had championed her disagreed. By 1930 it was almost unthinkable to produce a silent film, and Pickford's career was effectively over. Some say she never adapted to the very different method of acting required; it may simply be that she epitomized a style and an era that had passed as quickly as it had been born.

She retired from the business after only four sound films and lived the latter part of her life as an alcoholic recluse, speaking to visitors to Pickfair only by telephone from her bedroom. It was a decline as spectacular and tragic as anything her scriptwriters could have dreamed up, but like a supernova – a stellar explosion which outshines everything around it – her moment of glory has never been exceeded: she created a template for the career of every actor who followed her.

My career was planned – there was never anything accidental about it. It was planned, it was painful, it was purposeful. I'm not exactly satisfied, but I'm grateful.

Never get caught acting

LILLIAN GISH

Lillian Diana Gish
14 October 1893–27 February 1993

I never approved of talkies. Silent movies were well on their way to developing an entirely new art form. It was not just pantomime, but something wonderfully expressive.

Those little virgins. . . after five minutes you got sick of playing them. To make them more interesting was hard work.

I don't care for modern films – all crashing cars and close-ups of people's feet.

I've never been in style, so I can't go out of style.

[D. W. Griffith] inspired in us his belief that we were working in a medium that was powerful enough to influence the whole world.

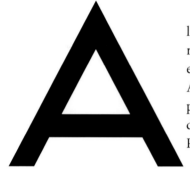

lfred Hitchcock famously pronounced that 'the length of a film should be directly related to the endurance of the human bladder'. In 1915, D. W. Griffith, one of early cinema's greatest directors, had challenged his audiences to sit through America's first twelve-reel (three-hour) epic about the American Civil War; it pioneered the form of visual narrative and editing that remains familiar to this day. One of its stars, Lillian Gish, later wrote in *Stage Magazine* of the evening President Woodrow Wilson watched it:

> *When it was learned that that a mere motion picture had the power to stir feeling so deeply,* The Birth of a Nation's *reputation was made, and motion pictures took their place as an important part of our daily life.*

Gish could hardly have known that her words were to prove an understatement. Fifty-five years later, when she was seventy-seven (and still acting), she received an honorary Oscar 'for superlative artistry and for distinguished contribution to the progress of motion pictures'.

Born into a poor family of itinerant theatre players, her first experience in front of the camera was something of a shock: without warning, Griffith fired a fake gun at her and chased her around the set to study her expression. As she would learn, almost all early directing techniques were crude. When she and her younger sister Dorothy were cast in *An Unseen Enemy* (1912), Griffith treated them just like props: he put differently coloured ribbons in their hair to distinguish them and would simply yell out as the cameras rolled: 'Red, you hear a strange noise. Run to your sister. Blue, you're scared too. Look toward me, where the camera is.'

Within four years of her first appearance, Gish was hailed as 'The First Lady of American Film'. Petite, beautiful, with Cupid's bow lips and Pre-Raphaelite hair, Gish radiated both innocence and determination. Better still, she knew exactly how to adapt her talents to the more intimate setting of the cinema: she scaled down her performance – including her body language – in such a way that her smallest gestures and expressions seemed passionate but absolutely natural. As she noted wryly, 'Never get caught acting'.

Despite her doll-like looks, Gish was a tough old bird – she had the longest career of any major star, spanning seventy-five years from her first appearance in 1912 to her last in 1987. She insisted on performing most of her own stunts, and in

Way Down East (1920) she spent so long lying on an ice floe that was drifting towards a waterfall that she froze – and permanently damaged – her wrist. Under Griffith's tutelage, she spent time studying such diverse characters as inmates of mental asylums and prize-fighters, and when playing opposite real-life train robber Al J. Jennings she made him teach her how to shoot with a pistol. She loved every minute of it: 'A happy life is one spent in learning, earning, and yearning.'

> *I can't remember a time when I wasn't acting, so I can't imagine what*
> *I would do if I stopped now.*

But if Gish was one of the earliest women in cinema to experience widespread acclaim and adulation, she was also among the first to suffer its prejudice. Well aware of her sex appeal, she once reprimanded a fan: 'Young man, if God had wanted you to see me that way, he would have put your eyes in your belly button' – but in 1925, when she was only thirty-two, her studio bosses at MGM deemed she was past her prime. They had decided that a new discovery, Greta Garbo, would be their principal protégé; adding insult to injury, they insisted Gish allow Garbo to study her methods on set as part of her training.

Gish subsequently pursued a successful career in radio and theatre, returning only infrequently to the big screen in later life. She had learned how the movie industry treats its women, now as then:

> *Lionel Barrymore first played my grandfather, later my father, and*
> *finally, he played my husband. If he'd lived, I'm sure I'd have played*
> *his mother. That's the way it is in Hollywood. The men get younger*
> *and the women get older.*

Her revenge, if a long time coming, was sweet. In 1987 she starred in Lindsay Anderson's *The Whales of August*; she was ninety-three, and remains the oldest screen actress ever to play a leading role. After one take, Anderson announced: 'Miss Gish, you have just given me a perfect close-up.' Bette Davis, Gish's co-star, tartly observed: 'She should. The bitch invented 'em.'

I think the things that are necessary in my profession are these: taste, talent and tenacity. I think I have had a little of all three.

'A genuine spark of divine fire'

CLARA BOW

Clara Gordon Bow
29 July 1905–27 September 1965

I'm almost never satisfied with myself or my work or anything. . . By the time I'm ready to be a great star I'll have been on the screen such a long time that everybody will be tired of seeing me.

Rehearsals sap my pep. Tell me what I have to do and I'll do it.

I worked in two and even three pictures at once. I played all sorts of parts in all sorts of pictures – it was very hard at the time and I used to be worn out and cry myself to sleep from sheer fatigue after eighteen hours a day on different sets.

When I decided to leave the screen, I told [my producer] I would not finish my contract or ever work again for anyone. He yelled and threatened to sue me and I said, 'Go ahead, Ben, sue me. I've fought a thief and a blackmailer and, if after such heartaches I am forced to fight you and the studio, so be it.'

The more I see of men, the more I like dogs.

n the 1920s, many a hard-working mother might have expressed dismay if her child had shown a desire to make a living in front of the new-fangled motion-picture camera, although few would try to slit their daughter's throat with a butcher's knife to thwart her ambition. When Clara Bow won her first screen role, her mother Sarah called her 'a whore' and warned she 'would be much better off dead'; shortly afterwards she tried to murder the sixteen-year-old Clara as she slept. Bow wrote later:

> *It was snowing. My mother and I were cold and hungry. We had been cold and hungry for days. We lay in each other's arms and cried and tried to keep warm. It grew worse and worse. So that night my mother – but I can't tell you about it. Only when I remember it, it seems to me I can't live.*

Bow fought off the attack and her mother was eventually committed to an asylum, but it was the culmination of a childhood filled with misery and tragedy. Clara's two sisters died as babies; the family moved home fourteen times in eighteen years; her father was constantly absent in search of work; and Sarah fell from a window and suffered psychotic episodes from the resulting epilepsy. 'As a kid, I took care of my mother, she didn't take care of me.'

Her mother's accident did not curtail her occasional spells as a prostitute, entertaining local firemen as clients at home while her daughter hid, terrified, in the wardrobe. At the age of eight, one of Clara's few close friends died in a horrific blaze, despite her efforts to cover him in a blanket to extinguish the flames. Her most adored relative was her grandfather, who died of a heart attack while pushing her on an indoor swing he had made so that Clara didn't have to play outside in the bitter winter weather. When his body was laid out in the coffin at home, Clara slept on the floor beside it to prevent well-wishers from making too much noise and disturbing him. Of her schooling, Bow said: 'I never had any clothes. . . and lots of times I didn't have anything to eat. We just lived, that's about all. Girls shunned me because I was so poorly dressed.' Her friends were mainly male, with all the attendant challenges: 'I could lick any boy my size. My right arm was quite famous. There was one boy who had always been my pal – he kissed me – I wasn't sore. I didn't get indignant. I was horrified and hurt.' Overall, she described her home life as 'miserable' and her school as 'heartache'.

Like so many of her contemporaries, Bow found movies a consolation and an escape, but it seems extraordinary, given that she described herself as a 'square, awkward, funny-faced kid', that she set her heart on a career as an actress. Of her earliest cinema visits she recalled:

> *For the first time in my life I knew there was beauty in the world. For the first time I saw distant lands, serene, lovely homes, romance, nobility, glamour. . . I always had a queer feeling about actors and actresses on the screen. I knew I would have done it differently. I couldn't analyze it, but I could always feel it. . . I'd go home and be a one-girl circus, taking the parts of everyone I'd seen, living them before the [looking] glass.*

In 1921, Bow borrowed a dollar from her father to get two photographs taken so that she could enter *Brewster* magazine's nationwide acting competition. It must have seemed a hopeless gamble – but she won, and the jury's verdict, published in *Motion Picture Classic* the following year, paints an astonishing picture of her raw talent:

> *She is very young, only sixteen. But she is full of confidence, determination and ambition. . . She has a genuine spark of divine fire. . . She screens perfectly. Her personal appearance is almost enough to carry her to success without the aid of the brains she indubitably possesses.*

When Bow's mother discovered she had skipped school to attend the audition, she fainted. Recovering, her first words were: 'You are going straight to hell. I would rather see you dead.'

Winning the competition brought interest from producers and set Bow on a path of further screen tests, but actual engagements proved elusive: 'There was always something. I was too young, or too little, or too fat. Usually I was too fat.' Her frustration was to be mercifully short-lived; within six years she was America's most popular female star: 'The It Girl'.

After a few modest successes, she appeared in *Grit* (1924), based on a story by F. Scott Fitzgerald, and a talent scout from Preferred Pictures invited her to California where Hollywoodland (as the sign still read) was fast becoming the epicentre of film production. The roles she was offered played to her natural exuberance and her lens-friendly gaze; audiences and critics admired her in equal measure. When Victor Fleming directed her in *Mantrap* (1926) he compared her to a Stradivarius violin: 'Touch her and she respond[s] with genius.' *Variety* concurred, writing in its review: 'Bow just walks away with the picture from the moment she walks into camera range.' Even so, it was not until she took the lead role in *It* (1927) that she became a phenomenon, with the nickname that endures to this day.

Elinor Glyn, the original author of *'It' and Other Stories* (1927), was a British novelist famous for her racy romantic fiction. With remarkable prescience, Glyn had moved to Hollywood in 1920 to capitalize on the appetite for her books and screenplays. Although Bow was by no means the only star whose career benefited from Glyn's work, the success of her role in the adaptation of the book was utterly transformative. The plot concerns Betty Lou Spence, a gamine, boisterous shop girl, who falls for her boss Cyrus only to suffer a series of setbacks as he comes to terms with her modest background and feisty nature. Bow's character, despite much obligatory flirting and girlishness, appears as a tough, principled and independent young woman: a remarkable role model, given the era.

Although 'It' is transparently a euphemism for sex – and the film did not disappoint audiences in its glimpses of camisoles, stocking-tops and shapely calves – Glyn claimed she was trying to make a subtler point about erotic power. A title card in the movie itself announced:

> IT is that quality possessed by some which draws all others by its magnetic force. The possessor of IT must be absolutely unself-conscious. With IT, you own all men if you are a woman – and all women if you are a man. IT can be a quality of mind as well as a physical attraction.

These aspects are perfectly united in a scene where Cyrus takes Betty Lou on a date to the fun fair at Coney Island and they ride the attractions together. Bow's flapper dress and dancing shoes prove something of a liability on the undulating slide and in the revolving tunnel, and in one episode she foreshadows the famous Marilyn Monroe air-vent sequence in *The Seven Year Itch* (1955) as her skirt billows around her waist. (Tellingly, one of the whirligig rides is called the 'Social Mixer'.)

Despite the capers and the titillation, Bow never loses her aplomb or her command of the situation: if she plays the fool, it is because she chooses to – and relishes it. The role – and Bow herself, since her real life was inescapably conflated with it – enchanted viewers and may have helped to encourage young women to liberate themselves from the lingering shadow of Victorian morality. Bow was triumphantly a woman proud of herself despite her background, confident in her femininity on her own terms, and without inhibition in her affections for men – both on screen and off. At the height of her fame, she was being sent 45,000 fan letters a week, still a record for any actor.

Sadly, these admirable qualities were to prove her downfall too. As audiences grew, Hollywood realized the advantages of managing a star's image, but Bow was resolutely opposed to playing along. Where other players from poor backgrounds took elocution lessons and carefully restyled themselves, Bow stood her ground: she was who she was. As stories of her exuberant love life became better known, her outspoken honesty came to seem less acceptable for the mores of the time. When the talkies arrived, her Brooklyn accent was deemed coarse, and, to make matters worse, she suffered terrible stage-fright when confronted with a microphone. Her stellar rise, it seemed, had reached its apex.

After her final role in *Hoop-La* (1933), she retired from the limelight to raise two sons with her husband Rex Bell, vanishing from the public gaze as quickly as she had appeared. In a final irony, given the extraordinary obstacles she had overcome and the millions of hearts she had won, she suffered a breakdown in the 1940s and was diagnosed with 'schizophrenia' – the very curse for which her mother had been committed to an asylum. Bow's last years were spent under the care of a nurse. As Monroe herself would later realize with equal poignancy: '[Being] a sex symbol is a heavy load to carry when one is tired, hurt and bewildered.'

We had individuality. We did as we pleased. We stayed up late. We dressed the way we wanted. Today, [stars are] sensible and end up with better health. But we had more fun.

*I will be every inch
and every moment
the star!*

GLORIA SWANSON

Gloria May Josephine Swanson
27 March 1899–4 April 1983

I have gone through a long apprenticeship. I have gone through enough of being a nobody. I have decided that when I am a star, I will be every inch and every moment the star!

I was twenty-five and the most popular celebrity in the world, with the possible exception of my friend Mary Pickford.

The fuss that actors began making about the difficulty of shifting to sound struck me as perfectly foolish.

All creative people should be required to leave California for three months every year.

It's amazing to find that so many people could have thought that *Sunset Boulevard* was autobiographical. I've got nobody floating in my swimming pool.

The public didn't want the truth, and I shouldn't have bothered to give it to them.

I've given my memoirs far more thought than any of my marriages. You can't divorce a book.

loria May Josephine Svensson, Gloria Mae Swanson, Josephine Swenson, Mrs Herbert Somborn, Mrs Henri the Marquis de la Falaise de la Coudraye – Gloria Swanson's private life (inasmuch as any of it remained private) was as glamorous as it was diverse, and even fans of *Sunset Boulevard* (1950) might be forgiven for underestimating the power she enjoyed – and exercised ruthlessly – during her heyday. Billy Wilder's masterpiece chronicles the vanity and fear of a fictional film star as she faces old age and obscurity; Swanson was fifty-one when she took the role and she always denied that her character was autobiographical, but nobody else could have portrayed a descent so tragic because few others had ever flown so high.

> *All they had to do was put my name on a marquee and watch the money roll in.*

As a teenager Swanson showed no overt ambition to act, but in 1914 her aunt took her on a visit to Essanay Studios in Chicago and she was hired as an extra for $13.50 [$320] a week. One of her colleagues was an Englishman by the name of Charles Chaplin. By 1919 Chaplin had co-founded the revolutionary United Artists and Swanson had been signed by Paramount. Within two years – after appearing in six films directed by Cecil B. DeMille – she had become one of America's most popular screen stars, with an equally stellar salary. According to archives at the Harry Ransom Center in Texas, by the early 1920s she was earning $20,000 [$280,000] a week, her studio was picking up the tab on all her expenditure and she spent $10,000 [$140,000] on lingerie in one year alone. She commissioned a solid gold bathtub for her black marble bathroom and employed four personal secretaries – presumably to help carry her luxurious, ever-changing wardrobe back from the ritzy boutiques of Los Angeles.

She was married six times, with varying degrees of success; actor Wallace Beery (who, according to Swanson, raped her on their wedding night and then tricked her into drinking a tincture that caused her to abort her pregnancy) claimed she had slept with thirteen men during their brief time together; in 1925 she married the Frenchman Henri, Marquis de la Falaise, only to cheat on him with Hollywood financier Joseph Kennedy, the father of John F. Kennedy. As her daughter later explained:

> *Men came into her life like machos and they left like poodles sitting up for a biscuit. She was incredibly feminine in appearance, but she*

had a masculine mind. She had a dominating personality.

By this stage Swanson was at the top of her game and the height of her fame. Clearly she knew how to manage her own career, noting later that 'after sixteen years in pictures I could not be intimidated easily because I knew where all the skeletons were buried'. But despite her power and her conspicuously constructed public image, she felt she had still not had the opportunity to reveal her talent as a serious actress. She had first caught the public eye as one of Mack Sennett's bathing beauties and her pictures with DeMille had largely been a succession of light-hearted love tangles; now she longed to find better material.

At twenty-six, I felt myself a victim rather than a victor in the realm of pictures.

In 1927 she turned down an offer of $1m [$13.5m] from Paramount to renew her contract and joined her old friend Chaplin at United Artists. The company had been started by Chaplin along with superstars Mary Pickford, Douglas Fairbanks and director D. W. Griffith to control their own projects and ensure they received a fair share of the revenue; one studio chief, on reading the press announcement, declared that 'the inmates are taking over the asylum'. When Swanson stepped into this more liberating environment she took full advantage of the possibilities it offered, and she quickly bought the rights to 'Rain', a short story by W. Somerset Maugham. It tells of a prostitute who flees prosecution and ends up waylaid on a tropical island where a missionary tries to convert her – and, when that fails, to blackmail her. The tale takes a twist when we realize that the preacher has become infatuated with her, with calamitous consequences. Swanson saw it as a perfect vehicle for her since it would allow her to blend her customary sexual playfulness with a more emotionally complex characterization.

Renaming Maugham's story after its protagonist, Swanson hired the gloweringly handsome Lionel Barrymore to play the missionary and Raoul Walsh to co-star and direct. *Sadie Thompson* (1928), shot in the last years of silent production, is lively, picturesque and intriguing, even if it feels a little unsophisticated for modern tastes. Not so with Swanson: no dialogue card could hope to capture her *joie de vivre* or her righteous fury, while her portrayal leaps from smouldering to blazing with the merest flicker of a mascara-laden eyelash. In a couple of scenes when she – literally – lets her hair down, she instantly escapes the formal, intensely photographed style of the period; she is wonderfully unforced yet stylish, foreshadowing the iconic looks of Rita Hayworth or Ava Gardner decades later. The film was released in 1928 with Swanson's name not only above the title but twice as large. It proved a huge hit, vindicating her ambitions to pursue a career on her own terms, and she was nominated for Best Actress in the first ever Academy Awards ceremony the following year.

> In those days they wanted us to live like kings. So we did – and why not? We were in love with life. We were making more money than we ever dreamed existed, and there was no reason to believe it would ever stop.

Twenty-two years later she would be nominated again for *Sunset Boulevard*, a film which recalled her glorious past as well as reinventing her for a younger generation of fans. The protagonist Norma Desmond, a movie icon long past her heyday, fantasizes hopelessly about a return to the silver screen, but her life begins to unravel when her young lover Joe Gillis (William Holden), an out-of-work, alcoholic screenwriter, is found dead in her swimming pool. Because the story satirizes a venal industry filled with egotistical stars and heartless moguls, the production team temporarily retitled the project *A Can of Beans* to deflect attention. Fearful of interference from censors and the studio itself, they handed the actors the script piecemeal as their scenes were typed up, in the hope that its full impact might be disguised. Swanson herself was willing to play the role of Desmond, but felt she was too grand to audition; director and friend George Cukor was convinced it would be an extraordinary opportunity, telling her: 'If they want you to do ten screen tests, do ten screen tests. If you don't, I will personally shoot you.'

On set, the framed publicity photos of the young Norma Desmond were genuine stills from the height of Swanson's career and Wilder surrounded her with colleagues from that era. Erich von Stroheim, a top director and actor from the 1920s, played Max, Desmond's butler, driver and projectionist; on one occasion he screens a movie of his in which Swanson actually starred (*Queen Kelly*, 1929). At the end of the film, Desmond descends her grand staircase only to find her house full of police officers and newsreel cameramen investigating Gillis's death. Mistaking the intruders for a studio crew and Max for Cecil B. DeMille, she prepares herself for her comeback and delivers the unforgettable line:

                  NORMA
All right, Mr DeMille, I'm ready for my close-
up.

Swanson was so moved by this moment that – when the scene was completed – she burst into tears. Whatever the actress really felt about the changes the industry had undergone, her character is obsessed by its decline and upbraids her lover bitterly:

                  JOE
You're Norma Desmond. You used to be in silent
pictures. You used to be big.

                  NORMA
I am big. It's the pictures that got small.

And again, later:

                  JOE
I'm not an executive, just a writer.

                  NORMA
You are, are you? Writing words, words, more
words! Well, you'll make a rope of words and
strangle this business! With a microphone there
to catch the last gurgles, and Technicolor to
photograph the red, swollen tongues!

The film was hugely successful and equally controversial, striking a chord with many who had grown up in the pre-talkie days; it won three Oscars, although Swanson lost out to Judy Holliday for *Born Yesterday* (1951). Graceful in defeat, she realized the voters had been unable to separate fact from fiction:

[The voters] wanted me to care. . . They expected scenes from me, wild sarcastic tantrums. They wanted Norma Desmond.

Fame was thrilling only until it became gruelling. Money was fun only until you ran out of things to buy.

*I just wanted
to survive and
eat and have a
nice coat*

BARBARA STANWYCK

Ruby Catherine Stevens
16 July 1907–20 January 1990

I knew that after fourteen I'd have to earn my own living, but I was willing to do that. . . I've always been a little sorry for pampered people, and of course, they're 'very' sorry for me.

Eyes are the greatest tool in film. Frank Capra taught me that. Sure, it's nice to say very good dialogue, if you can get it. But great movie acting – watch the eyes!

Put me in the last fifteen minutes of a picture and I don't care what happened before. I don't even care if I was in the rest of the damned thing – I'll take it in those fifteen minutes.

I'm a tough old broad from Brooklyn. I intend to go on acting until I'm ninety and they won't need to paste my face with make-up. . . I want to go on until they have to shoot me.

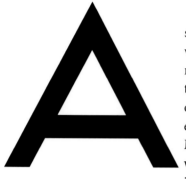

As rags-to-riches tales go, Barbara Stanwyck's ascent is surely unsurpassed. She was born Ruby Stevens in 1907 in Brooklyn, New York; four years later, her mother died when a drunken passenger accidentally shoved her from a moving tram. Two weeks after the funeral, her father left the family to join a work crew on the Panama Canal and was never heard from again. Orphaned before she had even started school, Ruby and her brother were raised by her nine-year-old sister Mildred. By 1944, she was not just the richest box-office star but the highest-paid woman in America and was eventually nominated for four Oscars for her roles in *Stella Dallas* (1937), *Ball of Fire* (1941), *Double Indemnity* (1944) and *Sorry, Wrong Number* (1948).

Mildred took care of her younger siblings until she got a job as a showgirl. The children passed the next few years moving between foster homes but Ruby spent summers touring with her sister, secretly learning all her routines. At fourteen she dropped out of school to take work variously as a shop girl, a telephone clerk, a dress-pattern cutter and a typist. Mildred tried to persuade her to stick with reliable employment but Ruby would not be swayed; aged only fifteen, she auditioned for a place in the chorus of the Strand Theatre in Times Square, and by the following year had won a place with the legendary Ziegfeld Follies.

By a stroke of luck almost poetic in its improbability, she was soon introduced to a theatre producer who hoped to cast a genuine showgirl to play 'herself' on stage. *The Noose*, which opened in 1926, was not a great success but Ruby had attracted good notices and the writers enlarged her part to lend the story more pathos; the revised version proved the hit of the season and ran on Broadway for nine months. The following year she was offered the lead in *Burlesque*, another smash. Arthur Hopkins, who produced it, cast her for her 'rough poignancy' and later lamented her move to Los Angeles: 'One of the theater's great potential actresses [has been] embalmed in celluloid.'

On arrival in Hollywood, Ruby adopted the stage name Barbara Stanwyck. Her first few pictures were modest affairs (she lost the lead in *Broadway Nights* (1927) because she couldn't cry on cue), but in 1930 Frank Capra, a young director also on the upswing, hired her to play good-time girl Kay Arnold in *Ladies of Leisure* (1930). The film, although finely directed and technically sophisticated, tells the familiar tale of two intersecting love triangles between high and low Manhattan society: love is declared, tears are shed, and tragedy looms before everything resolves happily. Jo Swerling, the screenwriter, described the original material he was paid to adapt as 'a putrid piece of Gorgonzola. . . inane, vacuous, pompous, unreal, unbelievable – and incredibly dull' – but he had not reckoned on Stanwyck as his leading lady. Kay's flirting, when she models for her portrait, is pitch-perfect:

>   BILL
>   Ever done any posing before?
>
>   KAY
>   I'm always posing.
>
>   BILL
>   How do you spend your nights?
>
>   KAY
>   Re-posing.

Film historian David Thomson celebrated her brazen exuberance as '[a] hard-boiled girl of easy virtue', with dialogue to match:

>   KAY
>   I feel like getting into trouble!

Capra wrote in his autobiography that '[Stanwyck] was destined to be beloved by all directors, actors, crews and extras. In a Hollywood popularity contest she would win first prize hands down.' However, he noticed one characteristic he had never come across in a performer before: it seemed she would never pace her work on set, preferring to deliver a killer first take and then losing steam – or, perhaps, interest. This made life hard for co-stars and technicians alike, so Capra was forced to rehearse her in private:

> *On the set I never let Stanwyck utter one word of the scene until the cameras were rolling. Before that I talked to her in her dressing room, told her the meaning of the scene, the points of emphasis, the pauses. . . I talked softly, not wanting to fan the smouldering fires that lurked beneath that somber silence. She remembered every word I said – and she never blew a line.*

A newspaper advertisement for the film's original release proclaims *Ladies of Leisure* as an 'All Dialog Drama of Nite Life – Zippy, Daring, Peppy, Gay!' This describes Stanwyck's turn as aptly as it does the movie itself, and indeed the rave reviews focused almost exclusively on the star. *Photoplay*, a hugely influential fan magazine, announced that audiences 'choked up' on seeing her, explaining 'something was happening. . . a real, beautiful, thrilling wonder had been born. . . It was Barbara Stanwyck, whose performance is one of the greatest yet given in the adolescent talkies. We are proud to cry her welcome. . . this beautiful young girl possesses emotional power and acting talent that are really amazing.'

Decades later, Pauline Kael of *The New York Times* confirmed the transformative effect Stanwyck was to have on a medium which had only recently embraced synchronized speech: '[she] seems to have an intuitive understanding of the fluid physical movements that work best on camera. The early talkies' sentimentality. . . only emphasizes Stanwyck's remarkable modernism.' Her later work grew in power as she gradually shed the mantle of ingénue, although she worried how she might escape the screen persona that had begun to feel too predictable:

> *My only problem is finding a way to play my fortieth fallen female in a different way from my thirty-ninth.*

In 1944 Billy Wilder met the challenge when he offered her the role of Phyllis Dietrichson in *Double Indemnity*. Phyllis is a Machiavellian femme fatale in one of the era's finest noir thrillers and the character was infinitely darker and more sophisticated than anything Stanwyck had played before. As she persuades Walter Neff (Fred MacMurray), an insurance salesman, to collude in the murder of her husband, her seduction is both irresistible and threatening:

> PHYLLIS
> Mr Neff, why don't you drop by tomorrow evening about eight thirty. He'll be in then.
>
> WALTER
> Who?
>
> PHYLLIS
> My husband. You were anxious to talk to him, weren't you?

```
                    WALTER
Yeah, I was, but I'm sort of getting over the
idea, if you know what I mean.


                    PHYLLIS
There's a speed limit in this state, Mr Neff.
Forty-five miles an hour.


                    WALTER
How fast was I going, officer?


                    PHYLLIS
I'd say around ninety.


                    WALTER
Suppose you get down off your motorcycle and
give me a ticket.


                    PHYLLIS
Suppose I let you off with a warning this time.
```

Once again, Stanwyck was ahead of her time in a role that was to become iconic in the history of film. Despite the acclaim she received she failed to secure an Oscar, although that oversight was rectified in 1982 when she was given an honorary award for the lasting influence of her performances. The citation that accompanied the statuette pulled no punches, praising her 'superlative creativity and [a] unique contribution to the art of screen acting'.

Career is too pompous a word. It was a job and I've always felt privileged to be paid for doing what I love doing.

I wasn't born an actress. Events made me one

JEAN HARLOW

Harlean Harlow Carpenter
3 March 1911–7 June 1937

Men like me because I don't wear a brassiere. Women like me because I don't look like a girl who would steal a husband. At least not for long.

I know I'm the worst actress that was ever in pictures.

I like to wake up each morning feeling a new man.

No one ever expects a great lay to pay all the bills.

I'm drinking only because I have to have something to keep me going. If I were leading a normal life, I'd drink only to be sociable.

To me, love has always meant friendship.

Must I always wear a low-cut dress to be important?

When you lie down with dogs, you get up with fleas.

Don't give me books for Christmas; I already have a book.

Many stars have talents or qualities that attain the status of hallmarks – Streep's versatility, Brando's mumble, Garbo's distant beauty – but few trade on a single physical attribute. Jean Harlow, with her unmistakable platinum blonde hair, was the first to admit she was not the world's finest actress, but that was to prove no hindrance to her becoming one of the great names of the 1930s. Along the way, however, she was to suffer many of the pitfalls that make a career in show business hazardous.

I turned to motion pictures because I had to work or starve.

Spotted by talent scouts while she was driving a friend to an audition, Harlow landed her first job as an uncredited extra for $7 [$100] a day. Her first memorable appearance was in a Laurel and Hardy short, *Double Whoopee* (1929), setting the tone for her image ever after: she steps out of a taxi, trapping her skirt in the door, and enters a hotel lobby wearing pretty much nothing. Unlike cinema's other early attempts at eroticism, so often compromised by a clumsy knowingness, her performance – as the hapless doormen try to cover her up – is gorgeously innocent. We feel guilty watching her, but we cannot turn our eyes away.

Harlow must have known the effect she was having on her audiences – she was reported to have rubbed ice cubes on her nipples just before a take to make them more prominent – and once famously let slip that 'underwear makes me uncomfortable. . . my parts have to breathe'. Unlike most of her male fans, Hollywood seemed unsure about what to do with this nascent star. But for another chance meeting – a fellow actor told producer Howard Hughes she might be right for a part he was casting – she might have languished in her lingerie until her looks faded.

Hughes was a hugely successful entrepreneur who had inherited a fortune from his family's oil companies and his two passions were aviation and film-making. He frequently combined business with pleasure, dating among others such leading ladies as Bette Davis, Ava Gardner, Olivia de Havilland, Katharine Hepburn, Ginger Rogers and Gene Tierney. Whether his infatuations influenced his choice of film projects will never be known, but his decisions were often mercurial and he pursued his aims with a fervour unfettered by corporate board members or shareholders. Today we realize he probably suffered from a severe case of Obsessive Compulsive Disorder (he commissioned a special fork to help sort the size of the peas on his plate, and later wore tissue boxes over his feet and refused ever to shake hands, to curtail the spread of germs), although at the time he was simply known as a precocious mogul who chose projects without recourse to petty concerns such as cost. He also, naturally, had the power to make or break the careers of those he picked to work with him. One famous story tells how he noticed that the bra Jane Russell wore in *The Outlaw* (1943) created unsightly wrinkles in her tight blouse, so he had new lingerie designed (using his engineering skills) to solve the problem. Ironically, Russell later revealed that the underwiring in his creation was so uncomfortable that she had reverted to her original undergarments; apparently, Hughes never noticed.

In 1927 Hughes had begun spending a colossal sum shooting *Hell's Angels,* an epic portrait of First World War fighter aces, but by the time it was finished Hollywood was in the throes of its transition to films with synchronized soundtracks. Hughes decided to replace a good deal of the original material with dialogue sequences, but the film's lead actress Greta Nissen had a Norwegian accent so strong that Hughes decided he needed to look for an American replacement. After a chance introduction to Harlow, he knew he had found his star – notwithstanding the minor disadvantage that nobody had heard of her. Her most distinctive attribute was clearly her unusually lustrous silvery hair, so Hughes's publicity director tried to launch a campaign proclaiming her the 'Blonde Landslide' or the 'Darling Cyclone'. Overruled, he then proposed 'Platinum Blonde'; Hughes approved, and ordered him to organize a national contest awarding $10,000 [$150,000] for any stylist who could match Harlow's shade for one of their clients. Nobody could, but the moniker stuck. Harlow later said of the stunt that if it hadn't been for her hair, 'Hollywood wouldn't know I'm alive'.

When she started filming, she was only eighteen and what little acting skills she had were undeveloped. James Whale, director of the dialogue sequences, realized he was going to have to work hard to elicit the performances he needed to justify the blockbuster $4m [$55m] budget: he shut the production down for three days to rehearse Harlow privately. As she confessed:

> *I was not a born actress. No one knows it better than I. If I had any*
> *latent talent, I have had to work hard, listen carefully, do things over*
> *and over and then over again in order to bring it out.*

Her speaking scenes are largely unmemorable, although she does at one point perfectly unwittingly sum up the raison d'être for her role:

HELEN
I wanna be free. I wanna be gay and have fun.
Life's short. And I wanna live while I'm alive.

What Hughes knew, and what Harlow came to understand, was that her effervescent presence brought sparkle and delight to every frame she graces. Only a few minutes of the production were shot in an early Technicolor process, prominently showcasing Harlow in a rose silk dress to complement her radiant locks; after decades of silent monochrome movies, often filled with stilted and typecast performances, her impact was startling and instantly propelled her to the front rank of stars. The film also contains the line forever associated with her sexy insouciance – 'Would you be shocked if I put on something more comfortable?' – leading *Variety* to exclaim: 'It doesn't matter what degree of talent she possesses. . . nobody ever starved possessing what she's got.' The film's opening at Grauman's Chinese Theatre attracted a crowd of 50,000 and the only sour note was the review from the *New Yorker* magazine, which described Harlow's performance as 'plain awful'.

Reviews from the highbrow press meant little to Hughes, who was busy trying to capitalize on Harlow's sudden fame. It was hardly a question of recouping his investment since he had signed her to a five-year deal on a salary of $100 [$1,400] a week, but he wanted to get her back on the screen as soon as possible. While he pondered her next project, he forced Harlow to go on national publicity tours (which terrified her) and loaned her out to other studios, pocketing the profits on the mark-up he demanded. This callous treatment of his prized asset reflected his business mentality, but some part of him still held a tender affection for his protégé. As Harlow recalled:

> *One day when he was eating a cookie he offered me a bite. Don't underestimate that. The poor guy's so frightened of germs, it could darn near have been a proposal.*

Hughes, with an unusual lack of imagination, finally cast his star in Frank Capra's 1931 production of *Gallagher* and simply renamed it *Platinum Blonde*. A modest hit, it gave the public exactly what they had paid to watch – according to the *New York Daily Mirror*, 'one of the gayest, sauciest comedies you've ever seen'. It seems Hughes's vision and marketing strategy had paid off; by 1933 women around the country were copying the platinum look as well as their stylists could manage and Harlow was a bigger box-office draw than either Greta Garbo or Joan Crawford. In 1937 she became the first ever film actress to be featured on the cover of *Time* magazine.

She starred in seventeen further pictures, including *The Public Enemy* (1931), *Dinner at Eight* (1933) and *Libeled Lady* (1936), but the very trademark that had launched her career was soon to prove a tragic liability.

> *I've always hated my hair, not only because it limited me as an*
> *actress, but because it limited me as a person. It made me look hard*
> *and spectacular.*

Decades after her death, *The Atlantic* magazine investigated the secret of her unusual hair colouring, citing an interview with celebrity stylist Alfred Pagano: 'I used to bleach her hair [with the formula she had devised]. . . We used peroxide, ammonia, Clorox, and Lux flakes. Can you believe that?' The reporter studied the likely chemical reactions and determined that the by-products of such a mixture would include hydrochloric acid and various gaseous poisons. The cumulative effect – Harlow had been using this home-brewed cocktail for over a decade – could not be calculated, but some sources claim that Harlow's hair was already falling out by 1935 (that year, while starring in *China Seas*, she wore wigs for the entire shoot).

In 1937, on the set of *Saratoga,* she keeled over in agony. When Clark Gable visited her in hospital, he reported 'it was like kissing a dead person, a rotting person'; her urinary functions had collapsed and her body was excreting waste through her lungs. On her death at the age of only twenty-six, the post-mortem cited uraemia (kidney failure), a condition for which she had been suffering for some time but which was almost certainly aggravated by the high doses of hydrochloric acid her scalp had absorbed.

Harlow had only one more lesson to learn about the vagaries of life as a star: that death is a good career move. Despite the fact that *Saratoga* had to be completed using a body double, it was Hollywood's most profitable release that year.

I love people to think I came up from the gutter.

I am at heart,
a gentleman

MARLENE
DIETRICH

Marie Magdalene 'Marlene' Dietrich
27 December 1901–6 May 1992

In Europe, it doesn't matter if you're a man or a woman – we make love with anyone we find attractive.

Most women set out to change a man, and when they have changed him they do not like him.

Once a woman has forgiven a man, she must not reheat his sins for breakfast.

In America, sex is an obsession; in other parts of the world it's a fact.

A country without bordellos is like a house without bathrooms.

Latins are tenderly enthusiastic. In Brazil, they throw flowers at you. In Argentina they throw themselves.

[My] legs aren't so beautiful. I just know what to do with them.

If there is a supreme being, he's crazy.

I am not a myth.

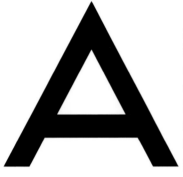

magisterial icon of early cinema whose sexual persona was notoriously fluid, Marlene Dietrich enjoyed a life closely mirroring her ground-breaking screen image. The daughter of a German police officer, she learned to admire discipline – she reputedly sucked lemons between takes to keep her cheeks taut – but to take its advantages wholly on her own terms: as a teenager, she had an affair with a teacher at school, which led him to be fired, and in later life one of her proudest achievements was to have bedded three prominent members of America's Kennedy clan as well as many of her most famous co-stars.

Born in 1901, Dietrich spent her formative years in Berlin and worked as a nightclub performer through her twenties while trying to break into the movies. Germany's capital city at that time was a pioneering centre of film-making as well as a nexus for avant-garde theatre, politics and sexuality, and all of these influences would prove crucial in the shaping of her personality. In 1929, after several years playing modest parts and at the ripe age of twenty-eight, Dietrich won the role of Lola in Josef von Sternberg's *The Blue Angel* (1930). Aptly, the story echoes her earlier adventures: a respectable schoolmaster (Emil Jannings) falls in love with her performance in a nightclub and his obsession causes him to spiral into madness. Her performance, as she sporadically encourages his devoted attentions, reflects every aspect of her screen image: she is at once compelling, haughty, provocative and tender. Even the scene where the teacher retrieves a letter from beneath her dressing-table – and where we see only Dietrich's legs demurely avoiding his fumblings – perfectly encapsulates her sexuality. For critics and historians of cinema, this was her breakthrough, distilling her unique skills and energy into a visual and musical archetype of intense eroticism. Erich Maria Remarque, author of *All Quiet on the Western Front* (1929), wrote of her:

> *The cool, bright face that didn't ask for anything, that simply existed, waiting – it was an empty face, he thought; a face that c ould change with any wind of expression. One could dream into it anything. It was like a beautiful empty house waiting for carpets and pictures. It had all possibilities – it could become a palace or a brothel.*

Being an electrifying new leading lady in Germany did not immediately establish Dietrich as a true star; it would take Sternberg, who quickly assumed credit for her success and set himself up as her mentor, to place her fully on the world stage. Paramount, desperate to find a rival for MGM's Swedish superstar Greta Garbo, were delighted when Sternberg brought his protégée to America and they went into production immediately with *Morocco* (1930). The story, transparently and simply a vehicle for Dietrich's talents, tells of cabaret singer Amy Jolly and a legionnaire (Gary Cooper) who fall in love; in a country where eighty million people were buying cinema tickets every week to escape the dreariness of their lives during the Depression, *Morocco* proved a stunning success. What Dietrich gave them, dressed in her impeccable top hat and man's tailcoat, was to be utterly transformative – not only for audiences but for cinema itself. Pacing a nightclub insouciantly while belting out classic *chansons* to an audience of soldiers and civilians, she scans the room as if sizing up her audience. She sings:

```
       AMY
What am I bid for my apple, the fruit that
made Adam so wise? On the historic night,
when he took a bite, they discovered a new
paradise. An apple, they say, keeps the doctor
away, while his pretty young wife has the time
of her life, with the butcher, the baker, the
candlestick maker... Oh, what am I bid for
my apple?
```

At the end of another show-stopper, 'Give Me the Man Who Does Things', she lights a cigarette and perches on a balustrade to enjoy the applause as a portly, pomaded admirer offers her a glass of champagne. She accepts politely, but already we see her eye has been drawn to one of his guests, a dark beauty in a shimmering dress. Dietrich asks if she may take the flower from the woman's hair – and when she consents, leans down with all the predatory grace of a Brando or Nicholson and kisses her full on the mouth before tipping her hat and sauntering away (the kiss, apparently, was Dietrich's suggestion).

It is easy to underestimate how powerful an image this must have been over eight decades ago, at a time when sexual self-expression in the cinema was largely a confused and hesitant business. Dietrich is suave and charming as she swoops on her prey, leaving the rest of the room in awe – at her brazen seduction, her absolute self-possession and her unshakeable elegance.

                    AMY
        Every time a man has helped me, there has been
        a price. What's yours?

                    LA BESSIÈRE
        My price? A smile.

                    AMY
        I haven't got much more.

As the critic Kenneth Tynan later remarked, 'She has sex but no positive gender. Her masculinity appeals to women, and her sexuality to men.' If American audiences found this androgyny challenging, it was a mystery they were intrigued to unravel.

Sternberg had taught her to embrace all the theatrical tricks that made her beauty distinctive: contoured make-up to accentuate her cheekbones, precise positioning of the camera to ensure the most flattering angles, and strong, chiaroscuro lighting (he once told Clark Gable that his hair would look better parted on the other side; Gable took his advice and kept it that way for the rest of his life). These techniques were becoming more common in Hollywood but Dietrich enforced them rigorously and kept a mirror on set so she could be confident her look remained consistent. Rumours spread that she commanded Max Factor to powder each of her wigs with half an ounce of real gold dust to guarantee their lustre – an extravagant diktat in the age of black-and-white film stock. But her passion for visual perfection was matched by that of her performances: one make-up assistant claimed that her screen kisses were so fiery that her lipstick had to be retouched after every take.

> *The relationship between the make-up man and the film actor is that of accomplices in crime.*

Although Dietrich had married assistant director Rudolf Sieber in 1924 – and they remained legally united until his death in 1976 – they pursued a famously open marriage: one of her lovers, the actor Maurice Chevalier, was great friends with both of them and sent cornflowers to Rudi whenever he gave Marlene her favourite white lilacs. Her other consorts included actors Jean Gabin, John Gilbert, Gary Cooper and Yul Brynner, newscaster Ed Murrow, General George

Patton, Erich Maria Remarque and, in 1963, the American president John F. Kennedy himself. Her most unlikely conquest was John Wayne, who is rumoured to have dodged the draft to avoid having to leave her, and who unchivalrously declared her 'the best lay I've ever had'. Wayne's biographer suggests Dietrich 'juicily sucked every last drop of resistance, loyalty, morality and guilt out of him, and gave him a sexual and moral cleansing'. The women she courted may have been less famous but seem to have been no less numerous. When a journalist enquired as tactfully as he could why she had taken so many lovers, she replied: 'They asked.'

> *Sex is much better with a woman, but then one can't live with a woman!*

Ernest Hemingway was never a sexual partner but the two adored and revered each other, and he wrote of her: 'If she had nothing more than her voice, she could break your heart with it.'

On her death in 1992, *The New York Times* added: 'Her sexuality was audacious, her wit was insolent and her manner was ageless.' *Morocco* earned Dietrich her only Oscar nomination and heralded a string of successes including *Dishonored* (1931), *Blonde Venus* (1932) and *Shanghai Express* (1932), all of which played to Dietrich's characteristic strengths and confirmed her as the pre-eminent femme fatale of her day. But this early success soon soured: with an irony almost too poignant to credit, she found that the American, Jewish and supposedly liberal Hollywood community she had embraced was as determined to clamp down on decadent performance as the Nazis she had so recently escaped. By 1934, the Hays Code (Motion Picture Production Code) was in full force and its censorship reduced Dietrich's smouldering roles to mere embers.

Although she continued to appear in films by celebrated directors Billy Wilder, Fritz Lang, Orson Welles and Alfred Hitchcock, she never again achieved the power of her early performances. In the 1950s she returned to the stage to rekindle a lucrative career as a cabaret star and chanteuse, ensuring that her trademark top hat and tails remained a key part of her costume changes; today she remains an icon not only for cineastes and style gurus but also for pioneers of sexual liberation, both straight and gay.

I was an actress.
I made films.
Finish.

I feel awkward,
shy, afraid

GRETA
GARBO

Greta Lovisa Gustafsson
18 September 1905–15 April 1990

[Hollywood] is boring,
incredibly boring, so boring I
can't believe it's true.

It is bitter to think of one's
best years disappearing in
this unpolished country.

Being a movie star means
being looked at from every
possible direction. You are
never left at peace, you're just
fair game.

I don't want to be a silly
temptress. I cannot see any
sense in getting dressed up
and doing nothing but
tempting men in pictures.

The story of my life is about
back entrances, side doors,
secret elevators and other
ways of getting in and out of
places so that people won't
bother me.

Your joys and sorrows – you
can never tell them. You
cheapen the inside of yourself
if you do.

Life would be so wonderful
if we only knew what to do
with it.

I live like a monk: with one
toothbrush, one cake of soap,
and a pot of cream.

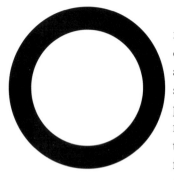ne thing had to happen before Greta Garbo could unleash herself on the world: cinema had to catch up with her. Viewers had grown used to a stylized medium all too often characterized by stilted acting, exaggerated make-up (because film stocks were still crude), clumsy directors who shouted instructions while the performances were taking place, and dialogue cards written as simply as possible for less literate audiences. By 1927 the advent of synchronized sound was set to revolutionize the movies: players would finally be liberated from mime, and from the two-dimensional performances that style demanded. But not all of the early stars would survive the transition; live speech put the emphasis firmly on acting ability – and on an attractive voice.

Garbo, as we now know, possessed these two qualities to an extraordinary degree. As a child she had dreamed of performing, and her path into that world proved both swift and straightforward: some modelling, drama school, a hit play in Sweden in 1924, one film in Germany in 1925, and by the end of that year a contract with an American studio. MGM brought her, along with her director and mentor Mauritz Stiller, to Los Angeles, where she caught the eye of the public for her turns in *The Temptress* (1926) and *Flesh and the Devil* (1926). The *New York Telegraph* declared: 'She has a glamour and fascination for both sexes which have never been equaled on the screen.'

Behind the scenes, MGM knew the clock was ticking. Short films had already been distributed showing actors speaking, and the success of *The Jazz Singer* (1927) confirmed for even the most reluctant producers that the 'talkies' were here to stay – but Garbo had arrived in Hollywood unable to speak more than a smattering of English, and her Swedish accent was proving hard to soften. The studio delayed the premiere of *Anna Christie* (1930), her first sound picture, as long as they dared, finally heralding its release under the daring banner: 'Garbo Talks!' Her first ever spoken line remains a classic:

> ANNA
> Gimme me a whisky, ginger ale on the side. And don't be stingy, baby!

Her sultry tones were utterly captivating, and the accent only served to add to her alluring mystique. Even more entrancing was her face, which had a natural stillness perfectly suited to the intimacy of close-ups. She had already established her working method:

*[Before filming begins] I allow only the cameraman and lighting man
on the set. When people are watching, I'm just a woman making faces
for the camera. It destroys the illusion. If I am by myself, my face will
do things I cannot do with it otherwise.*

Indeed, her nicknames included 'The Face', 'The Swedish Sphinx' and 'La Divina'.
Rouben Mamoulian, the Armenian-American who directed her in *Queen Christina*
(1933), took her technique one step further, encouraging her at crucial moments to
think of 'nothing at all', allowing the audience to project onto her ravishing close-
ups whatever stirred their souls – or other parts of their anatomy. But the film
that most perfectly captured her beauty and her extraordinarily modern presence
was *Mata Hari* (1931). A bold retelling of the real-life story of dancer, courtesan
and First World War spy Margaretha MacLeod, it provided passion and intrigue
in equal measure. Any viewer today would find it compelling, and would have no
difficulty imagining Meryl Streep or Cate Blanchett in the lead role.

As much as anything, the dialogue enables Garbo to shine; her ability to
counterpoint overt expression against emotional subtext is unerring. Here, she
meets Rosanoff, a suitor from whom she hopes to steal military secrets:

```
        ROSANOFF
I saw you once in the Bois. You were so lovely.
I watched you till you drove out of sight among
the chestnut blossoms... Oh, Paris in the
spring.

        MATA HARI
Spring...

        ROSANOFF
And now I'm here. With you.

        MATA HARI
But it's autumn.

        ROSANOFF
But perhaps next spring the war will be over...
you and I...
```

                    MATA HARI
        I never look ahead. By next spring, I shall
        probably be quite alone.

Prefiguring her best-known line from *Grand Hotel* (1932) – 'I want to be alone'
– Garbo radiates a heart-stopping wistfulness. Yet she is equally capable of
ruthlessness; when she finally seduces Rosanoff in order to copy the dispatches
he carries, she forces him to extinguish his votive candle before they make love.

                    ROSANOFF
        I love you as one adores sacred things.

                    MATA HARI
        What sacred things?

                    ROSANOFF
        God... country... honour... You.

                    MATA HARI
        I come last?

                    ROSANOFF
        You come first. Before anything.

                    MATA HARI
        Before... anything?

                    ROSANOFF
        Yes.

She hesitates before kissing him.

                    MATA HARI
        There is so much light in here. Put out that
        one too.

                    ROSANOFF
        The Madonna's lamp?

```
          MATA HARI
    Yes.
```

Garbo knows exactly what it will cost Rosanoff to obey her; she forces him simply because she can. Conflicted by her love for him and by the terrible burden of her task, it seems she needs to confront the vilest truth about herself – that she will sacrifice everything, including her life, to achieve her ends. No title card or silent gaze could convey the bitterness or the agony of her words: Garbo transfixes us.

Her outward remoteness – and her talent for persuading us that beneath the tranquil exterior beats the most passionate heart – remained her hallmark, off screen as well as on, throughout successive hits including *Grand Hotel* (1932), *Queen Christina* (1933), *Anna Karenina* (1935), *Camille* (1936) and *Ninotchka* (1939). Nominated three times for an Oscar, she received an honorary award in 1954 for her 'luminous and unforgettable screen performances'; she did not attend the ceremony, and the statuette was mailed to her.

By then she had been a recluse for over a decade, and remained so until her death in 1990. She had abandoned the industry at the age of thirty-five in 1941, seeming to vanish as suddenly as she had arrived. Few were surprised, since she had long shunned interviews, autographs, fan mail and galas. Her absence from the screen only served to magnify her legacy and she remains an icon: sacred to her fans, if not to herself. As to her most private feelings, it seems she never recovered from the death of her earliest mentor and first love, Mauritz Stiller; some of her correspondence also suggests she was homosexual, with partners including Marlene Dietrich and Louise Brooks. Whatever the truth, it seems she had always yearned to experience the emotions she conveyed so powerfully on screen:

> *I never said, 'I want to be alone'. I only said, 'I want to be left alone'.*
> *There is a whole world of difference.*

If only those who dream about Hollywood knew how difficult it all is.

*If you use your im-
agination, you can
look at any actress
and see
her nude*

HEDY
LAMARR

Hedwig Eva Maria Kiesler
9 November 1914–19 January 2000

I must quit marrying men
who feel inferior to me.
Somewhere there must be a
man who could be my
husband and not feel inferior.
I need a superior inferior
man.

My problem is, I'm a hell of a
nice dame. The most horrible
whores are famous. I did
what I did for love. The others
did it for money.

I hope to make you use your
imagination.

The ladder of success in
Hollywood is usually agent,
actor, director, producer,
leading man. And you are a
star if you sleep with them in
that order. Crude but true.

Jack Kennedy always said to
me: 'Hedy, get involved.
That's the secret of life. Try
everything. Join everything.
Meet everybody.'

[On receiving a 1997 EFF
(Electronic Frontier
Foundation) award for her
patent] It's about time.

ext time you take a call on your mobile phone or search for a wi-fi signal, think of a gorgeous Austrian girl running naked through the woods by a tranquil lake – in black-and-white – eighty-two years ago. Hedy Lamarr, the star of *Ecstasy* (1933), once described by impresario Max Reinhardt as 'the most beautiful woman in Europe', has won more awards for her achievements as an inventor than as an actress, despite the fact that she starred in some of Hollywood's most successful movies of the 1940s.

Born Hedwig Eva Maria Kiesler in 1914 in Vienna, she was – with little previous dramatic experience – cast by director Gustav Machatý to play Eva Hermann, a young woman in a loveless marriage who has an affair with Adam, a handsome engineer. The plot of *Ecstasy* is unremarkable, although it must have inspired countless soft-porn movies with their equally unconvincing story lines: the first time Adam sees Eva, she has been skinny-dipping in a lake only to find that her lusty stallion has bolted with all her clothes in the saddlebag. As if to underscore the unimportance of the plot, the script ran to a mere five pages. The film proved hugely controversial even though it was not the first mainstream film to contain full nudity (that landmark almost certainly belongs to a 1911 adaptation of Dante's *Inferno*). What caused the furore was the forthright depiction of Eva's seduction and her subsequent orgasm – in close-up. It is almost certainly the first film with widespread distribution to have featured sexual intercourse; Lamarr was seventeen when the cameras rolled, although she had told the producers she was nineteen.

> I remember all too well the premiere of Ecstasy *when I watched my bare bottom bounce across the screen and my mother and father sat there in shock.*

Despite the fact that we have already seen Eva fully naked, the camera does not reveal much in the key scene (indeed, Adam keeps his primly stylish sleeveless sweater on throughout their moments of passion); by today's standards, the photography simply offers a starkly expressionist portrait of a woman yielding to absolute pleasure. Lamarr's facial contortions as she is transported were reportedly prompted by the director jabbing her bottom with a safety pin ('You will lie here. When I prick you a little on your backside, you will bring your elbows together and you will react!'), and the crowning visual metaphor for the orgasm is, somewhat unfortunately, a shot of her pearl necklace lying broken on the floor beside them.

Machatý fully anticipated that the film would be controversial and he shot versions in German, Czech and French to ensure the largest possible audience; in Vienna, 71,000 people paid to see it in the first two weeks of its release. Lamarr was quickly courted by the Hollywood studios and signed a deal with MGM. Studio chief Louis B. Mayer, a stern moralist, was initially wary of his new protégé's notoriety and cautioned her about her contract obligations: '[You'll] never get away with that stuff in Hollywood. Never. A woman's ass is for her husband, not theatre-goers.' Joseph Breen, principal censor with the Motion Picture Producers and Distributors of America (MPPDA), called the picture 'highly – even dangerously – indecent' and delivered the verdict:

> I regret to have to advise you that we cannot approve [the] production
> Ecstasy *that you submitted for our examination yesterday for the*
> *reason that. . . it is a [story] of illicit love and frustrated sex, treated*
> *in detail without sufficient compensating moral values.*

Little did Breen know that Lamarr's personal life was even more startling than this fictional narrative. In 1933, echoing the plot of *Ecstasy* itself, Lamarr had married Friedrich Mandl, a wealthy Austrian weapons manufacturer fourteen years her senior. Pedantic and controlling, Mandl so hated the fact that the public had seen his wife making love to another man that he kept her virtually locked away in his twelfth-century moated castle while he tried to buy up and destroy all copies of the movie. Luckily for cinema-goers he failed – and, understandably, so did their marriage. In her 1966 autobiography *Ecstasy and Me*, Lamarr tells how she tried to flee Mandl's home and found herself hiding in a brothel. With her husband hot on her heels, she claims she had no choice but to offer her services to the client who approached her, in order to prevent her spouse from searching the room. As if this were not brazen enough, she also claims she hired a maid who looked like her only to drug her and steal her uniform as a ruse to facilitate her eventual escape.

Despite being denounced by Pope Pius XII, as well as by the MPPDA, *Ecstasy* was eventually released in America in 1940 for a limited run, and its star's subsequent life in Los Angeles – where she adopted the surname Lamarr, in homage to silent screen actress Barbara La Marr – must have seemed a walk in the park compared to her adventures in Austria. The '*Ecstasy* Lady' was soon taking leading roles alongside such luminaries as Lana Turner, Clark Gable, Spencer Tracy, Judy Garland and Bob Hope, although her one mistake was to turn down the part of Ilsa Lund, the character Ingrid Bergman made famous in *Casablanca* (1942).

Even so, her fame continued to grow; seven years later she portrayed Delilah in Cecil B. DeMille's *Samson and Delilah* (1949), the most financially successful film of that year and Paramount's biggest hit since *The Ten Commandments* (1923). As one of history's great temptresses, Delilah offered Lamarr yet another role in which the public were encouraged to see her as a scarlet woman, transgressing religious as well as moral barriers. The film's reception was not always as reverent as the producers might have hoped; when director Cecil. B. DeMille asked Groucho Marx what he thought of it, the comedian replied: 'Well, there's just one problem, C.B. No picture can hold my interest where the leading man's tits are bigger than the leading lady's.'

> *American men, as a group, seem to be interested in only two things*
> *– money and breasts. It seems a very narrow outlook.*

Eventually Lamarr tired of her typecasting, but if the legacy of *Ecstasy* continued to shadow her, she had plenty of other talents to deploy. A talented mathematician, she was also an inventor. She had a design office in her home and the projects that rolled off her drawing-board included a luminous pet collar, a more efficient traffic light, an instant fizzy drink in tablet form and a cosmetic cream. A chance meeting with avant-garde composer George Antheil, however, was to lead to her most important patent. Antheil was an expert in the field of hormones as well as harmony, and Mayer had sent Lamarr to meet him to see if anything could be done to enlarge her bust. After discovering a mutual interest in technical matters, Hedy raised the matter of remotely controlling torpedoes, a thorny problem she had heard her former husband discussing with his Nazi paymasters. The composer and the actress shared their ideas, sitting on the floor at Lamarr's home and mapping out the technical wiring for their prototype using household matches.

In 1942 they were granted Patent number US2292387, headed 'SECRET COMMUNICATION SYSTEM'. Lamarr and Antheil devised a method for disguising the control signal used by submarines to direct the missiles they fired, employing the mechanism of a player piano, which uses perforated paper rolls to automate its performance. The 'frequency-hopping', or spread-spectrum broadcasting, prevented enemy craft from blocking or jamming this signal. The second paragraph of their introduction to the patent reads:

An object of the invention is to provide a method of secret
communication which is relatively simple and reliable in operation,
but at the same time is difficult to discover or decipher.

And so it proved, although it was 1962 before the US Navy implemented the technology – and longer still until the telecoms industry realized it held the key to many of the technologies we take for granted in today's mobile, connected world.

Rightfully proud of her achievement, Lamarr hoped to become a member of the National Inventors Council, but the governing members declined her application, suggesting patronizingly that her feminine charms would be more usefully employed selling war bonds. Thus Lamarr appeared on the front page of the *Stars and Stripes* newspaper under the headline 'Hedy Adds New Twist to War' – beside a photograph of her in a bikini. *The New York Times*, more tactfully omitting her breasts from the story, still could not resist a pun:

> *HEDY LAMARR INVENTOR: Actress Devises 'Red-Hot' Apparatus*
> *for Use in Defense.*

But if the film business offers transitory pleasures and fickle fame, intellectual achievements endure: though she failed to win any significant acting awards, Lamarr was posthumously inducted into the US National Inventors Hall of Fame in 2014.

Any girl can be glamorous. All you have to do is stand still and look stupid.

The joy of dancing is conversation

GINGER ROGERS

Virginia Katherine McMath
16 July 1911–25 April 1995

When two people love each other, they don't look at each other, they look in the same direction.

The only way to enjoy anything in this life is to earn it first.

Intelligence, adaptability and talent. And by talent I mean the capacity for hard work. Lots of girls come here with little but good looks.

Rhythm is born in all of us. To be a desirable dancing partner you don't have to do all the intricate fancy steps that happen to be in vogue. All you have to do is be a good average dancer and anybody who spends the time and effort can accomplish this.

The kids today, they think they can dance with their faces.

inger Rogers and. . . Well, it may take two to tango (or swing, foxtrot, or waltz) but we are here to celebrate the actress, not the couple. Although fans clamour to rank her legendary performances with Fred Astaire in *Top Hat* (1935), *Follow the Fleet* (1936), *Swing Time* (1936) and many others, it is invidious – and impossible – to single out any one movie. Instead, we should begin at the beginning.

> *My mother told me I was dancing before I was born. She could feel*
> *my toes tapping wildly inside her for months.*

Rogers had originally hoped to become a schoolteacher. Her mother was involved with the local theatre, and the young Ginger used to keep herself occupied by dancing along with the performers; she had a natural talent and was soon touring in a vaudeville act. By the time she was nineteen she had hit the big time playing Molly Gray in the Gershwin brothers' musical *Girl Crazy* on Broadway; the choreographer for the show happened to be Astaire.

In 1933 RKO brought them together again to shoot *Flying Down to Rio* (1933); 'Carioca', its main dance number, was the moment the match really lit the blue touchpaper. Sheathed in a black ball gown, with a perfectly weighted hem to ensure that her silhouette cast eddies as she spun, Rogers danced as if a Matisse painting had leapt to life to pour its curves across the screen, and the moment when she and Astaire touch foreheads as they skitter together in perfect harmony adds an unexpected intimacy to their partnership. As critics and choreographers have since noted, Rogers brought the entirety of her performance – her character and its emotions – into every step she took.

The screen partnership with Astaire lasted until 1949, when they played in *The Barkleys of Broadway*. But Rogers had long been restless in her career:

> *Over the years, myths were built up about my relationship with Fred*
> *Astaire. The general public thought he was a Svengali, who snapped*
> *his fingers for his little Trilby to obey; in their eyes, my career was his*
> *creation. . . I just couldn't stand being typed or pigeonholed as only a*
> *singing and dancing girl. I wanted to extend my range.*

Kitty Foyle (1940) gave her the perfect chance to do so. The film – a romantic drama about a girl from the wrong side of the tracks who is forced to choose between a rich suitor and a hard-up lover – is a classic post-Depression morality tale about passion, ambition and integrity. It wears its heart – and its politics – on its sleeve:

```
            KITTY
How do you know when you're falling in love?


            MARK
Well, I don't make very much dough, and when I find
myself wanting to spend ten bucks on a girl then I
know.
```

The film did not involve Astaire, and featured only the most demure of ballroom waltzes. But the tirade Kitty delivers as she spurns the family of her snobbish beau Wyn Strafford had Academy Award written all over it:

```
            KITTY
Let's get a few things straight here! I didn't ask
to marry a Strafford, a Strafford asked to marry
me. I married a man, not an institution or a trust
fund or a bank. Oh, I've got a fine picture of your
family conference here. All the Straffords trying to
figure out how to take the curse off of Kitty Foyle.
Buy the girl a phony education, polish off the
rough edges. And make a Mainline doll out of her!
Aww, you oughta know better than that! It takes six
generations to make a bunch of people like you. And
by Judas Priest, I haven't got that much time.
```

It was a smash hit, and did indeed win Rogers her only Oscar. *Life* magazine promoted the film with an unprecedented eight-page spread, largely because Ginger wasn't dancing throughout, but for her there was no real distinction between her talents. As she explained, quite simply:

Part of the joy of dancing is conversation.

Beauty is a valuable asset, but it is not the whole cheese.

When women go wrong, men go right after them

MAE WEST

Mary Jane 'Mae' West
17 August 1893–22 November 1980

Good girls go to heaven. Bad girls go everywhere else.

When caught between two evils I generally pick the one I've never tried before.

I used to be Snow White, but I drifted.

Ten men waiting for me at the door? Send one of them home, I'm tired.

A hard man is good to find.

I believe in censorship. After all, I made a fortune out of it.

I only like two kinds of men: domestic and foreign.

To err is human, but it feels divine.

Is that a gun in your pocket or are you just glad to see me?

Marriage is a great institution, but I'm not ready for an institution yet.

Sex is emotion in motion.

I'm the lady who works at Paramount all day. . . and Fox all night.

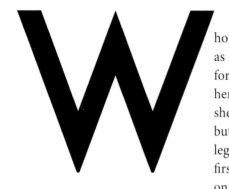

ho could fail to be delighted by tributes as diverse as Salvador Dalí's sofa shaped as a pair of lips, the inflatable life vest for an entire branch of the US armed forces, and the iconic shape of the Coca-Cola bottle itself? Even the Beatles put her on the cover of their album *Sgt. Pepper's Lonely Hearts Club Band* (at first she objected, declaring she would never be a member of a 'Lonely Hearts Club', but the band professed their admiration for her and she relented). Mae West, legendary siren and wit – and emulated by many lesser actresses ever since she first appeared on celluloid – was every bit as powerful a woman off screen as on. Intelligent, uncompromising and politically engaged, she championed a form of feminism absolutely familiar to today's audiences.

I'm no model lady. A model's just an imitation of the real thing.

Cultivate your curves – they may be dangerous but they won't be avoided.

You only live once, but if you do it right, once is enough.

A dame that knows the ropes isn't likely to get tied up.

It isn't what I do, but how I do it. It isn't what I say, but how I say it, and how I look when I do it and say it.

Born in 1893, she began her career as a child actor before turning to vaudeville; after a period of growing fame on stage, she persuaded Broadway producers in 1926 to let her write, direct and star in the play *Sex*. The production was quite as shocking as its title suggests. Arrested on charges of obscenity, West served ten days in jail on Welfare Island where, she delighted in telling reporters, she had worn silk underwear throughout her stay. Her follow-up creation *The Drag,* which dealt with homosexuality, had its opening run in the provinces but when West announced she would be bringing it to New York the Society for the Prevention of Vice had it banned. Even so, the mixture of success and controversy ensured her – at the age of thirty-eight – a contract with Paramount.

During the production of her first film, playing Maudie Triplett in *Night After Night* (1932), West insisted on rewriting many of her scenes, prompting her co-star George Raft to declare 'she stole everything but the cameras'. Her characteristic witticisms were already well established and her talent, as well as her notoriety, translated perfectly to the silver screen. Glorious one-liners abounded:

> HAT CHECK GIRL
> Goodness, what beautiful diamonds!

> MAUDIE
> Goodness had nothing to do with it, dearie.

Or, equally celebrated:

> MABEL
> Maudie, do you believe in love at first sight?

> MAUDIE
> I don't know, but it saves an awful lot of
> time.

But the film which cemented her reputation and provided a wider showcase for her talents – dancing, singing and acting, as well as writing the entire screenplay – was *I'm No Angel* (1933). With rumours already growing about pressure being brought to bear on Hollywood to enforce a stricter moral code, West's script is a glorious swan song (no pun intended for fans of *Sunset Boulevard*) to those early, heady days of cinematic freedom – and it exploits flirtation and sexual innuendo to the full. The story itself is both racy and tender. It tells of Tira, a cage dancer and lion-tamer (in the days before sophisticated special effects, the circus scenes are jaw-dropping), who tries to escape her boyfriend and boss in the hope of marrying a rich patron. After a succession of high jinks and misunderstandings the path to true love is uncovered, and although the plot's convolutions are predictable enough, West's role is cosmopolitan, sparkling and persuasive. Her banter remained pitch-perfect:

> JACK
> You were wonderful tonight.

> TIRA
> I'm always wonderful at night.

                    JACK
          Tonight, you were especially good.

                    TIRA
          Well... When I'm good, I'm very good. But,
          when I'm bad...

She winks at Jack.

                    TIRA
          I'm better.

Although Tira freely admits she is a gold-digger, she is genuinely open to love
when it happens, and when millionaire Jack Clayton (Cary Grant) breaks off
their engagement she is so heartbroken she sues him for breach of promise. In
court, Jack's lawyer has assembled a line-up of witnesses who testify, as openly as
they dare, that they have all spent intimate evenings with Tira in the past. Jack's
lawyer hopes to paint Tira as a sexually voracious predator on rich men's hearts
– and on their wallets – but West, holding the twinkly-eyed old judge in the
palm of her well-manicured hand, captivates the courtroom just as surely as she
thrilled the punters under the big top. She denies nothing, but brings the motives
of the men – sex, naturally – under scrutiny with such wily charm that it is their
reputations, not hers, which lie in tatters by the end.

                    JACK
          Oh I'm crazy about you.

                    TIRA
          I did my best to make you that way.

                    JACK
          Look darling, you need a rest, and so do I. Let
          me take you away somewhere, we'll...

                    TIRA
          Would you call that a rest?

                    JACK
What are you thinking about?

                    TIRA
Same thing you are.

West's performance is suave, perspicacious and extremely funny; more impressively, it is far ahead of its time in its portrayal of a woman wholly in charge of her life and utterly unashamed of her appetites, who feels entirely entitled to behave as she likes – especially if it involves beating her male admirers at their own game. The whole film foreshadows the verbal style of the best screwball comedies; it is filled not only with West's famous double entendres but with a cornucopia of wisecracks, zingers and asides which prove that pretty much everyone else in the cast is just playing straight-man to her wit and verve.

                    TIRA
    Always remember, honey, a good motto is: take
    all you can get and give as little as possible.
    Don't forget, honey: never let one man worry
    your mind... find 'em, fool 'em, and forget 'em.

Though she preferred the term 'women's liberation' to 'feminism', West's beliefs were clear and her insistence that her maid Beulah in *I'm No Angel* be played by a black woman (Gertrude Howard, much against the studio's wishes) further proves she was not about to let anyone or anything stand in her way. As the original trailer for *Night After Night* proclaimed before her title card:

   No use talking. . . I'm a woman of action.

Those who are
easily shocked should
be shocked more often.

'She did it the hard way'

BETTE DAVIS

Ruth Elizabeth 'Bette' Davis
5 April 1908–6 October 1989

From the moment I was six I felt sexy. And let me tell you it was hell, sheer hell, waiting to do something about it.

I am a woman meant for a man, but I never found a man who could compete.

What a fool I was to come to Hollywood where they only understand platinum blondes and where legs are more important than talent.

There was more good acting at Hollywood parties than ever appeared on the screen.

Attempt the impossible in order to improve your work.

I have been uncompromising, peppery, intractable, monomaniacal, tactless, volatile and oftentimes disagreeable. I suppose I'm larger than life.

An affair now and then is good for a marriage. It adds spice, stops it from getting boring. . . I ought to know.

I will never be below the title.

Until you're known in my profession as a monster, you're not a star.

Bette Davis was revered for her ruthless and uncompromising performances, and her 'private' life – not that it was ever much hidden from the public eye – was no different. It's hard to imagine any of her screen creations outshining a woman who once sent her brother-in-law, a recovering alcoholic, a case of spirits for his wedding present. Extraordinarily ambitious, tenacious and focused, she was unafraid to take on any role that genuinely interested her, no matter how unappealing it might seem to audiences; as a result she was nominated for ten Academy Awards, winning twice for *Dangerous* (1935) and *Jezebel* (1938). To date, her tally of nominations has only been surpassed by Meryl Streep, Katharine Hepburn and Jack Nicholson.

> *Acting should be bigger than life. Scripts should be bigger than life. It should all be bigger than life.*

Davis was inspired to become an actress after seeing Mary Pickford in *Little Lord Fauntleroy* (1921), although the first drama school she applied to rejected her for being 'insincere' and 'frivolous'. By the time she was twenty-one she was playing modest roles on Broadway, and before long a talent scout from Universal Studios had invited her to Hollywood for a screen test: she hated the results so much that she fled the projection room screaming. Even so, Universal signed her and put her to work in a largely unremarkable run of twenty-three films in her first three years alone.

Reactions to her talent were already polarized: while the *Saturday Evening Post* wrote of her in *The Man Who Played God* (1932), 'she is not only beautiful, but she bubbles with charm', director William Wyler commented to his crew: 'What do you think of these dames who [just] show their chests and think they can get jobs?'

Caught between faint praise and disdain, it seems hardly surprising that Davis jumped at the chance to show her true capabilities in *Of Human Bondage* (1934), the first of several versions of W. Somerset Maugham's celebrated but bleak novel. Certainly the role transformed public and critical perception of her; *Life* magazine at the time declared it 'probably the best performance ever recorded on screen by a U.S. actress'.

Thus vindicated, Davis began to be offered increasingly powerful scripts and her journey towards stardom with *Dark Victory* (1939), *Now, Voyager* (1942) and *All*

About Eve (1950) began in earnest. To modern audiences, those pictures remain moving, insightful and stylish; *Of Human Bondage* – in startling contrast – feels overblown, inept and mawkish. Perhaps it should serve to remind us quite how young an art form screen acting still was, less than a decade after the first 'talkie', but our first reaction is one of baffled awe. How could such a ham-fisted piece of story-telling have provoked such admiration?

With a numbing relentlessness, the film tells of the infatuation felt by impoverished English medical student Philip Carey (Leslie Howard) for callous, shrewish London waitress Mildred Rogers (Davis). We are offered almost nothing for an hour and twenty-three minutes but forlorn and strangled declarations of love, grimly predictable betrayals, vile indifference, a gallery of class caricatures and an accent (from Davis) that makes Dick Van Dyke in *Mary Poppins* sound like John Gielgud. Howard's performance is hypnotically charmless and he does little to prevent us from thinking him a gutless sap (while his club foot, miraculously cured at the end, proves a metaphor worthy of the *Titanic*'s iceberg); Davis's introductory scenes are breathtakingly contrived, two-dimensional and lacking in redeeming virtue (or even defect).

To some degree, this can be excused by the script, which is simultaneously florid and vapid and reads like a spoof travellers' guide to a backward European country. The direction is a little more contemporary in its avant-garde dissolves and snappy elisions of time and location, and once or twice the camera catches the fire in Davis's expression, but for the first two thirds of the film nothing seems to come alive at all. Even at the point where Mildred cynically acknowledges Philip's generosity the dialogue is grimly wooden:

> MILDRED
> I don't know what would have become of me and
> baby if you hadn't taken us in.
>
> PHILIP
> Oh, you'd have got on, I expect.
>
> MILDRED
> You've always been much nicer to me than I
> deserved. I'm beginning to realize how silly
> I've been.

> PHILIP
> Well, you couldn't help how you felt. Let's not
> talk about it, shall we?

Quite how Davis believed she could make anything credible or compelling from this kind of material is astonishing. Only in her final tirade, after Howard admits he has grown to hate her, does anything remotely approaching a classic Davis line appear:

> PHILIP
> You disgust me.

> MILDRED
> Me? I disgust you?... You cad, you dirty swine!
> I never cared for you, not once! I was always
> making a fool of you! You bored me stiff — I
> hated you! It made me sick when I had to let
> you kiss me. I only did it because you begged
> me, you hounded me and drove me crazy! And
> after you kissed me, I always used to wipe my
> mouth!... Griffiths and me, we laughed at you
> because you were such a mug, a mug, a mug! You
> know what you are, you gimpy-legged monster? A
> cripple, a cripple, a cripple!

And suddenly she is there – Bette Davis as the cinema would always remember her and making the scene so terrifyingly real that the idea she might simply be acting seems absurd. Her performance turns on the proverbial dime, bursting onto the screen as if she and the hapless Philip have been sleepwalking for the first hour of the film. She trembles, she stares, she screams; her eyes sparkle and her body shakes, and poor Leslie Howard looks (in a series of almost idiotically static close-ups) as if he has been hit by a train. Clearly that's how Hollywood felt, too; so many Academy members were outraged that Davis was not among the contenders for an Oscar that year that the president – for the only time in the institution's history – decreed 'any voter. . . may write on the ballot his or her personal choice for the winner'. In the end Claudette Colbert carried home the statuette for *It Happened One Night* (1933), but the furore caused a permanent change in the way future nominations were determined.

Everything about Davis's turn in *Of Human Bondage* foreshadowed her later style and working method: an unwillingness to compromise no matter what her co-stars felt about her (she was initially snubbed by Howard until he realized she was stealing the show), a meticulous attention to detail (she designed the make-up for her death scene herself so as to make it as realistic as possible), and a fearless self-awareness. Looking back on the role in later years, she remembered:

> *My understanding of Mildred's vileness – not compassion, but*
> *empathy – gave me pause. . . I was still an innocent. And yet Mildred's*
> *machinations I miraculously understood when it came to playing her.*
> *I was often ashamed of this. . . I suppose no amount of rationalization*
> *can change the fact that we are all made up of good and evil.*

This duality informed all of her subsequent performances and remained a compelling part of her private life too. Married four times, alienated from her adopted daughter, and frequently feuding with her great rival Joan Crawford, Davis was rarely out of the limelight. When an interviewer suggested as tactfully as he could that 'at one time' she had a reputation for being difficult to work with, she laughed:

> *'At one time?' I've been known as difficult for fifty years, practically!*
> *And it's always to make it the best film I can make it.*

Not for nothing did she have her sarcophagus engraved with the words: 'She did it the hard way'.

Today everyone is a star – they're all billed as 'starring' or 'also starring'. In my day, we earned that recognition.

*It matters more
what's in a woman's
face than what's
on it*

CLAUDETTE
COLBERT

Émilie 'Lily' Chauchoin
13 September 1903–30 July 1996

Hollywood was not my dream, you know. I only left Broadway when the crash came. The Depression killed the theatre, and the pictures were manna from heaven.

I just went right onstage, and I learned by watching. I've always believed that acting is instinct to start with; you either have it or you don't.

Audiences always sound like they're glad to see me, and I'm damned glad to see them. If they want you, you want to do it.

It took me years to figure out that you don't fall into a tub of butter – you jump for it.

I think there was more sex in those old films than in all that thrashing around today. I'm tired of sex scenes.

**N**ot blessed with poster-winning good looks, the young Claudette Colbert was tactfully promoted by her producers as 'apple-faced'. More galling still, in an anecdote she happily related herself, Noël Coward said during their rehearsals for *Blithe Spirit* in 1955: 'If she had a neck, I'd wring it.' But her gutsy determination and her impeccable, if fortuitous, timing during cinema's evolution assured her a place in history.

Born Émilie 'Lily' Chauchoin in a Paris suburb in 1903, she emigrated with her family at the age of three to the United States (to this day the French still loyally claim her as one of only five native actors to have won an Oscar, alongside Juliette Binoche, Marion Cotillard, Simone Signoret and Jean Dujardin). Studying in New York to be a painter and fashion designer, she took bit parts in local stage productions and eventually signed a Broadway contract. Though the work kept her in demand, all too often she found herself cast as a maid or ingénue:

> *In the very beginning, they wanted to give me French roles. . . That's why I used to say my name Col-bert just as it is spelled, instead of Col-baire. I did not want to be typed as 'that French girl'.*

In 1927 she was given a small role in *For the Love of Mike*, an early Frank Capra picture. Now lost, the silent film was not a success; Capra described it in his autobiography as 'my first flop', and even *The New York Times* review was pointedly lukewarm: 'Claudette Colbert. . . [merely] lends her charm to this obstreperous piece of work.' Frustrated, Colbert vowed publicly: 'I shall never make another film.' Thank heavens her resolution did not last. She had a strong, clear voice, perfect for the incoming era of sound pictures, and the following year she signed a five-year contract with Paramount.

One early hit, Ernst Lubitsch's *The Smiling Lieutenant* (1931), brought good notices, but the film itself seems laboured and old-fashioned. Lubitsch had not yet hit his stride with the masterpieces we remember him for (*Ninotchka* (1939) and *To Be or Not To Be* (1942)) and Colbert's acting style is broad and unsophisticated – it feels like a silent film with dialogue added only as an afterthought. But it did well, and Colbert – despite her earlier threat of returning to Broadway – hung on. In 1934 she teamed up with Cecil B. DeMille to play Cleopatra in a film of the same name, and her performance is transformed. The histrionics and over-acting are gone, replaced by a gamine enthusiasm and a knowing sexiness as the Egyptian queen parlays her feminine charms into political power games.

CLEOPATRA
Together we could conquer the world.

JULIUS CAESAR
Nice of you to include me.

The epic nature of DeMille's production delivers a stunning backdrop to Colbert's set-pieces and, in the last few months before the Motion Picture Production Code forced decency upon its signatories, her performance is delightfully flirtatious as well as intelligent.

The same year, as if from nowhere, came *It Happened One Night*, the film that put Capra, Clark Gable, Colbert and Columbia Pictures firmly on the map. Hailed as the progenitor of all 'screwball comedies' (a term that came to mean a lively battle between classes and sexes, shot through with zany plot twists and zippy, memorable dialogue), it thrilled audiences and gave Colbert the chance to show her true mettle. In it she plays Ellie Andrews, the runaway daughter of a millionaire who is recognized (and pursued) by ne'er-do-well newspaperman Peter Warne (Gable, on terrific form). In retrospect, it is easy to imagine that Capra and his co-writer Robert Riskin were simply finessing a winning formula but cinema historians agree that the film invented – and instantly perfected – the genre straight off the bat. Everything we would subsequently come to know and adore about sparkling repartee, sublimated sexuality and star-crossed love found its genesis here, and Colbert excels as the woman who loses her heart without losing her head.

The fact that she was not the most smouldering of stars worked to her advantage, giving her the air of a woman who (were it not for her unfortunate millions) could be any one of us, battling circumstance and curmudgeonly relatives as she steers her way to honesty, freedom and true love. Her predicament is exquisite, her poise perfection itself and her performance – even though Gable has the more proactive role – a joy. She is by turns sharp, sappy, bullish, afraid, defiant, desperate and devoted, but she never misses a trick or a beat and is utterly winning throughout. The evolution in her acting style across a mere three years is astonishing. The role marked a turning-point for audiences as the epic but stilted style of films from the twenties gave way to the fresher, more natural form that heralded Hollywood's golden age – and Colbert was now its poster girl.

After the debacle of Capra's *For the Love of Mike* seven years earlier, it was no surprise that Colbert wasn't the director's first choice for the role and the shoot itself was not entirely a smooth ride; knowing that the part had been offered to several other stars, Colbert initially demurred, and only agreed to accept on condition she was paid $50,000 [$875,000] and that filming be completed within four weeks to allow her to take a vacation she had already booked. Trickier still, Colbert had decided she no longer wanted to capitalize on her sexuality in portraying her characters. As Capra noted ruefully, 'Claudette refused to even partially undress before the camera. She wanted to feature her acting, not her sex appeal.' Even so, one of the film's most memorable moments came as a result of the director's canny understanding of human vanity. In a scene where Peter fails to get passing cars to stop and offer him and Ellie a lift, she takes matters into her own hands, stepping into the road to see if she will have more luck. The script demanded that she lift her skirt and flash her leg, but Colbert refused. Capra – as wise with his actors as he was with his screenplays – noted later in his autobiography: 'We waited until the casting director sent us a chorus girl with shapely underpinnings to "double" for Colbert's. When she saw the double's leg, she said: "Get her out of here. I'll do it. That's not my leg!"'

Ellie and Peter ride in the back of the car.

                    ELLIE
        Aren't you going to give me a little credit?

                    PETER
        What for?

                    ELLIE
        I proved once and for all that the limb is
        mightier than the thumb.

                    PETER
        Why didn't you take off all your clothes?
        You could have stopped forty cars.

                    ELLIE
        Well, I'll remember that when we need forty
        cars.

Later, their reluctant banter continues as they are forced to share a motel room:

                    ELLIE
          You've got a name, haven't you?

                    PETER
          Yeah, I got a name. Peter Warne.

                    ELLIE
          Peter Warne. I don't like it.

                    PETER
          Don't let it bother you. You're giving it back
          to me in the morning.

                    ELLIE
          Pleased to meet you, Mr Warne.

                    PETER
          The pleasure is all mine, Mrs Warne.

Capra claimed afterwards that Colbert had 'many little tantrums, motivated by her antipathy toward me', but that 'she was wonderful in the part'. His star, somewhat less gracefully, told friends later: 'I've just finished the worst picture in the world.'

Within months, however, the film had won all five main Oscars (best picture, best writer, best director, best actor and best actress) – the first in Hollywood's history to do so – and Colbert, who had little faith in its success, had to be fetched from the train she was leaving on and hurriedly brought to the ceremony to accept her award. To her credit, she raised the statuette aloft and said simply: 'I owe Frank Capra for this.'

I know what's best for me; after all, I've been in the Claudette Colbert business longer than anybody.

*My name doesn't
sell tickets to serious
pictures*

CAROLE
LOMBARD

Jane Alice Peters
6 October 1908–16 January 1942

I've lived by a man's code designed to fit a man's world, yet at the same time I never forget that a woman's first job is to choose the right shade of lipstick.

I love living, I love life. Eating, sleeping, waking up again, skeet-shooting, sitting around an old barn doing nothing, my work, taking a bath, talking my ears off, the little things, the big things, the simplest things, the most complicated things – I get a kick out of everything I do while I'm doing it.

Your mind rather than your emotions must answer for the success of matrimony. It must be friendship – a calm companionship which can last through the years.

The time-tested technique for an actor playing a drunk is to focus absolutely on *not* seeming squiffy. No such reliable method exists, however, for an actress who plays an actress who cannot act – but Carole Lombard, as Lily Garland in her first great screwball comedy *Twentieth Century* (1934), nails it. After an excruciating rehearsal for his new play, director Oscar Jaffe (John Barrymore) loses his patience – and his temper – with his leading lady:

> JAFFE
> You squalling little amateur! On your feet. Get up. Take that hump out of your back. You're not demonstrating underwear anymore.

> LILY
> I've taken all the bullying from you I'm going to. No man living can kick me around for eight hours until I can't see straight. I'm a human being, do you hear? A human being. I wanted to be an actress, but I won't crawl on my stomach for any man. You find somebody else.

Jaffe is astonished by Lily's intensity.

> JAFFE
> She's marvelous, just as I thought! Fire, passion, everything. The gold is all there, but we must mine it...

Born to a well-to-do family in Fort Wayne, Indiana, Lombard was both smart and athletic and landed her first screen role playing a tomboy who could swing a baseball bat. She quickly established herself as a fine actress and a good sport both on screen and off, and she was quite happy to play the hapless ingénue – as well as the nightmare diva she becomes as the film unfolds. Her greatest skill was to balance broad jokes and expansive acting with more nuanced and intimate humour, perfect for the movies of the time which cherished feisty, independent women with a tender heart. In 2005, critic Rhoda Koenig praised the 'platinum blonde with a heart-shaped face, delicate, impish features and a figure made to be swathed in silver lamé', while novelist Graham Greene had earlier noted that her glamour and universal appeal were rooted in an unmistakably distinctive style: 'It is always a pleasure to watch those hollow Garbo features, those neurotic elbows and bewildered hands. . . her voice [evokes] heart-breaking and nostalgic melodies.'

After her success in *Twentieth Century*, Lombard sought more serious roles, but after a run of classic melodramas failed to draw the crowds, she grew to understand – and accept – where her true talents lay; further classics like *My Man Godfrey* (1936) and *To Be or Not to Be* (1942) confirmed her reputation as the Queen of Comedy. At peace with her fame, she was noted for her easy, open manner and often shunned her opulent dressing room, preferring to hang out on the set with other cast members and the crew – and entertain them with her notoriously filthy repartee. *Life* magazine reported that 'her conversation, often brilliant, is punctuated by screeches, laughs, growls, gesticulations and the expletives of a sailor's parrot'. She acted opposite Clark Gable in several pictures; after reading Margaret Mitchell's 1936 hit novel *Gone with the Wind*, she sent him a copy with a note suggesting 'Let's do it'. Gable, a notorious womanizer, assumed it was a flirtatious gambit on Lombard's part and invited her on a date. They married in 1939. Lombard was under no illusions about her husband's ability to remain faithful (although she once described him as 'a lousy lay') and they led a contented off-screen life on a ranch in California. Good humour was the bedrock of their union; they referred to each other as Ma and Pa, and when Lombard gave Gable a large ham with his name on it he responded by buying her a fire truck. The couple remained devoted to one another until Lombard was killed in a plane crash at the age of thirty-three.

Some say Lombard herself coined the term 'dumb blonde' to describe her screen persona, but in her view it was a term of approbation for the subversive humour she brought to the roles she played. Nobody doubted her talent; the precociously gifted Orson Welles wanted her to play the lead in what would have been his first Hollywood picture, *Smiler with a Knife,* but when she declined his offer he dropped the project without so much as considering another star. But Lily's director Jaffe in *Twentieth Century* had seen it all along:

                    LILY
    Was I all right? Was I what you wanted?

                    JAFFE
    I came to pay my respects to a great actress.

I love my work and I take it seriously. As I love everything I do and give everything I've got to whatever I'm doing. But I do not go about clutching my career to an otherwise naked bosom.

It's much easier to make people cry than to make them laugh

VIVIEN LEIGH

Vivian Mary Hartley
5 November 1913–8 July 1967

I don't know what that Method is. Acting is life, to me, and should be.

Sometimes I dread the truth of the lines I say. But the dread must never show.

Some critics saw fit to say that I was a great actress. I thought that was a foolish, wicked thing to say because it put such an onus and such a responsibility onto me, which I simply wasn't able to carry.

Scorpios burn themselves out and eat themselves up and they are careless about themselves – like me. I swing between happiness and misery and I cry easily. I am a mixture of my mother's determination and my father's optimism. I am part prude and part non-conformist and I say what I think and don't dissemble.

Am I finished with Hollywood? Good heavens, no! I shall certainly go back there if there is a film to make.

I have just made out my will and given all the things I have and many that I haven't.

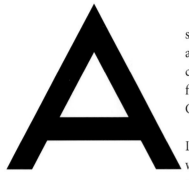

A sophisticated and beautiful Englishwoman with a fine theatrical pedigree and a reverence for Shakespeare, in love with Laurence Olivier, the finest British classical actor of his day, wins the greatest role Hollywood has to offer – her first role in America – against established stars such as Tallulah Bankhead, Joan Crawford and Lana Turner. What could possibly go wrong?

Later in her life, after Vivien Leigh had won two Oscars, and despite long battles with alcoholism, bipolar disorder and tuberculosis, the most bizarre verdict on her career came from the British Cabinet Office when the Honours and Appointments Secretariat assessed her suitability for the highest accolade the monarch can bestow: 'There are contrary opinions about her merits as an actress. Personally I think she is underrated and see no reason why she should not have a CBE (Commander of the British Empire) but certainly not a DBE (Dame Commander).' The distinction expressed an unspoken feeling that although the establishment was happy to tip its hat to a national (and international) treasure, Leigh was somehow not reliable enough to be recognized with its fullest approbation.

Leigh had been a complex character from the start. Following a handful of minor stage and screen roles, she was accepted at the Royal Academy of Dramatic Art; her talent was undeniable and quickly acclaimed, but she was intense, determined and outspoken. A *Daily Express* review of *The Mask of Virtue* (1935) praised her animation in the play ('a lightning change came over her face'), and this ability to convey mercurial emotional shifts would become the cornerstone of her success.

As a professional actress negotiating the white-water rapids of the Hollywood studios, such mutability was less helpful; even the way she won the role of Scarlett O'Hara was as magnificent as it was improbable. Her US agent was Myron Selznick, brother of producer David who had recently bought the rights to Margaret Mitchell's bestselling book of love and war in the American South, *Gone with the Wind*. When Leigh asked Myron to consider her for the part, he baulked, claiming she was 'too British', but Leigh was undaunted. She told various reporters, 'I've cast myself as Scarlett O'Hara. . . [Olivier] won't play Rhett Butler, but I shall play Scarlett. Wait and see.' Leigh flew to Los Angeles where Olivier was shooting *Wuthering Heights* (1939) – she had also lobbied for the part of Catherine Linton in that film – and when Myron met her he realized he had underestimated her. Introducing her to David, he simply declared: 'Hey, genius, meet your Scarlett O'Hara.' David screen-tested her and was immediately won over, remarking on her 'incredible wildness'. Whether he – or anyone else who was to live and work alongside Leigh in the coming years – was ready for the ride is another matter.

Leigh had garnered a reputation for being difficult on set and fell out with both co-star Leslie Howard and director Victor Fleming, who seemed to her only interested in portraying Scarlett as an 'out-and-out bitch'. She believed the character deserved a more nuanced interpretation, but when she sought his advice for one tricky scene, he just told her to 'ham it up'. She consulted him again about another performance detail and he responded by telling her to 'take the script and stick it up [your] royal British ass'. Whether or not these stories are true, her friend Olivia de Havilland (playing Melanie Hamilton) maintained: 'Vivien was impeccably professional, impeccably disciplined... She had two great concerns: doing her best work in an extremely difficult role and being separated from Larry.' Struggling to cope with a protracted and complicated production schedule, while also dealing with unprecedented interest from the press, left Leigh miserable. She wrote to Olivier:

> *Puss, my puss, how I hate film acting! Hate, hate, and never want to do another film again!*

The passionate relationship with her fellow actor and occasional co-star was as much a challenge as a comfort; they had met in 1937 filming *Fire Over England*, but remained married to their current partners until their divorces went through in 1940. Social decorum as well as studio publicity departments undoubtedly hampered what was by all accounts a most torrid affair. Leigh's sexual appetite was apparently insatiable; Olivier himself wrote to a friend after the couple finally married that '[she is] bloody wearing me out... it's every day, two, three times'. Before long she was flirting with others to provoke Olivier's jealousy (he was frequently unfaithful to her) and she embarked on a series of extramarital flings herself.

She also suffered from bipolar disorder, formerly known as manic depression, and it must have been almost impossible for her friends and colleagues to help her given the extraordinary (and very public) pressures of her life. For the filming of *Gone with the Wind*, Leigh was required on set for 125 days between January and September 1938, and even director Fleming had to absent himself for two weeks as a result of exhaustion. Scarlett appears on screen for 143 minutes out of a total of 238; the result earned Oscars for both of them, and vindicated Leigh's conviction that she was destined to be the film's star.

Leigh can hardly have known that the picture would become one of the most celebrated and beloved of all time, but it seems clear from her energy in every scene that she sensed it. The book ran to over a thousand pages and the movie lasts almost four hours, so there was no shortage of material with which to express herself; portraying the most epic of battles, social and political intrigue and surrounding its heroine with suitors, lovers and husbands, the story is encyclopaedic in its emotions – a gift to any actor. Almost every key moment that Leigh played is canonical and the diversity of her performance still astonishes today.

> SCARLETT
> As God is my witness, as God is my witness
> they're not going to lick me. I'm going to live
> through this and when it's all over, I'll never
> be hungry again. No, nor any of my folk. If I
> have to lie, steal, cheat or kill. As God is my
> witness, I'll never be hungry again.

With a backdrop of a flame-red sky on a desolate hillside, Scarlett's speech is one of the most acclaimed in the film and yet is the least representative of Leigh's talents; the *mise en scène* and even the performance, with her clenched fist raised, are overtly theatrical. Where Leigh excels are the moments where she quivers, explodes or turns to ice – frequently within seconds of each other. Sensibly, the camera tends to frame her upper body as well as her face, to allow her full physicality to echo her expression: it is a very different technique from the more focused close-ups of which, say, Garbo and Bergman were masters. When Scarlett climbs the staircase in the barbecue sequence, she glances down at a stranger who continues to stare at her:

> SCARLETT
> Cathleen, who's that?

> CATHLEEN
> Who?

```
            SCARLETT
That man looking at us and smiling. The nasty,
dark one.


            CATHLEEN
My dear, don't you know? That's Rhett Butler.
He's from Charleston. He has the most terrible
reputation.


            SCARLETT
He looks as if... as if he knows what I look
like without my shimmy [chemise].
```

Scarlett is, as so often, conflicted; shocked and indignant while still fascinated to discover more. The whole film depends on her ability to convey these paradoxes of longing, regret, fear and determination. Living in the moment, and acknowledging only the truth she experiences in that instant, is everything that makes Scarlett – and Leigh – so compelling. As she says herself, unaware of the irony:

```
            SCARLETT
I can shoot straight, if I don't have to shoot
too far.
```

When Rhett scandalously bids 'one hundred and fifty dollars in gold' for the first dance with the newly widowed Scarlett, the expressions that pass over her face are like a time-lapse film of a tornado; many actresses, renowned for more one-dimensional turns, would need a dozen movies to convey such a spectrum of emotion. Ultimately, the warning of the story that Mitchell, Selznick, Fleming and Leigh shaped together was that Scarlett's passion would consume her – as it did all those around her:

```
            SCARLETT
I only know that I love you.


            RHETT
That's your misfortune.
```

People think that if you look fairly reasonable you can't possibly act, and as I only care about acting I think beauty can be a great handicap.

A kiss is a lovely trick designed by nature to stop speech when words become superfluous

INGRID BERGMAN

Ingrid Bergman
29 August 1915–29 August 1982

People didn't expect me to have emotions like other women.

I was the shyest human ever invented, but I had a lion inside me that wouldn't shut up.

You must train your intuition – you must trust the small voice inside you which tells you exactly what to say, what to decide.

It is not whether you really cry. It's whether the audience thinks you are crying.

When a job is finished, relax and have fun.

Until forty-five I can play a woman in love. After fifty-five I can play grandmothers. But between those ten years, it is difficult for an actress.

Happiness is good health and a bad memory.

If you took acting away from me, I'd stop breathing.

I work so hard before the camera and on the stage that I have neither the desire nor the energy to act in my private life.

Be yourself. The world worships the original.

Today, publicizing a film star and her latest production is a pretty straightforward business. The studio tells the media they may have an interview with their leading lady on condition that the list of questions (and forbidden topics) is contractually pre-approved. The result is not so much an interview as a promotional feature in which no money – nor even interesting information – changes hands. Carefully crafted titbits of acceptable gossip are drip-fed into the media machine, and publications which refuse to toe the line are blacklisted.

By the 1930s, when the Hays Code had come into force to safeguard the morals of cinema-going audiences, the studios had already learned plenty of techniques for sanitizing their output. They persuaded their errant players to have abortions, sent them away from the public eye to be married in secret, forced them to undergo plastic surgery and elocution lessons, supplied drugs (prescribed and otherwise) and paid for rehab under the guise of rest cures. Once they had removed any whiff of scandal, they had to supply a manageable and memorable identity for marketing their protégés: The Platinum Blonde (Jean Harlow), The Sweater Girl (Lana Turner), The Peekaboo Girl (Veronica Lake), The Girl with the Curl (Mary Pickford), The Swedish Sphinx (Greta Garbo), The It Girl (Clara Bow), The First Lady of Film (Bette Davis), The Profane Angel (Carole Lombard), The Queen of Scream (Fay Wray), The Pin-Up Girl (Betty Grable) and The Million Dollar Mermaid (Esther Williams). When studio chief David O. Selznick brought twenty-three-year-old Ingrid Bergman from Sweden to appear in *Intermezzo: A Love Story* (1939), he hoped to mould her as a conventionally appealing newcomer. Unfazed by the Hollywood machine, Bergman refused all of his demands – that she change her name, cap her teeth and pluck her eyebrows – and simply threatened to return to her husband and child in Europe.

Selznick backed down, but the battles continued on set. Cinematographer Harry Stradling, who would win two Oscars and be nominated for a further twelve during his career, could not seem to make Bergman look as radiant as she had in her continental pictures. Selznick fired him and asked replacement Gregg Toland (*Wuthering Heights* (1939) and *Citizen Kane* (1941)) what the problem was. Toland said simply: 'In Sweden they don't make her wear all that make-up.' They reshot Stradling's scenes under Toland's guidance, thereby establishing the look that would make Bergman an overnight star; Selznick, turning a crisis into an opportunity, dubbed his new discovery 'The Nordic Natural' and his publicity team hurried to their typewriters to churn out a supporting script for her image.

*[Bergman] is completely unaffected and completely unique and I
should think [this] would make a grand angle of approach. . . so that
her natural sweetness and consideration and conscientiousness
become something of a legend.*

In contrast to her fellow Swede Greta Garbo, Bergman was presented not as
mysterious or aloof, but open and uncomplicated in all ways. The press was fed
stories of her unaffected lifestyle, printing such eulogies as 'she has committed
the Hollywood faux pas of being ecstatically married. . . She has no maid, no car,
doesn't own a lipstick; she likes to wash dishes, has a complexion like Shirley
Temple and bites her nails.' Her agent produced a six-page list of startlingly dull
attributes to be celebrated, including a fondness for ice cream, a penchant for
singing show tunes when alone, and the ability to 'outwalk anyone in Hollywood
in speed and distance'. Never, it seems, can a star have been conjured from so
little – aside from her innate ability to mesmerize audiences.

Intermezzo tells the story of Holger Brandt, a concert violinist (Leslie Howard
– considerably more wooden than his prized instrument), who abandons his
family when he falls in love with pianist Anita Hoffman (Bergman). The film
is gloriously sentimental, a warm bathtub of platitudes in which we are only
too happy to immerse ourselves. The yearningly romantic chamber music they
play (for close-ups, Howard's left arm was doubled by a professional musician
kneeling beside him) segues seamlessly into the passionate dialogue:

> ANITA
> What am I? Your shadow. I don't exist without
> you.

> HOLGER
> You're not a shadow. How can you talk such
> nonsense?

> ANITA
> But it's enough. Let me be with you like
> this... always.

> HOLGER
> And will that be enough always?

```
                    ANITA
          The tour is over. Now we can rest awhile. It
          has been the greatest happiness I've ever
          known... and the greatest I'll ever know. Such
          happiness couldn't come more than once in one's
          life. I know it couldn't. Could it?
```

Toland's photography is indeed spectacular and it shapes Bergman's face to perfection, allowing her to radiate a poignant bliss. She seems to exist in a world of ideals, her everyday travails falling away in the face of her tranquillity: a Mona Lisa of her time.

If *Intermezzo* brought her fame, *Casablanca* (1942) made it immortal – but despite the film's enduring success, there was little chemistry behind the scenes. Bergman and Humphrey Bogart remained indifferent to one another (not helped, apparently, by the fact that Bergman was 5′ 10″ and Bogart had to wear lifts in his shoes on camera); when actress Geraldine Fitzgerald persuaded the two to join her for lunch one day, she noted that all they talked about was 'how they could get out of that movie. They thought the dialogue was ridiculous and the situations were unbelievable.' Production was hasty and muddled; the screenwriters were still turning in fresh drafts long after shooting had begun and nobody knew right up until the filming of the last scene whether Ilsa (Bergman) would end up with Rick (Bogart) or Victor Laszlo (Paul Henreid). When Ingrid Bergman repeatedly asked director Michael Curtiz which man she loved more, he just suggested: 'Play it in between'.

> *I had no idea how I should play the character. I kept begging them to give me the ending but they'd say, 'We haven't made up our minds. We'll shoot it both ways.' We did the first ending and they said, 'That's good, we won't bother with the other.'*

Many actresses later trained under the rigours of the Method school might have baulked at this laissez-faire approach, but Bergman learned a lesson she passed onto her daughter Isabella Rossellini:

> *Keep it simple. Make a blank face, and the music and the story will fill it in.*

Once, when working with Alfred Hitchcock, she admitted: "'I don't think I can give you that kind of emotion". And [he] sat there and said, "Ingrid, fake it!" Well, that was the best advice I've had in my whole life.' This is not to say that Bergman was lazy about her performance; she was perfectly aware of the power of her gaze and she capitalized on her iconic close-ups with consummate professionalism. She favoured the left side of her face and benefited from the use of diffusion filters on the lens and supplementary lighting to add sparkle to her eyes; the latter undoubtedly allowed her to convey mood through the subtlest shifts of expression.

Howard Koch, one of several contributors to the screenplay of *Casablanca*, was surprised by the acclaim the film received, ruefully admitting that it was filled with 'more corn than in the states of Kansas and Iowa combined. But when corn works, there's nothing better.'

```
            ILSA
Kiss me. Kiss me as if it were the last time...
```

Some of Bergman's lines are as overwrought as those in *Intermezzo,* but somehow she transcends mawkishness; her talent for evoking a heartbreaking past infuses her present and future moments with an energy that words are ill-equipped to deliver.

Even so, a huge hit can occasionally prove a curse and, despite three Oscars for *Gaslight* (1944), *Anastasia* (1956) and *Murder on the Orient Express* (1974), Bergman never quite recaptured the fame *Casablanca* brought; in later life, she dismissed it coolly.

> *I made so many films which were more important, but the only one people ever want to talk about is that one with Humphrey Bogart.*

I've gone from saint to whore and back to saint again, all in one lifetime.

*No one can be
Gilda twenty-four
hours a day*

RITA
HAYWORTH

Margarita Carmen Cansino
17 October 1918–14 May 1987

I haven't had everything from life. I've had too much.

After all, a girl is. . . well, a girl. It's nice to be told you're successful at it.

All I wanted was just what everybody else wants. . . to be loved. What surprises me in life are not the marriages that fail, but the marriages that succeed.

Basically, I am a good, gentle person, but I'm attracted to mean personalities.

I think all women have a certain elegance about them which is destroyed when they take off their clothes.

I never really thought of myself as a sex goddess.

I was certainly a well-trained dancer. I'm a good actress: I have depth. I have feeling. But they don't care. All they want is the image.

Increasingly, stars are recruited from the ranks of professional models, with the result that today's starlets are better dressed and better groomed than ever before, though it is doubtful if they are better actresses.

pstaging' is an age-old theatrical tactic for stealing the audience's attention. The rake, or slope, of the stage means that the rear is higher than footlights; historically, an actor delivering an important line might move to the front – downstage – to be closer to the crowd at key moments of a performance. But ambitious actors with smaller roles soon learned that if they moved *upstage* during a dialogue with their fellow players, the others would all be forced to turn away from the audience, leaving only the 'upstager' facing the front. It is a low trick, and much frowned upon. 'Stealing the show', however, has less pejorative connotations. One can do it deliberately – as Raquel Welch is said to have done when shooting *One Million Years B.C.* (1966), when she shortened the hem of her fur skirt by a tiny amount each day – or one can simply be so compelling that one's co-stars are left trailing in one's wake. There can be no better feeling for an actor, and audiences love to witness it. When Rita Hayworth played an aviator's wife in Howard Hawks's production of *Only Angels Have Wings* (1939), her presence was so electrifying that even Cary Grant seemed unable to take his eyes off her.

Born Margarita Carmen Cansino in Brooklyn, New York, in 1918, Hayworth was the daughter of two dancers who were only too keen to see her take to the stage.

> As soon as I could stand on my own feet, I was given dance lessons. . .
> I didn't like it very much, but I didn't have the courage to tell my
> father. Rehearse, rehearse, rehearse, that was my girlhood.

Her first turn on screen came at the age of eight; the following year, the family moved to Los Angeles where her Spanish father guessed a burgeoning film industry would be eager to discover new talent. He was right: between 1934 and 1939 Hayworth appeared in thirty films, mostly in minor roles, although the titles themselves suggest the nature of the work: *Charlie Chan in Egypt* (1935), *Under the Pampas Moon* (1935), *Dancing Pirate* (1936) and *Hit the Saddle* (1937). Her Latin features were not conspicuous, but for Hollywood exotic meant foreign, and directors had her play Russians and Egyptians as well as Argentines and Mexicans. (The tendency towards unlikely casting endured for decades, most bizarrely with Mickey Rooney as the Japanese Mr Yunioshi in *Breakfast at Tiffany's* (1961) and Alec Guinness as the Arab Prince Faisal in *Lawrence of Arabia* (1962).)

In 1937 Columbia's president Harry Cohn offered Hayworth a seven-year contract and immediately broached the subject of her looks. Specifically, he wanted her to have electrolysis to raise her hairline and broaden her forehead, and to dye her hair a dark red. She signed, and the transformation was astonishing – imagine Jennifer Lopez disappearing for a month and returning as Julianne Moore; Cohn even made the make-over a shameless aspect of his marketing strategy. Having invested in a new star, he set out to find a suitable vehicle to showcase her reinvention.

Howard Hawks's *Only Angels Have Wings* (1939) tells the story of Geoff Carter (Cary Grant) heading up a troupe of gung-ho pilots on a treacherous mail route through remote South American mountains where the only things trickier than the flying and the weather are the women who pitch up in the local bar. One day Judy MacPherson (Hayworth) walks in with her airman husband, who does not know she was formerly married to Geoff. Later, Judy visits Geoff alone in his office:

                    JUDY
  Busy?

She closes the door and leans against it.

                    JUDY
  Do you like my hair this way?

                    GEOFF
  I thought it was different.

                    JUDY
  I could hardly believe my eyes. I had no idea
  that you...

                    GEOFF
  Pretty small world. Hello Judy.

He kisses her on the lips. She holds his gaze.

                    JUDY
  I'm not sure you should have done that.

If any woman's middle name was trouble it is Judy, as volatile as the nitroglycerine cargo in her husband's plane. She is demure, yet she smoulders; she gives nothing away, but everything is to play for. Later in the movie she flirts more overtly with Geoff, but he spurns her drunken advances and reprimands her for turning her back on her new husband:

```
                    GEOFF
      Did you ever hear the word 'trust'?


                    JUDY
      I did once, but I forgot it.
```

Hayworth is shameless, with a pout that could bring ordinary mortals to their knees, and her ardour is only cooled when Geoff pours a jug of water over her head – at which point every man in the audience must have been shouting, 'If you won't have her, I will!' Within weeks she was inundated with fan mail from admirers of both sexes, and Cohn had his new star. Director Rouben Mamoulian was one of the first to note her intense physical presence: 'Hayworth moved better than anyone else I have ever seen in film. The camera responded to her movement as it did to Garbo's intelligence and Chaplin's mime.'

As an icon, Hayworth had few peers. She appeared on the front cover of *Time* magazine seven times, and her name was inscribed on one of the atomic bombs detonated in 1946 in the Bikini Atoll. Countless US troops cherished her as a pin-up during the Second World War and one publicity photo was even discovered in an abandoned trapper's hut in the far Canadian wilderness. She provided the inspiration for Jessica Rabbit's lissom curves and sultry voice in *Who Framed Roger Rabbit* (1988) and her poster hid Tim Robbins's escape route in *The Shawshank Redemption* (1994). In 1943 she married Orson Welles (but soon divorced him, claiming 'I can't take his genius any more') and then, in 1949, Prince Aly Khan, son of the Aga Khan. Ultimately her convoluted love life compromised her stellar trajectory (she barrelled through five husbands in twenty-one years, three of whom abused her and squandered her money), but not before she had consolidated her reputation with Charles Vidor's noir classic *Gilda* (1946). Reprising her role as a wife – the eponymous Gilda – unexpectedly reunited with her ex-husband, Hayworth here burns an even bigger hole in the celluloid than she had done in *Only Angels Have Wings*. This was a much larger part and she exploits it to the full: her overt sexuality is matched only by her dancing, the costumes and the unforgettable dialogue. In a glorious nod to the audience's expectations, when Gilda's husband Ballin Mundson (George Macready) knocks at the door of her boudoir, she welcomes him with a purr:

```
                MUNDSON
     Gilda, are you decent?

                GILDA
     Me?
```

The subsequent shot reveals Hayworth in a thousand-dollar gown and a million-dollar smile, tossing her long hair coquettishly. She knew just what the public wanted; when asked once what held Gilda's famous strapless dress up, she replied, 'two things'. But nothing could capture her fiery intensity better than the scene where she confronts her former spouse, Johnny Farrell (Glenn Ford):

```
                GILDA
     You do hate me, don't you, Johnny?

                JOHNNY
     I don't think you have any idea of how much.

                GILDA
     Hate is a very exciting emotion. Haven't you
     noticed? Very exciting. I hate you too, Johnny.
     I hate you so much I think I'm going to die
     from it. Darling...

They kiss passionately.

                GILDA
     I think I'm going to die from it.
```

It remains one of the most memorable kisses in cinema history, although Hayworth later remembered it with a wistful regret:

Every man I have ever known has fallen in love with Gilda and awakened with me.

Sensitive, shy – of course I was. The fun of acting is to become someone else.

THE
CLASSICS

KATHARINE HEPBURN

JANE RUSSELL

LAUREN BACALL

TALLULAH BANKHEAD

JOAN CRAWFORD

AVA GARDNER

LANA TURNER

DEBORAH KERR

ELIZABETH TAYLOR

GRACE KELLY

AUDREY HEPBURN

JUDY GARLAND

KIM NOVAK

BRIGITTE BARDOT

JEANNE MOREAU

MARILYN MONROE

*I don't know
what it is, but
whatever it is,
I've got it*

KATHARINE
HEPBURN

Katharine Houghton Hepburn
12 May 1907–29 June 2003

I'm a personality as well as an actress. Show me an actress who isn't a personality, and you'll show me a woman who isn't a star.

I strike people as peculiar in some way, although I don't quite understand why. Of course, I have an angular face, an angular body and, I suppose, an angular personality, which jabs into people.

I welcome death. In death there are no interviews.

Once a crowd chased me for an autograph. 'Beat it,' I said, 'go sit on a tack!' 'We made you,' they said. 'Like hell you did,' I told them.

I find a woman's point of view much grander and finer than a man's.

Plain women know more about men than beautiful ones do.

If you want to sacrifice the admiration of many men for the criticism of one, go ahead, get married.

Life's what's important. Walking, houses, family. Birth and pain and joy. Acting's just waiting for a custard pie. That's all.

odie Foster keeps them in her study, Juliette Binoche prefers hers in the bathroom and Cate Blanchett chooses the living room (on her piano). Katharine Hepburn, the only actress ever to win four Oscars in a leading role, once stumbled across the statuette she won for *The Lion in Winter* (1968), in which she played one of her direct forebears Queen Eleanor of Aquitaine, at the bottom of an old paper bag in her shoe closet.

Hepburn had two magnificent careers: one as a contracted player to her studio, and one – even more impressive – entirely on her own terms. Tall, elegant, smart and uncompromising, blue-blooded and nobody's fool, she compelled and baffled in equal measure. If one tiny detail can suggest an entire personality, try this: she said she performed her own stunts not because she enjoyed it, but because none of her stand-ins ever showed good enough posture. Her disdain for the industry matched her penchant for good manners and discretion: she never once attended the Academy Awards in all the years she was nominated.

Born into a well-to-do liberal family, Hepburn was encouraged to be healthy, to think for herself and to speak her mind. As she noted towards the end of her career, 'I never realized until lately that women were supposed to be inferior'. Appearing in student plays at the prestigious Bryn Mawr College confirmed her desire to perform – 'I always wanted to be a movie actress. I thought it was very romantic. And it was' – but her early years on stage were tough going. Fired from a number of productions for turning up late and fumbling her lines, she sought the advice of drama teachers and voice coaches but the poor notices continued: 'She looks a fright, her manner is objectionable, and she has no talent.' But perseverance was another feature of the Hepburn family ethos, and before long she enjoyed her first proper success on Broadway with *The Warrior's Husband* (1932).

Hollywood took notice, and she was quickly signed by RKO after some tricky negotiations about the appropriate salary for a new face. Hepburn stuck out for an astonishing $1,500 [$25,000] a week – and won. But if that was a result of her sheer chutzpah, her next step was pure luck: she was cast in *A Bill of Divorcement* (1932), to be directed by George Cukor. In his autobiography he recalled: 'There was this odd creature... she was unlike anybody I'd ever heard'. Her voice, as much as her classical beauty and her dignified bearing, was to become one of her hallmarks and she would collaborate with Cukor on many great pictures in the future, including *Little Women* (1933), *Holiday* (1938) and *Adam's Rib* (1949).

In the meantime, she would have to content herself with the headline in the *Hollywood Reporter*: 'a new star on the cinema horizon'.

Hits such as *Morning Glory* (1933) and *Stage Door* (1937) brought her increasing success and wealth, but neither Hollywood nor her audiences could quite get a handle on what kind of star she really was. Her life then, and later, was filled with delightful paradoxes, all of which seemed to make perfect sense to her, if to nobody else. She was brazen, refusing to wear make-up or skirts; she once paraded around the studio lot in her underwear until the costume department returned the trousers they had stolen from her dressing room. She was tender, declining to attend the funeral of her long-time lover Spencer Tracy in order to allow his family to mourn without a media frenzy. She was snobbish, persuading her first husband Ludlow Ogden Smith to change his name to S. Ogden Ludlow on the grounds that there was already a frumpy radio star by the name of Katharine Smith – and that she could not bear to take such a dull surname. She disliked photo shoots and interviews, earning herself the moniker 'Katharine of Arrogance'. Though she enjoyed sticking to her guns, she was heading for a fall.

Hepburn longed to balance her screen career with more frequent theatre appearances, perhaps keen to prove to herself that she could transcend her early disappointments on stage. In 1933 she signed up for the lead role in *The Lake* by Dorothy Massingham and Murray MacDonald. It opened in Washington DC and was greeted by one of the most damning reviews in show-business history when critic and wit Dorothy Parker wrote: 'Katharine Hepburn runs the gamut of emotions from A to B.' Back in Hollywood, she later lobbied David O. Selznick for the part of Scarlett O'Hara in *Gone with the Wind* (1939), but he deemed her not sexy enough, claiming: 'I can't see Rhett Butler chasing you for twelve years.' If her family had taught her forbearance, Hepburn would need it in abundance now.

Studio producers, who had become adept in marketing their players, still had no clue what to do with this troublesome figure. So long as the hits continued, they just had to sit back and let her be. . . Hepburn. But the power wielded by stars was to prove a double-edged sword; the higher they flew, the easier it became for the PR and accounting departments to track the bottom line of cinema receipts. When Harry Brandt, an outspoken member of the Independent Theater Owners of America, wrote an open letter in 1938 entitled 'Dead Cats', he cited Hepburn as 'Box Office Poison' – along with Greta Garbo, Mae West, Fred Astaire and John Barrymore. RKO seized the opportunity to reassert its control, but when it offered Hepburn the patently demeaning *Mother Carey's Chickens* she baulked and paid $75,000 [$1.25m] to buy herself out of her contract. Professionally insulted, publicly panned, and now bewildered, Hepburn did what she did best: she turned her back and walked away.

> *They say I'm a has-been. If I weren't laughing so hard, I might cry.*

Though the remark sounds like a parting shot, it was actually the opening line of the greatest second act in cinema history. Hardened – and sharpened – by her recent setbacks, Hepburn's eye for material was now shrewder; she took the role of socialite Tracy Lord in the 1939 theatre debut of *The Philadelphia Story*, which Philip Barry had written for her. Fast-forward. . . she was perfect in it, and it was perfect for her; it was a huge smash; her lover Howard Hughes bought the rights for her as a present; she returned to Hollywood and sold the play to MGM for $250,000 [$4.25m] – on condition she had absolute creative control. Roll camera. . .

Directed by Hepburn's long-time friend and collaborator George Cukor, the film is one of the most exquisite romantic comedies ever committed to celluloid. It showcased every talent Hepburn had always wanted to display, and it did so on her own terms. Before production started, she had confessed: 'I don't want to make a grand entrance in this picture. Moviegoers think I'm too la-di-da or something. A lot of people want to see me fall flat on my face.' Gracious (and perceptive) as ever, she gave her audience exactly what they desired. In the very first scene, on the porch of the grandest house imaginable and in a dress to match, Tracy Lord is knocked flat on her ass in a comic tussle with her ex-husband (played by Cary Grant). The rest of the story – in which three very different men (Grant as C. K. Dexter Haven, James Stewart as Macaulay 'Mike' Connor and John Howard as George Kittredge) woo the prim, rich Tracy – unfolds in a seamless cascade of witticisms, misunderstandings and yearnings in a brilliantly moving and modern journey of self-discovery for all concerned. No confection was ever so magical, no cast so perfectly united – but Hepburn is the movie, and the movie is Hepburn.

MACAULAY
It can't be anything like love, can it?

> TRACY
> No, no, it can't be.

> MACAULAY
> Would it be inconvenient?

> TRACY
> Terribly.

Her formal reserve is softened by the men circling her and her glamorous façade soon begins to crack:

> GEORGE
> You're like some marvelous, distant, well, queen, I guess. You're so cool and fine and always so much your own. There's a kind of beautiful purity about you, Tracy, like a statue.

> TRACY
> George...

> GEORGE
> Oh, it's grand, Tracy. It's what everybody feels about you. It's what I first worshipped you for from afar.

> TRACY
> I don't want to be worshipped. I want to be loved.

If ever a star was (re)born, it was in this moment. We adore her, we forgive her everything we misunderstood in her, and we realize that the real Hepburn had been there all along. Despite a career studded with sixteen Oscar nominations as well as four wins, she had only one regret:

> *With all the opportunities I had, I could have done more. And if I'd done more, I could have been quite remarkable.*

Who is Katharine Hepburn? It took me a long time to create that creature.

*'What are the
two reasons for
Jane Russell's rise
to stardom?'*

JANE

RUSSELL

Ernestine Jane Geraldine Russell
21 June 1921–28 February 2011

Publicity can be terrible. But only if you don't have any.

All it was about was some cleavage! Today they're doing cleavage in the back.

I like a man who can run faster than I can.

They held up [the release of] *The Outlaw*. . . And Howard Hughes had me doing publicity for it every day, five days a week for five years.

I learned that without [Christian] faith I'd do anything that came into my head. And a lot can come into my head.

Not so much an icon as a purely man-made object, Jane Russell hit cinema screens like a bolt from the blue. Everything about her impact was manipulated: her physique, her publicity and even her viewers themselves. The unwilling co-stars in the story are Russell's natural endowments, and the villain Howard Hughes – oil millionaire, aviation genius and movie mogul. His infatuation with statuesque starlets and his adolescent lasciviousness combined to reach their joint apex (no pun intended) in the furore surrounding *The Outlaw* (1943).

The film itself is an unmemorable Western with Russell playing Rio, the two-dimensional love interest. The most famous anecdote about the production recounts that Hughes had noticed the bra Russell wore created unsightly wrinkles in her tight blouse, so he called together his team of aircraft designers and announced: 'Time for another engineering feat – the world's first cantilevered brassiere.' A complex arrangement of steel rods connected to the shoulder straps reputedly allowed the largest possible area of permissible cleavage to be displayed, although the device was hardly revolutionary since the first patent for an underwired bra had been filed in 1863. Russell found the contraption 'ridiculously uncomfortable' and discarded it in favour of the time-honoured solution of tissue paper to pad the cups of her own brassiere: 'He never knew. He wasn't going to take my clothes off to check if I had it on. I just told him I did.' The entire rigmarole was unnecessary in any case since the camera crew had plenty of tricks of its own: 'Sometimes the photographers would pose me in a low-necked nightgown and tell me to bend down and pick up the pails. They were not shooting the pails.'

The film took three years to complete, but the buzz started early. Introducing his new star to the press, Hughes played the rags-to-riches card claiming that he had discovered Russell working as a dental assistant, although she later confessed she had simply been spotted by an agent while she was having her photograph taken. The poster for the film's release was aimed well below the belt, with Russell ('Mean, Moody, Magnificent!') lying in a hay barn with the caption 'How Would You Like to Tussle With Russell?' Inevitably, the real tussle proved to be with Joseph Breen of the Motion Picture Producers and Distributors of America, responsible for enforcing the moral code agreed upon by Hollywood studios, who wrote: 'In my more than ten years of critical examination of motion pictures, I have never seen anything quite so unacceptable... In the picture the girl's breasts, which are quite large and prominent, are shockingly emphasized'.

At least Hughes knew he had successfully established Russell's credentials. One step ahead of Breen, he had slyly briefed his publicists to whip up a frenzy among women's clubs and church groups, warning them that the film was deeply provocative, so that when Breen allowed the picture to be released (after cutting the most flagrant sequences) the film was already in the headlines. It ran for a week before being shut down, but its uncensored re-release in 1946 more than sated the public's desire for a risqué spectacle and turned Hughes a handsome profit.

Unsurprisingly, Russell's career never really had a chance to develop. She was voted the country's most popular star long before most people had actually seen her on screen, and despite a couple of hits with *The Paleface* (1948) and *Double Dynamite* (1951) she never found a director who understood how to reconcile her public image with her acting abilities. Only in *Gentlemen Prefer Blondes* (1953), playing Dorothy, the cool, pragmatic foil to Marilyn Monroe's ditzy Lorelei, did she find a role in which she could be smart, charming and self-assured:

```
Lorelei is holding a tiara.

            LORELEI
    How do you put it around your neck?

            DOROTHY
    You don't, honey, it goes on your head.

            LORELEI
    You must think I was born yesterday.

            DOROTHY
    Well, sometimes there's just no other possible
    explanation.
```

The film offered a frustratingly brief glimpse of what Russell might have been had her reputation not, as it were, preceded her. Sadly, not even *The New York Times* could resist a final swipe as it grudgingly recognized her charisma:

Call it inherent magnetism. Call it luxurious coquetry. Call it whatever you fancy. It's what makes this a – well, a buoyant show.

Sex appeal is good — but not in bad taste. Then it's ugly. I don't think a star has any business posing in a vulgar way.

I am not a
has-been.
I am a will be

LAUREN
BACALL

Betty Joan Perske
16 September 1924–12 August 2014

I was this flat-chested,
big-footed, lanky thing.

Stardom isn't a profession, it's
an accident.

Patience was not my strong
point.

The big rule is that you must
never get mixed up with a
married man – never even
look sideways at another
woman's fella. Boy, I really
was terrific at obeying that
rule, wasn't I?

I put my career in second
place throughout both my
marriages and it suffered.
I don't regret it. . . You can't
have it all.

We live in an age of
mediocrity. Stars today are
not the same stature as Bogie,
James Cagney, Spencer Tracy,
Henry Fonda and Jimmy
Stewart.

A legend involves the past.

A woman isn't complete
without a man. But where do
you find a man – a real man
– these days?

T o *Have and Have Not* (1944) – based on a novel by Nobel Prize winner Ernest Hemingway, co-written for the screen by Nobel Prize winner William Faulkner, directed by Oscar winner Howard Hawks and starring Oscar winner Humphrey Bogart – looked to be a hit from the moment the clapperboard snapped shut. All the producers needed was an irresistible leading lady. Ava Gardner? Rita Hayworth? Lana Turner? Nope. Instead, Hawks cast nineteen-year-old Lauren Bacall, who had appeared in. . . precisely nothing.

Bacall had taken a few modest roles on Broadway before appearing on the cover of *Harper's Bazaar* in March 1943. The image is now considered iconic and it caught the eye of Hawks's wife Nancy, a glamorous and well-connected socialite. She suggested that Bacall should be screen-tested; Hawks immediately adored her, signed her to a modest contract and left it to Nancy to refine their protégé's dress sense, style and manners. Bacall's trademark sultry voice was the result of hours of coaching to lower its pitch, but both Nancy and Howard knew which parts of Bacall to leave well alone: her feline grace and her sexual confidence. All that remained now was to see if their creation would really play on the big screen. Bacall recalls one key moment of the shoot: 'My hand was shaking, my head was shaking, the cigarette was shaking, I was mortified. The harder I tried to stop, the more I shook. I realized that one way to hold my trembling head still was to keep it down, chin low, almost to my chest, and eyes up at Bogart. It worked and turned out to be the beginning of The Look.'

The Look was only one of her distinctive qualities. Apart from being drop-dead gorgeous, she was smart, sassy and super-cool. Bogart had been Hollywood's go-to bad guy for several years now and was not used to coming second best to anyone, but Bacall had him wrapped around her perfectly manicured little finger before their first scene was in the can. He later described her as 'steel with curves', which translated roughly as 'I am insanely in love with this woman'. Bacall returned the compliment by confessing: 'Was he tough? In a word, no. Bogey was truly a gentle soul.' The dialogue between them is an endless stream of zingers, but Bacall leads the dance when she kisses Steve:

```
                    STEVE
          What did you do that for?


                    SLIM
          I've been wondering if I'd like it.
```

```
                    STEVE
          What's the decision?

                    SLIM
          I don't know yet.
```

Later – after another embrace that must have melted the camera lens – the couple flirts as Slim prepares to leave Steve's room. She turns back:

```
                    SLIM
          I liked that, except for the beard. Why don't
          you shave it and we —
```

```
She slaps his cheek playfully.
```

```
                    SLIM
          — we'll try again.
```

The effect on Bogart – and on us – is electrifying. Our first thought is surely that if Ingrid Bergman as Ilsa in *Casablanca* (1942) had tried slapping him, he would have punched her right back. It goes without saying that in the following scene between them Bogart's cheeks are smoother than silk, but the extraordinary thing is that his character does not seem weak or in any way diminished – just utterly in thrall to her. Richard Brody of the *New Yorker* summed it up perfectly:

> *Hawks filmed tough women because he filmed tough men; he invented female characters to knock his leading men down in a way that other men couldn't.*

It is one of the greatest on-screen romances ever portrayed and nobody was more delighted than the American public to discover that the couple were to be married – and stayed so until Bogart's death in 1957. Bacall went on to make many other acclaimed movies, including *The Big Sleep* (1946), *Key Largo* (1948) and *How to Marry a Millionaire* (1953), but few can have been such a thrill for her as her first. As Bogart said during rehearsals:

> *I think we're going to have a lot of fun making this picture, kid.*

I think your whole life shows in your face and you should be proud of that.

*Say anything about
me, darling, as long
as it isn't boring*

TALLULAH
BANKHEAD

Tallulah Brockman Bankhead
31 January 1902–12 December 1968

[on seeing a former lover
for the first time in years]
I thought I told you to wait
in the car.

I read Shakespeare and the
Bible, and I can shoot dice.
That's what I call a liberal
education.

The only thing I regret about
my past is the length of it.
If I had to live my life again,
I'd make the same mistakes,
only sooner.

Acting is a form of confusion.

I have three phobias which,
could I mute them, would
make my life as slick as a
sonnet, but as dull as ditch
water – I hate to go to bed,
I hate to get up, and I hate to
be alone.

I'm the foe of moderation,
the champion of excess.

I want to try everything once.

I've played *Private Lives*
everywhere except
underwater.

Here's a rule I recommend.
Never practice two vices
at once.

For an actress so celebrated that she was cited 'first choice among established stars' to play Scarlett O'Hara in *Gone with the Wind* (1939) by its producer David O. Selznick, the most glorious thing about Tallulah Bankhead's career is that she didn't give a damn about it. Despite a fondness for performing (she claimed her earliest appearance was at a private party for the aviators the Wright brothers, where she improvised a skit lampooning her kindergarten teacher), she wanted only to live life to the fullest – and soon realized that a fee of $50,000 [$750,000] per film was the perfect way to support her heedless, decadent pursuits.

Bankhead was born into a powerful political family in Alabama, and her father (later to be chosen as Speaker of the House of Representatives) spotted her as trouble from an early age and packed her off to a Catholic boarding school. At this stage she showed no sign of her later svelte good looks; somewhat overweight, she was described as 'an extremely homely child'. But she had been bitten by the acting bug, and as she began to blossom as a teenager she won a prize in a movie magazine contest. Amazingly, she persuaded her parents to let her move to New York, where she began to be offered bit parts in off-Broadway shows; within a year – aged sixteen – she was playing fully credited roles. Her penchant for the high life and her reputation as a wickedly lively companion were equally quickly established; she became a member of the celebrated Algonquin Round Table, a literary salon whose luminaries included writers Robert Benchley, George S. Kaufman and Dorothy Parker, as well as Harpo Marx and editor of the *New Yorker,* Harold Ross. Her quick tongue was welcome there – and doubtless also at the increasingly libertine parties she was reputed to be hosting. She remarked at the time that:

> *My father warned me about men and booze, but he never mentioned*
> *a word about women and cocaine.*

She later added: 'Cocaine isn't habit-forming. . . I know because I've been taking it for years.'

She continued to support herself through stage work before moving to London in 1923, where she established herself as a true leading lady. Her new-found acclaim did nothing to change her view of her profession as merely a congenial and convenient way to earn her pay cheques; on the opening night of *Conchita*, her co-star – a monkey – snatched her wig and cavorted about the stage brandishing his trophy. Bankhead simply joined in the fun, performing cartwheels until the thief was captured; she earned a standing ovation.

As in New York, her reputation soon extended beyond the stage door; she bought a Bentley but had an extremely poor sense of navigation, so she frequently had to hail a black cab and follow it to her destination. Her charming eccentricities did occasionally overstep the mark; recently released MI5 files detail allegations that she enjoyed underage lovers, especially those with good pedigree.

> *The charge against Miss Tallulah Bankhead (an American aged twenty-six) is quite simply (a) that she is an extremely immoral woman and (b) that in consequence of her association with some Eton boys last term, the latter have had to leave the school. As regards (a) according to [our] informant, she is both a Lesbian and immoral with men. [Our] informant believes she comes from a respectable American family, her father, a senator, having turned her out of the house when she was young owing to immoral proclivities.*

Whether or not the titled schoolboys in question would have considered the afternoons they spent with this charming star of the theatre to be 'indecent and unnatural' we shall never know; Eton's headmaster adroitly quashed any proper inquiry, admitting only that several boys had been expelled for 'riding in a car'.

Luckily for the reputation of England's landed gentry, Bankhead was lured back to America in 1931 to try her hand at films – although she found the experience disappointing. Meeting producer Irving Thalberg, she expressed her frustration: 'How do you get laid in this dreadful place?' The mogul replied: 'I'm sure you'll have no problem. Ask anyone.' In 1932, despite the fact that she had still not appeared in any notable pictures, her fame was sufficient to ensure that when playing a cameo role as herself in *Make Me a Star* – alongside such legends as Gary Cooper, Maurice Chevalier and Claudette Colbert – she still received top billing. Dismissive as ever, she later admitted: 'the main reason I accepted [the part] was to fuck that divine Gary Cooper'.

Her sexual appetite had already been widely acknowledged, but now it seems she did not even take the trouble to be discreet about it in a very public – and prurient – industry. As with Mae West, her comments became her trademark:

> *It's the good girls who keep diaries; the bad girls never have the time.*

> *I'm as pure as the driven slush.*

I've tried several varieties of sex, all of which I hate. Going down on a woman gives me a stiff neck, going down on a man gives me lockjaw and conventional sex gives me claustrophobia.

I'll come and make love to you at five o'clock. If I'm late, start without me.

In her thirties she began to notice that her lifestyle might not be the healthiest, not least because she admitted to smoking seven packs of cigarettes every day. She told a friend that her doctor had suggested she eat an apple every time she was tempted to have a drink; her reply was succinct: 'But really, darling, sixty apples a day?' When she narrowly escaped death after an emergency hysterectomy necessitated by a severe case of gonorrhoea, she thanked the surgeon who had saved her life with the parting remark: 'Don't think this has taught me a lesson!'

She made a modest total of only eight pictures during the 1930s, but the self-indulgent lifestyle continued at full pace; her parties were reputed to have 'no boundaries', and when she started to tally her lovers for her autobiography, she claims she reached 185 before she was interrupted by the doorbell.

I've had many momentary love affairs. A lot of these impromptu romances have been climaxed in a fashion not generally condoned. I go into them impulsively. I scorn any notion of their permanence. I forget the fever associated with them when a new interest presents itself.

Some said her overtly sexual behaviour began to grow tiresome (she would frequently disrobe at parties just to jolly things along) and others claimed she never received as much pleasure as she gave. Whether or not this is true, her career began to slump as her excesses – particularly her drinking – continued to grow. Despite the fact that her first love was the theatre, she began to receive lousy reviews, most notably for her title role in *Antony and Cleopatra* when *New York Evening Post* critic John Mason Brown wrote: 'Tallulah Bankhead barged down the Nile last night as Cleopatra – and sank.'

But in 1944, aged forty-two, she was offered the role of Connie Porter in Alfred Hitchcock's *Lifeboat*. Stranded in the Atlantic after their warship is torpedoed, a party of survivors shares the small craft with Willy (Walter Slezak), the captain of the German U-boat which attacked them. The role was perfectly suited for Bankhead, playing to her callous, arch glamour while subverting it with glimpses of fear and neediness. As always, Hitchcock was probing the character of his actors just as much as he was exploring their story, but the result is Bankhead's finest screen moment and the only film of hers which endures.

Willy fixes Connie's diamond bracelet.

                    WILLY
Looks like bits of ice.

                    CONNIE
I wish they were.

                    WILLY
They're really nothing but a few pieces of
carbon crystallized under high pressure at
great heat.

                    CONNIE
Quite so, if you want to be scientific about it.

                    WILLY
I'm a great believer in science.

                    CONNIE
Like tears, for instance. They're nothing but
H2O with a trace of sodium chloride.

Even here, though, her controversial behaviour could not be contained. Climbing the stepladder into the studio-built lifeboat each morning, she seemed keen to prove to the stagehands that she never wore underwear. When the matter was referred to the director, he simply shrugged and suggested he was unsure whether the issue should be dealt with by the costume or the hairdressing department. Marlon Brando later lamented that Bankhead had never had a chance to show her true talent – and that she could have been a fine actress had she not chosen her twin gods of sex and alcohol. Remaining true to herself, unrepentant and seemingly unsated, Bankhead's dying words were simply:

Codeine. . . Bourbon. . .

Nobody can be
exactly like me.
Even I have trouble
doing it.

Don't fuck with me, fellas. This cowgirl has been to the rodeo before

JOAN CRAWFORD

Lucille Fay LeSueur
23 March 23 1904–10 May 1977

I need sex for a clear complexion, but I'd rather do it for love.

I think the most important thing a woman can have – next to talent, of course – is her hairdresser.

Women's Lib? Poor little things. They always look so unhappy. Have you noticed how bitter their faces are?

Send me flowers while I'm alive. They won't do me a damn bit of good after I'm dead.

If I can't be me, I don't want to be anybody.

You have to be self-reliant and strong to survive in this town. Otherwise you will be destroyed.

I love playing bitches. There's a lot of bitch in every woman – and a lot in every man.

Nobody can imitate me.

Damn it. . . Don't you dare ask God to help me.

n the early years of the twentieth century, the new-fangled theories of Sigmund Freud were making their way into the most fashionable books and films, and it can be tempting to apply homespun psychology to the career of Joan Crawford, crowned 'Queen of the Movies' by *Life* magazine in 1937. Celebrated but reviled, exuberant yet heartless, beautiful but bitter, she polarized those around her, just as she led a life of extraordinary extremes. She even had two bites at the cherry of fame, with a wave of success in the silent era and a renaissance in the 1940s. But as screenwriter Frederica Sagor Maas (*Flesh and the Devil*, 1926) observed: 'No one decided to make Joan Crawford a star. Joan Crawford became a star because Joan Crawford decided to become a star.'

Born Lucille Fay LeSueur in 1904 or 1905, her drive was evident from the very beginning. Her stepfather ran a local opera house, something of a curiosity in Lawton, Oklahoma, and Crawford was drawn to the theatre. As a child she jumped out of a window to avoid her weekly piano lesson and cut her foot so badly she had to miss a year of school and suffer three operations. Told she would never walk properly again, she forced herself to dance every day until she conquered the pain. Returning to school, she found herself in the hands of a vicious teacher who beat her and forced her to do housework instead of studying; she forged Crawford's grades to cover up for her absences.

> I never had any close friends. I was 'different' because my mother wasn't a very good seamstress, so my dresses were always too long or too short. I yearned to be famous, just to make the kids who had laughed at me feel foolish.

There is plenty of material for any shrink's couch here, and Crawford was perfectly candid about her demons. She helped her mother run the local laundry, but was terrified that her classmates could smell the chemicals on her; she cultivated a lifelong habit of frequent showers (never baths) and scrupulous cleanliness:

> I used to wash my hands every ten minutes. I couldn't step out of the house unless I had gloves on. I wouldn't smoke a cigarette unless I opened the pack myself, and I would never use another cigarette out of that pack if someone else had touched it.

She married four times and every time she took a new husband she changed the name of the Hollywood estate where they lived and replaced all the lavatory seats. Indeed, her 1962 autobiography, *A Portrait of Joan*, reveals considerably less about show business than it does about sewing and food storage. Obsessive compulsions notwithstanding, she found work as a chorus girl in the Midwest and then in New York, but her ambition still outpaced her opportunities; canny and persistent, she befriended a publicity agent who agreed to arrange a screen test with MGM. She arrived in Hollywood in 1925, signed to a salary of $75 [$1,000] a week. Renamed Joan Crawford as a result of a national competition, Lucille LeSueur had arrived.

After a year of uncredited roles, she grew frustrated. Determined to boost her profile, she started entering dance competitions and won several prizes. Finally, MGM began to pay her closer attention. Her profile as romantic co-lead grew but in 1928 she hit pay dirt as Diana Medford in *Our Dancing Daughters*. The flapper craze was at its height, and Crawford's skills with the Charleston and the Black Bottom were ready to thrill the public. The film starts with a close-up of her feet shimmying as she dresses in front of a triple mirror. Frilly undergarments slide up impeccable legs until the camera reveals the hem of a sequinned dress that leaves virtually nothing to the imagination; an opulent fur coat complete the sequence, perfectly crowning the arrival of a new star. *The New York Mirror* wrote 'Joan Crawford. . . does the greatest work of her career', and even the Jazz era's pre-eminent novelist F. Scott Fitzgerald declared:

> *Crawford is doubtless the best example of the flapper, the girl you see in smart night clubs, gowned to the apex of sophistication, toying iced glasses with a remote, faintly bitter expression, dancing deliciously, laughing a great deal, with wide, hurt eyes.*

Real life, however, proved less of a fairy tale. Although Crawford married the dashing Douglas Fairbanks Jr in 1929, his mother dismissed her as 'a chorus girl fling'. The comment cut deep, and doubtless rekindled much of her childhood fears:

> *I was always an outsider. I was never good enough. Not for the Fairbanks tribe, not for Louis B. Mayer, not for so-called film society.*

Even her frequent casting as that audience favourite, 'the hard-working young woman who finds romance and success', seemed to reinforce the feeling that she was out of her league. But the social challenge had one unexpected benefit:

Crawford decided to work on her elocution. 'I would lock myself in my room and read newspapers, magazines and books aloud. At my elbow I kept a dictionary. When I came to a word I did not know how to pronounce, I looked it up and repeated it correctly fifteen times'. She learned to shed her strong Southern accent just in time for the transition to 'talking pictures', an upheaval which saw many stars fade as microphones revealed their less-than-mellow tones. *Our Blushing Brides* (1930), *Paid* (1930) and a trio of movies with Clark Gable propelled her to still greater heights, and yet with great courtesy she spent two days a week replying personally to her endless stream of fan mail.

> *If you're going to be a star, you have to look like a star, and I never go out unless I look like Joan Crawford the movie star. If you want to see the girl next door, go next door.*

Whether this remark constituted professionalism, good manners, bitchiness or simply amour propre is unclear. But when Crawford's success faltered in 1937 with a handful of underperforming pictures, she – along with Greta Garbo, Marlene Dietrich, Mae West, Katharine Hepburn, Fred Astaire and John Barrymore – was shunned by a powerful cabal of distributors as 'Box Office Poison'. Times and tastes were changing all too fast in an already capricious industry. Good roles dried up, reinforcing the problem, but Crawford's drive – inseparable from her ego, as Freud might have pointed out – ensured that when she was offered a fresh start with Warner Brothers she declined their first script, firmly reminding her new bosses that 'Joan Crawford never dies in her movies, and she never ever loses her man to anyone'.

Luckily, her nerves of steel held. In 1945 she took the eponymous lead role in *Mildred Pierce*, a film that overturned her previous screen persona and allowed her to reinvent herself as an emotionally complex woman fighting to survive amid a maelstrom of betrayal and heartache. She was delighted by the project:

> *The character I played was a composite of the characters I'd always played, and there were a few elements from my own personality and character, too. . . It rescued me from what was known at MGM as the Joan Crawford formula.*

Mildred first appears at night on a rain-swept pier with a tear-streaked face, preparing to end her life in the ink-black ocean.

```
        COP
What's on your mind, lady? You know what I
think? I think you maybe you had an idea you'd
take a swim.

        MILDRED
Leave me alone.
```

Crawford, by now in her forties, radiates a cool beauty very different from that of her flapper days and the terse dialogue feels perfectly shaped to capture both her toughness and her tenderness. The picture, which she loved above all her others, won her an Oscar and remains her greatest legacy.

But Freud still lingered in the shadows. The film is about the sacrifices a mother makes for her family; in 1940 Crawford, unable to have children, had adopted the first of several babies, a girl whom she named Christina. One film historian described the act as an 'unconscious attempt to save those she saw as mirrors of her childhood self'. Psychology aside, what we do know is that the relationship between mother and children (four in total) was fraught and hugely damaging for all concerned. Christina published her autobiography *Mommie Dearest* after Crawford's death, describing her as a 'monstrously abusive and alcoholic tyrant'; by the time the book came out, Crawford had already disinherited her daughter.

As her own looks faded she became increasingly reclusive, a tendency only encouraged by a remark she overheard in the lobby of her apartment building when another resident pointed her out to a friend: 'See her? She used to be Joan Crawford.'

Most poignantly of all, Crawford herself once admitted: 'We actresses wanted to be mothers, but it was a lousy idea. The biggest part of us wanted the career, and we had to live up to the demands of that career'. But whatever it was that she longed for, fought for, or struggled to escape, her determination never left her. Despite the fame and riches, one friend confessed that throughout her life Crawford had remained 'utterly lonely'. But as the Queen of the Movies herself once said:

> *Love is fire. But whether it is going to warm your hearth or burn down your house, you can never tell.*

Learn to breathe, learn to speak, but first. . . learn to feel.

*It's a pity nobody
believes in simple
lust any more*

I was a nobody, a starlet —
not even a nobody.

I made it as a star dressed,
and if it ain't dressed, I don't
want it.

I've made so many fucking
mistakes in my life. I wake up
at night thinking of all the
fuck-ups I've made.

Deep down, I'm pretty
superficial.

I wish to live until 150 years
old but the day I die, I wish it
to be with a cigarette in one
hand and a glass of whiskey
in the other.

AVA
GARDNER

Ava Lavinia Gardner
24 December 1922–25 January 1990

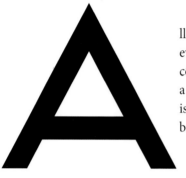

All stars have their looks, but nobody ever had a killer look like Ava Gardner. Not even the most carefully crafted photography by Hollywood's greatest cameramen could soften her raw sexuality – the fact that, despite her cool elegance, she was a red-blooded woman, vital in every smile and glance. She was so feisty that it is almost impossible to reproduce any of her more candid interviews without a bucketful of asterisks:

When I lose my temper, honey, you can't find it any place.

Born the youngest of seven children to cotton farmers in North Carolina, she got her first showbiz break when visiting her brother-in-law in New York. He was an established photographer and put a shot he had taken of her in his studio window; almost instantly an MGM talent scout saw the picture and arranged a screen test. Tactfully aware that Gardner's Southern accent might deter his bosses, the director arranged for the film to roll without sound. On seeing the result, Louis B. Mayer immediately cabled: 'She can't sing, she can't act, she can't talk – she's terrific!'

Gardner was nineteen when she hit Hollywood, a town notorious for signing small-town beauties to pitiful contracts only to drag them to the casting couch and then send them home. Gardner may have been innocent, but she was nobody's fool and – just as she was to do in her greatest screen role – she used her sexuality to take command. For the next five years she was assigned relatively minor parts; she made twenty-one uncredited appearances in the first three years. But while she waited for her moment, she used her wiles (and her curves) to play the studio system at its own game. The story is not pretty, but it is revealing.

In 1941 Gardner met Mickey Rooney, a short, boyish comedy actor two years her senior. He was also – despite being a relentless seducer – America's most wholesome actor and earned a fortune for MGM. He pursued the far more attractive Gardner ceaselessly; eventually she agreed to marry him, but insisted on remaining a virgin until their honeymoon. MGM were so horrified at the union – Gardner was a nobody, and of little use to their publicity machine – that they forced the couple to wed in secret, far from Los Angeles. But it was worth the wait. As Gardner admitted to an interviewer:

I'd been holding back a lot of emotions, honey. We screwed each other silly for the whole year we were married. We did it for a bit longer than that, actually. I was making up for lost time. Everybody was fucking everybody in those days.

The marriage ended in 1943 after continued philandering on Rooney's part. Unforgivably, while drunk one night, he taunted Gardner by reading aloud in front of her and various friends the explicit contents of his Little Black Book. On hearing that the couple were to separate, MGM were even more furious – and terrified of compromising Rooney's innocent public image. Much to her credit, although possibly fearing she would never again work for Louis B. Mayer, Gardner declined to sue for adultery and agreed to a quiet divorce. In gratitude, the studio doubled her salary, but she would have to wait a further two years before she landed the role that made her an instant – and enduring – success.

The Killers (1946), based on a short story by Ernest Hemingway, and co-starring Burt Lancaster, was an early example of a now-familiar genre: film noir. Characterized by shadowy photography, gritty plot lines and hardball dialogue, the format offered the perfect showcase for tough guys and cool dames alike, and – in her first major role, playing Kitty Collins – no dame was cooler nor any femme more fatale than Gardner. Toughened by her poor childhood, inured to the studio system, fully liberated in her sexuality and instinctively talented, she played the gangster's moll to perfection. No woman ever looked more ruthless or irresistible with a cigarette in her hand and a man to toy with:

```
        KITTY
I'm poison, Swede, to myself and everybody
around me. I'd be afraid to go with anyone I
love for the harm I'd do them.
```

The acclaim she garnered from that single appearance was matched only by her subsequent marriage to Frank Sinatra in 1951 – which would make a fine film noir in itself. She continued to make notable pictures for the next three decades, but if she never quite burned as brightly as she did as Kitty then Humphrey Bogart's response to the film must have felt better than any Oscar:

Whatever it is, whether you're born with it or catch it from a public drinking cup, she's got it.

What I'd really like to say about stardom is that it gave me everything I never wanted.

*I liked the boys and
the boys liked me*

LANA
TURNER

Julia Jean 'Lana' Turner
8 February 1921–29 June 1995

A successful man is one who makes more money than a wife can spend. A successful woman is one who can find such a man.

I find men terribly exciting, and any girl who says she doesn't is an anaemic old maid, a streetwalker, or a saint.

I planned on having one husband and seven children, but it turned out the other way around.

I would rather lose a good earring than be caught without make-up.

It was romance I wanted, kisses and candlelight, that sort of thing. I never did dig sex very much.

I'm so gullible. I'm so damn gullible. And I am so sick of me being gullible.

[Hollywood] was all beauty and it was all talent, and if you had it they protected you.

Lana Turner, whose chance discovery while enjoying an ice-cream soda in a diner across the street from her school inspired a million young women across the globe to dream of fame, had never aspired to be an actress but by the mid-1940s she was a major star.

MGM had initially placed her in a series of pictures aimed at the younger crowd but Turner now had her heart set on more serious scripts – and as her career flourished, the disagreement continued to fester. The company's view was that 'If it ain't broke, don't fix it'; once the public knows what it wants – and is contentedly getting it each time the auditorium lights dim – all a studio needs to do to keep cinemas full is to feed and pay its tame screenwriters to dream up the next 'vehicle' for its contracted players. MGM wanted Turner to keep the show on the road, but Turner was determined to take the scenic route.

> *I finally got tired of making movies where all I did was walk across the screen and look pretty. I tried to persuade the studio to give me something different. But every time I went into my argument about how bad a picture was, they'd say, 'well, it's making a fortune'. That licked me.*

Eventually, Turner dug in her famous four-inch heels. Refusing 'four pretty-pretty parts in a row', she was finally assigned to shoot *The Postman Always Rings Twice* (1946), an adaptation of James M. Cain's controversial 1934 novella notorious for its violent and sexual subject matter.

Producer Louis B. Mayer had bought the film rights to the book on its publication but had not yet dared do anything with it because he felt sure its content would fall foul of the Motion Picture Production Code, which proscribed depiction of '[the] technique of committing murder by whatever method' as well as 'sympathy for criminals' and 'excessive or lustful kissing'. Films based on the book had already been made in the more liberal France (*Le Dernier Tournant*, 1939) and Italy (*Ossessione*, 1943), but it was only after *Double Indemnity* (also based on a novel by Cain about adultery and murder) was successfully released in 1944 that Mayer decided he had sat on his investment long enough.

In the film, Frank – a drifter, played by James Garfield – stops at a diner where Cora Smith, the waitress, catches his eye. The two embark on an affair and eventually murder Cora's husband, but before they can enjoy a new life together,

Cora dies in a car accident. Frank is tried and wrongly found guilty of staging the crash; he is sentenced to death. (The phrase 'the postman always rings twice' was Cain's oblique explanation of his belief that fate tends to avenge wrongdoing.)

Turner was admired as much as a pin-up girl as an actress, and nothing in her career so far had prepared her for the role of Cora. To the surprise of many, she captured the character brilliantly and the film remains a powerful and brooding critique of the American Dream, stylish but somehow jagged – as if startled by its own brutal, venal content.

```
        CORA
I'm not what you think I am. I wanna keep this
place and work hard and be something. That's
all. But you can't do it without love — at
least, a woman can't... I've made a big mistake
in my life, and I've got to be this way just
once to fix it.


        FRANK
They hang you for that.


        CORA
Not if we do it right.
```

Critic Stephen MacMillan Moser wrote that 'her character [is] so enticingly beautiful and insidiously evil that the audience is riveted', while *The New York Times* said: 'Miss Turner is remarkably effective as the cheap and uncertain blonde who has a pathetic ambition to "be somebody" and a pitiful notion that she can realize it through crime'.

Two years later, in a dark echo of this breakthrough role, she was involved in a sensational scandal when her daughter Cheryl Crane stabbed Turner's mobster lover Johnny Stampanato to death. Crane was acquitted on the grounds of self-defence, and Turner used her notoriety to secure an impressive deal with Universal studios for her next picture, Douglas Sirk's *Imitation of Life* (1959). No longer a contract player, she negotiated an agreement guaranteeing her 50 per cent of the film's profits. She earned $2m [$17m] in the first year alone of its release – enough for ten million ice-cream sodas.

I haven't had an easy life, but it sure hasn't been a dull one. And I'm pretty proud of the way this gal has held up.

*All I had to do was
to be high-minded,
long suffering,
white-gloved and
decorative*

Personally, I think if a woman hasn't met the right man by the time she's twenty-four, she may be lucky.

All successful people these days seem to be neurotic.

I [act] because it's exactly like dressing up for the grown-ups. . . I'm like a child when I'm out there performing. . . enchanting them, making them laugh or cry.

[autobiographies] are all the same – it's always rags-to-riches or I-slept-with-so-and-so. I'm damned if I'm going to say that.

[on the famous kiss in *From Here to Eternity*] We were like surfers, waiting for the perfect waves. Between each take, we had to do a total clean-up. When it was all over, we had four tons of grit in our mouths – and other places.

DEBORAH
KERR

Deborah Jane Kerr-Trimmer
30 September 1921–16 October 2007

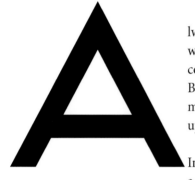

Always the bridesmaid, never the bride; between 1950 and 1961 Deborah Kerr was nominated six times for an Oscar. She never won, but she is in excellent company: the same is true of Peter O'Toole across his career (eight), Richard Burton (seven) and Glenn Close (also six). Thank God she was not a sound mixer: Kevin O'Connell has been in the running twenty times without picking up a statuette.

In interviews she was disarmingly modest – she once referred to herself as a Jersey cow because her eyes turned down at the corners – and yet she was the star of such classics as *From Here to Eternity* (1953) *The King and I* (1956) and *The Innocents* (1961). In 1994 she was finally given an honorary Academy Award as 'an artist of impeccable grace and beauty, a dedicated actress whose motion picture career has always stood for perfection, discipline and elegance'. And how.

Born in Glasgow, Kerr trained as a dancer at the prestigious Sadler's Wells ballet school but soon began acting in London's West End, where critic Beverley Baxter offered a particularly perceptive review: 'She has the rare gift of thinking her lines, not merely remembering them. The process of development from a romantic, silly girl to a hard, disillusioned woman in three hours was moving and convincing'. This ability to encompass the paradox of conflicting emotions, evident in her physicality as much as her technique, was to prove a mainstay of Kerr's acting. But to gain access to the best scripts, she understood she would have to win Hollywood's attention:

> *I studied voice for three months to get rid of my English accent. I changed my hair to blonde. I knew I could be sexy if I had to.*

In the meantime, Michael Powell and Emeric Pressburger cast her in one of their most extraordinary creations, *Black Narcissus* (1947). It tells the story of five Anglican nuns sent to a remote outpost near Darjeeling to bring Christianity and education to a largely unwilling population. Despite its austere premise, the film is about the repressed emotions of the women as they confront their beliefs and the lives they abandoned in order to pursue their vocation. Kerr plays Sister Clodagh, who reveals in a series of flashbacks that she only took the veil following a failed relationship with a caddish local landowner in the Irish village where she grew up. Those scenes are evocative and tender, and throw into sharp relief the stark setting and purpose of the mission the nuns now face.

What unfolds is a masterpiece both of storytelling and of acting, largely because the epic scale of the backdrop could so easily have overwhelmed the intense intimacy of the various personal journeys. As if that challenge were not enough, Kerr's character wears her missionary garb – full white linen habit and wimple – throughout, ensuring that at no point do we ever see more of her than her tightly framed face. Prim but unmistakably sexy, her performance is never less than compelling, and always wholly human. As the nuns come into increasingly close contact with the only European man in the area (Mr Dean, played by David Farrar) passions and jealousies stir, and Kerr articulates to perfection the knife-point balance between devotion and abandonment – to both heavenly and earthly feelings. As Sister Philippa (Flora Robson) realizes:

> PHILIPPA
> There are only two ways of living in a place
> like this — either ignore it or give yourself
> up to it.

Despite the story's overt chastity, Martin Scorsese described it as 'one of the earliest erotic films'. Powell himself agreed: 'It is all done by suggestion, but eroticism is in every frame and image from beginning to end. It is a film full of wonderful performances and passion just below the surface, which finally, at the end of the film, erupts'. Kerr's reputation as an 'English rose' never quite disappeared, but producers and directors were intrigued by the energy that lay beneath this demure surface. The conclusion of *Tea and Sympathy* (1956), where she seduces a seventeen-year-old schoolboy, is as shocking now as it was then:

> LAURA
> Years from now, when you talk about this — and
> you will — be kind...

Equally controversial was the kissing scene in the surf with Burt Lancaster in *From Here to Eternity*. Kerr's famous line 'I never knew I could be like this! Nobody ever kissed me the way you do' and her heedless sexuality caused a furore at the time, but her characteristic modesty remained and she simply said of the episode:

I don't think anyone knew I could act until I put on a bathing suit.

When you're young, you just go banging about, but you're more sensitive as you grow older.

If someone's dumb enough to offer me a million dollars to make a picture, I'm certainly not dumb enough to turn it down

ELIZABETH TAYLOR

Elizabeth Rosemond Taylor
27 February 1932–23 March 2011

My mother says I didn't open my eyes for eight days after I was born, but when I did, the first thing I saw was an engagement ring. I was hooked.

You find out who your real friends are when you're involved in a scandal.

I believe in mind over matter and doing anything you set your mind on.

I, along with the critics, have never taken myself very seriously.

I've come through things that would have felled an ox. That fills me with optimism, not just for myself but for our particular species.

**M**any actresses reach the stage and hold their award aloft only to disappoint us in the moment of glory. In tears, contritely self-effacing, they thank their agent and their dog, praise their co-nominees and remind us sanctimoniously that art is not about winners. However much we may have loved their performance in the movie, their lustre fades as they hurry to remind us of their humility. Not so with Elizabeth Taylor, who was too sensible to pretend any modesty – she knew exactly what her public (and peers) expected, and she was courteous enough to give it to them. On receiving her first Oscar for *Butterfield 8* (1960), she spoke for only fourteen seconds:

> *I don't really know how to express my gratitude for this and for everything. I guess all I can say is thank you. Thank you with all my heart.*

Taylor grew up in Los Angeles, where her mother grew tired of people praising her daughter's beauty and insisting she should seek a screen test. When Louis B. Mayer finally met the young Elizabeth, he simply yelled at his staff: 'Sign her up, sign her up! What are you waiting for?' She appeared in ten pictures before she was eighteen, although she later regretted Hollywood's eagerness to make her a star: 'I have the emotions of a child in the body of a woman. I was rushed into womanhood for the movies. It caused me long moments of unhappiness and doubt'.

Thankfully – unlike many of her contemporaries – she survived the transition to adult roles without undue trauma. In 1951 George Stevens, who had seen beyond her success alongside dogs (*Lassie Come Home,* 1943) and horses (*National Velvet,* 1944), decided to try her with Montgomery Clift instead. Theodore Dreiser's hit novel and play *An American Tragedy* had finally been adapted for the screen as *A Place in the Sun* (1951), and Stevens cast Taylor as Angela Vickers, a captivating rich socialite. Clift plays George Eastman, a restless, ambitious fellow reluctantly engaged to a young woman who works alongside him in the local factory. After being invited to a smart soirée, George falls in love with Angela, and following a melodramatic whirlwind of yearning, class conflict, starched shirt-fronts and mawkish professions of undying devotion, he takes his fiancée out on a boat trip, where she drowns. Whether the death is murder or (un)fortunate accident is ambiguous, but the ending calculatedly yanks every heartstring we possess as Angela wistfully bids farewell to George on death row:

ANGELA
Seems like we always spend the best part of our
time just saying goodbye.

The film was a huge success, earning six Oscars, and was hailed by Charlie Chaplin as 'the greatest movie ever made about America'. Taylor is radiant in a white ball gown that proved a huge fashion hit, and her flirtation with George is demure but irresistible. She creates a character who is svelte, charming, bright and filled with a magnetic energy – and a maturity surprising in someone who had barely turned nineteen.

What happened next is more complex. Great roles followed, but Taylor the star was already outshining Taylor the actress: almost everything in her subsequent life loomed larger in the public's imagination than any part she played. Howard Hughes, reclusive millionaire and movie mogul, arrived in a helicopter scattering diamonds and promised Taylor's parents he would set up a studio solely to produce her movies if she agreed to marry him (Taylor's mother agreed; Taylor refused). She met Richard Burton on the set of *Cleopatra* (1963) and their burgeoning affair was so widely reported (they both had spouses, although they subsequently married each other – twice) that it was condemned by the Vatican as 'erotic vagrancy'. Burton later explained their doomed romance by admitting 'you can't keep clapping a couple of sticks of dynamite together without expecting them to blow up', but Taylor remained an unrepentant romantic. In 1996 she appeared in a cameo role in a television sitcom where – cheerfully acknowledging her then spouse, as well as seven previous husbands – she let herself be introduced as Elizabeth Taylor-Hilton-Wilding-Todd-Fisher-Burton-Burton-Warner-Fortensky.

Remarkably, the roller-coaster ride of her personal life never compromised her professionalism as an actor. When she played Martha in *Who's Afraid of Virginia Woolf?* (1966) – perhaps her most famous role, and one which won her a second Oscar – she deliberately gained weight, added grey to her hair and deepened the shadows beneath her eyes. On being interviewed about the disparity between this and her glamorous media image, she told the simple truth:

> *The Elizabeth Taylor who's famous, the one on film, really has no depth or meaning to me. She's a totally superficial working thing, a commodity.*

I don't entirely approve of some of the things I have done, or am, or have been. But I'm me. God knows, I'm me.

*'She's too perfect. . .
too everything but
what I want'*

GRACE
KELLY

Grace Patricia Kelly
12 November 1929–14 September 1982

Hollywood amuses me.
Holier-than-thou for the
public, and unholier-than-
the-devil in reality.

I hated Hollywood. It's a
town without pity. Only
success counts. I know of no
other place in the world
where so many people suffer
from nervous breakdowns,
where there are so many
alcoholics, neurotics, and
so much unhappiness.

As an unmarried woman
I was thought to be a danger.

I don't want to dress up a
picture with just my face.

The freedom of the press
works in such a way that
there is not much freedom
from it.

The idea of my life as a fairy
tale is itself a fairy tale.

I never say 'never', and I never
say 'always'.

When Ava Gardner gets in a
taxi, the driver knows at once
she's Ava Gardner. It's the
same for Lana Turner or
Elizabeth Taylor, but not for
me. I'm never Grace Kelly.
I'm always someone who
looks like Grace Kelly.

race Patricia Kelly was a sensational star until her early death in 1982; she also, for a brief period, happened to act in films. But which role endures? Born to a wealthy, prominent Philadelphia family, she expressed a desire to act from an early age, an ambition not hindered by her head-turning beauty and several show-business relatives, including an uncle (George Kelly) who was a Pulitzer Prize-winning playwright. Her ascent – by way of modelling and television appearances – was swift; by the age of twenty-two she had landed her first leading role and the following year the prestigious director Fred Zinnemann cast her as Gary Cooper's wife in *High Noon* (1952).

Prim and decorous, in keeping with her own background, Kelly plays Amy Fowler Kane, the newly married young wife of a lawman (Marshal Will Kane) who is challenged by a paroled killer he has recently turned in. Amy pleads with her husband to walk away from the encounter, and her most famous speech rings powerfully:

```
                AMY
    I've heard guns. My father and my brother
    were killed by guns. They were on the right
    side but that didn't help them any when the
    shooting started. My brother was nineteen.
    I watched him die. That's when I became a
    Quaker. I don't care who's right or who's
    wrong. There's got to be some better way for
    people to live.
```

The film remains a classic and established her fame, but the role failed to showcase the qualities that would make her truly shine. Alfred Hitchcock, a more sophisticated master of character, would soon cast her in three films – *Dial M for Murder* (1954), *Rear Window* (1954) and *To Catch a Thief* (1955) – which captured her lightness of touch as well as the effortless confidence that was her greatest talent. Hitchcock also exploited a quality few had dared confront:

> *The subtlety of Grace's sexuality – her elegant sexiness. . . conveyed much more sex than the average movie sexpot. With Grace, you had to find it out – you had to discover it.*

Kelly, equally admiring of her new collaborator, said:

Mr Hitchcock taught me everything about cinema. It was thanks to him that I understood that murder scenes should be shot like love scenes, and love scenes like murder scenes.

Camille Paglia suggests that 'what [Hitchcock] records is the agonized complexity of men's relationship to women – a roiling mass of admiration, longing, neediness and desperation'. Audiences in 1954 may not have agreed with the claim, but they would surely have sensed that the director was offering them a version of Kelly far more nuanced and perceptive than anything they had known before.

Kelly's love life was largely kept from the public eye. She is rumoured to have had affairs with many of her leading men, including Gary Cooper, Ray Milland and William Holden; it seems clear she had a lively sexual appetite, but found the social mores of both her class and her profession frustrating. Her comments about the role of women in the 1950s are contradictory, declaring that 'I'm basically a feminist. I think that women can do anything they decide to do', but also that 'emancipation of women has made them lose their mystery. . . Women's natural role is to be a pillar of the family.'

A decade before the Swinging Sixties hit with full force, few cared about such inconsistencies. Kelly's radiance had already cast its spell on audiences everywhere and it seemed that nothing – neither fact nor gossip, screen appearances or her myriad magazine portraits – could alter what her fans believed: she was perfect, unassailable, a walking fairy tale. It was a cross many other actresses might have found hard to bear, but Kelly, as with everything else, simply smiled and carried on being herself – whoever that really was. *Rear Window* (1954), Hitchcock's second film with her, captures the paradox of this iconic status and wryly mocks her public image in the character of Lisa Fremont, a rich socialite:

> LISA
> A woman never goes anywhere but the hospital
> without packing make-up, clothes, and jewelry.

Lisa is dating L. B. (Jeff) Jefferies (James Stewart), a curmudgeonly photographer laid up after breaking his leg. Trapped in his apartment with nothing to survey but the communal courtyard below, he is obsessed with the activities of his neighbours and becomes convinced he has witnessed a murder – but he depends on Lisa to help him investigate it. Despite the ensuing high jinks, the most thrilling element of the story is the relationship between the two. The film begins with him telling his nurse Stella, played by Thelma Ritter, why he shies away from marrying Lisa:

>   JEFF
>   She's too perfect, she's too talented,
>   she's too beautiful, she's too sophisticated,
>   she's too everything but what I want.

Lisa, rather implausibly, seems hopelessly devoted to her glum companion. The more she tries to woo him with canoodling, persuasion, luxurious dinners, and even on one controversial occasion the promise (or threat) of staying the night, Jeff remains implacably committed to his amateur investigation. Hitchcock teases his male star too, suggesting he is impotent in every physical sense, though his real objective is to satirize Kelly. She wears the most outrageous couture outfits at all hours, carries herself like an angel and speaks with a cut-glass accent: under any other circumstances it would be a grotesquely two-dimensional portrait of a shallow, vain, dumb blonde.

Jeff pretends he has never set eyes on Lisa before
now.

>   JEFF
>   The Lisa Fremont who never wears the same dress
>   twice?

>   LISA
>   Only because it's expected of her.

She twirls, showing off the gown.

>   LISA
>   Right off the Paris plane. Think it will sell?

>   JEFF
>   Depends on the quote. Let's see... there's
>   the plane tickets over, import duties, hidden
>   taxes, profit markups...

>   LISA
> A steal at eleven hundred dollars.

>   JEFF
> That dress should be listed on the stock
> exchange.

Even her dialogue, as she overhears a beautiful melody being composed by the songwriter next door, seems calculated to make her sound vapid:

>   LISA
> It's enchanting. It's almost as if it were
> being written especially for us.

>   JEFF
> No wonder he's having so much trouble with it.

Like a proper princess in a fairy tale, she remains undaunted by impossible odds and by the end of the film even Hitchcock relents, allowing her to become a key part of the action as she willingly puts herself in the murderer's path and gamely scrambles up and down fire escapes (still in an exquisite silk dress) to flee him.

If her director had seen beyond her façade, did Kelly recognize the portrait he had so cunningly crafted? Certainly none of the roles she took on in her few remaining appearances suggest so; although she won an Oscar for the downbeat *The Country Girl* (1954), it was not a movie many remember, and *High Society* (1956) was greeted by *The New York Times* as merely 'bright but synthetic'. Six years after her screen debut, she abandoned Hollywood – without much apparent regret – to take on the role that ultimately defined her: Princess Grace, wife of Prince Rainier of Monaco. Her wedding was more lavish than any Hollywood production and was broadcast live to thirty million viewers in Europe. No box-office opening was ever bigger.

She died at the age of fifty-three when she suffered a stroke and lost control of the car she was driving on a narrow mountain road; the only reason her usual chauffeur was not at the wheel was that there was no room, as the princess had laid her new season's dresses on the back seat to prevent them from becoming creased. Not even Hitchcock could have achieved so rich an irony.

I came to success very quickly. Perhaps too quickly to value its importance.

I never thought
I'd land in pictures
with a face like
mine

AUDREY
HEPBURN

Audrey Kathleen Ruston
4 May 1929–20 January 1993

There must be something
wrong with those people who
think Audrey Hepburn
doesn't perspire, hiccup or
sneeze, because they know
that's not true. In fact, I
hiccup more than most.

My look is attainable. Women
can look like Audrey
Hepburn by flipping out their
hair, buying the large
sunglasses, and the little
sleeveless dresses.

I'm an introvert. . . Playing
the extroverted girl in
Breakfast at Tiffany's was the
hardest thing I ever did.

There are certain shades of
limelight that can wreck a
girl's complexion.

Only the absolutely
determined people succeed.

f we care to learn who the true arbiters of aesthetics are, we must ignore Plato, Aquinas and Kant. In 2004, a panel of fashion experts voted Audrey Hepburn 'the most naturally beautiful woman ever' out of a list of 100 gorgeous faces compiled by water company Evian. On hearing their announcement, *Elle* magazine confirmed: 'Audrey Hepburn is the personification of natural beauty'. Of course, these media polls are nonsense – were it not for the fact we might be tempted to agree.

Extraordinarily cosmopolitan and later fluent in seven languages, Hepburn was born in Brussels in 1929 to a British businessman and his Dutch aristocrat wife. After a brief stint as a model, she was spotted by a studio talent scout and appeared in only six films (in one she was billed as 'hotel receptionist'; in another as 'cigarette girl') before being cast by director William Wyler as Ann, a princess of an unspecified European royal family, in *Roman Holiday* (1953). Wyler was unable to direct Hepburn's screen test himself and delegated the task to an assistant. Perhaps sensing her nervousness, he ordered the cameraman to keep the camera rolling after he had called 'cut', ensuring he captured Hepburn off her guard. The footage proved to be so electrifying that some of it was eventually included in the trailer for the film.

A classic romantic comedy, *Roman Holiday* shows Hepburn escaping from the tedious chaperoning of her royal visit to Italy only to be rescued by journalist Joe Bradley (Gregory Peck), who becomes too fond of her to betray her disappearance. Peck recognized at once that here was a star in the making: although Hepburn was virtually unknown, he insisted to the producers that she would win an Academy Award and that they should put her name above the title. They did, and Peck was proved right about the statuette she held aloft the following year (after receiving it, she absent-mindedly left it in the cloakroom). The film perfectly captures Hepburn's charming mix of innocence and knowingness:

                    ANN
        Have I been here all night, alone?

                    JOE
        If you don't count me, yes.

                    ANN
        So I've spent the night here — with you?

                    JOE
Well now, I — I don't know that I'd use those
words exactly, but uh, from a certain angle,
yes.

She smiles radiantly.

                    ANN
How do you do?

When Hepburn bids farewell to Joe, who has both protected and entranced her, the script required her to cry. Perhaps because she had so little acting experience, she found herself unable to do so. When Wyler complained about the amount of film stock that had been wasted on failed takes, Hepburn burst into tears and the crew got the shot they needed.

Roman Holiday made her a star, but the movie that guaranteed her enduring fame came eight years later. *Breakfast at Tiffany's* (1961), based on the novella by Truman Capote, proved a magical evocation of the freedom and excitement of the 1960s; ditzy, sexy, funny and gorgeous, Hepburn is the epicentre of New York's hip new social whirl as Holly Golightly. Elegant and self-possessed, while remaining both vital and vulnerable, she inspired a generation of women to lead their lives on their own terms; the only prop they would need, the film suggested, would be the LBD (little black dress) designed by Givenchy she wears throughout.

She captivated audiences again in *Charade* (1963) and *My Fair Lady* (1964), but grew so contented at home ('If I get married, I want to be very married') that she turned down roles in such hits as *Goodbye, Mr. Chips* (1969), *Nicholas and Alexandra* (1971), *The Exorcist* (1973) and *One Flew Over the Cuckoo's Nest* (1975). Few who conquered Hollywood have done so with such grace:

> *I never think of myself as an icon. What is in other people's minds is not in my mind. I just do my thing.*

I know I have more sex appeal on the tip of my nose than many women in their entire bodies. It doesn't stand out a mile, but it's there.

If I'm a legend,
then why am I so
lonely?

JUDY
GARLAND

Frances Ethel Gumm
10 June 1922–22 June 1969

You think you can make me sing?. . . I sing for myself. I sing when I want to, whenever I want to, just for me. I sing for my own pleasure, whenever I want. Do you understand that?

I can live without money, but I cannot live without love.

I'm a woman who wants to reach out and take forty million people in her arms.

In the silence of night I have often wished for just a few words of love from one man, rather than the applause of thousands of people.

I have the unfortunate habit of not being able to have an affair with a man without being in love with him.

It's lonely and cold on the top. . . lonely and cold.

Hollywood is a strange place if you're in trouble. Everybody thinks it's contagious.

How strange when an illusion dies. It's as though you've lost a child.

udy Garland was seventeen when she made *The Wizard of Oz* (1939). Perhaps the greatest story ever told about the longing for home, the film contains two unforgettable lines as Dorothy begins – and ends – her adventure in Oz:

> DOROTHY
> Toto, I've a feeling we're not in Kansas any
> more...

And, on her return, exclaimed with an unfeigned childlike wonder:

> DOROTHY
> Toto, we're home. Home! And this is my room, and
> you're all here. And I'm not gonna leave here
> ever, ever again, because I love you all, and —
> oh, Auntie Em — there's no place like home!

But the most poignant moment of all is Dorothy's lament, a shadow at the very start of the film which darkens everything yet to unfold:

> DOROTHY
> Somewhere over the rainbow, Bluebirds fly...
> Birds fly over the rainbow. Why then, oh why
> can't I?

Many an actress would have killed for the opportunity to sing these words, but as Garland discovered – along with many stars signed to long contracts under the Hollywood studio system – there were fewer bluebirds flying when she got there than the dream had promised.

> *I've never looked through a keyhole without finding someone was looking back.*

Garland – born Frances Ethel Gumm in 1922 in Grand Rapids, Minnesota – was the daughter of two vaudevillians and appeared at the astonishing age of two with her siblings as the Gumm Sisters. Legendary director and choreographer Busby Berkeley saw one of their teenaged performances and persuaded Louis B. Mayer of MGM to sign her up. Like Shirley Temple and Elizabeth Taylor, Garland would now be working under the auspices of a hard-nosed production empire and MGM had doubts about whether her childish radiance would evolve into a sufficiently alluring maturity.

Charles Walters, who directed her in *Easter Parade* (1948) and *Summer Stock* (1950), admitted 'Judy was the big money-maker at the time, a big success, but she was the ugly duckling. . . I think it had a very damaging effect on her emotionally for a long time. I think it lasted forever, really.' Mayer himself referred to his protégé as 'my little hunchback', which was more than uncharitable since Garland was already earning a fortune for him in a string of successes with Mickey Rooney. Not only did she suffer the indignity of wearing prosthetic teeth and a padded nose, but she would later be forced to have an abortion to avoid scandal, and subjected to a régime of drugs to cope with the punishing schedule of MGM's shooting and publicity machine. The stress – and the eventual addiction – would dog her all her life.

> *I was born at the age of twelve on a Metro-Goldwyn-Mayer lot. . .*
> *From the time I was thirteen, there was a constant struggle between*
> *MGM and me – whether or not to eat, how much to eat, what to eat.*
> *I remember this more vividly than anything else about my childhood.*
> *MGM had us working days and nights on end. They'd give us pep-up*
> *pills to keep us on our feet long after we were exhausted. Then they'd*
> *take us to the studio hospital and knock us cold with sleeping pills. . .*
> *Then after four hours they'd wake us up and give us the pep-up pills*
> *again so we could work another 72 hours in a row. I started to feel*
> *like a wind-up toy.*

Denied any semblance of a childhood, and with her very identity polarized between the constructs of the studio marketing department and the public's perception of her, Garland inevitably found herself confused and lonely as she faced life as an adult. She went on to appear in a string of hits including *Ziegfeld Girl* (1941) and *Meet Me in St. Louis* (1944) and was celebrated for her dancing and singing talents; Fred Astaire, who played opposite her in *Easter Parade* (1948), praised her as 'the greatest entertainer who ever lived'. But her personal life became increasingly challenging; already on her third marriage at the age of thirty-two, she added alcohol and morphine to her diet of uppers and downers and retreated periodically to various clinics to escape her addictions. By 1950 her unreliability had caused MGM to terminate her contract and friends reported she had made a half-hearted suicide attempt. Garland later wrote of the episode:

All I could see ahead was more confusion. I wanted to black out the future as well as the past. I wanted to hurt myself and everyone who had hurt me.

Abandoning the screen, she returned to her roots as a singer and vaudevillian. Her tour of the United Kingdom in 1951 was one of many periodic comebacks, and one particularly successful appearance prompted her to declare: 'I suddenly knew that this was the beginning of a new life... Hollywood thought I was through; then came the wonderful opportunity to appear at the London Palladium, where I can truthfully say Judy Garland was reborn.'

Hollywood, as jealous as it is fickle, was quick to woo her back. In 1954 the cameras rolled on George Cukor's lavish Technicolor remake of *A Star is Born* and the opening credits suggested all was forgiven:

> *TITLE CARD*
> *The Great Voice... The Great Heart... The Great Personality of the Most Beloved Entertainer of Our Time. Judy Garland... She Made a Hundred Songs Live on Her Lips and Sang Them All to the One Man Who Lived in Her Heart.*

Today's audiences would run a mile from such hyperbole, but it turned out to be a wonderful production with accomplished turns by Garland as Vicki Lester and James Mason as Norman Maine. Garland plays a nightclub singer whose act is rudely derailed one evening by Maine, a film actor whose career is in decline as his alcoholism becomes known. The two fall in love and marry, and Maine helps Lester get a screen test; the rest of the story depicts the challenges they face as Lester's star waxes and Maine's wanes.

```
                VICKI
    Now, all I need is just a little luck.


                NORMAN
    What kind of luck?


                VICKI
    Oh, the kind of luck that every girl singer
    with a band dreams of... One night a big talent
```

scout from a big record company might come in
and he'll let me make a record.

                    NORMAN
Yes, and then?

                    VICKI
Well, the record will become number one on the Hit
Parade, it'll be played on the jukeboxes all over
the country... and I'll be made. End of dream.

                    NORMAN
There's only one thing wrong with that.

                    VICKI
I know... It won't happen.

                    NORMAN
No, it might happen pretty easily - but the
dream isn't big enough.

The irony, of course, is that it was Garland herself who was suffering from a variety of dependence issues (Cary Grant turned down the part of Maine as he was worried about her unreliability as a co-star), but the film showcases Garland's charisma and talents to the full: though she was no Garbo or Dietrich in terms of her raw beauty, she lights up the screen and the lens loves her. The film brought her first Oscar nomination (she had previously won a juvenile award) and reignited her screen career, prompting *Time* magazine to write: 'Garland gives what is just about the greatest one-woman show in modern movie history'. But was it the homecoming she had dreamed of? Showered with nominations and awards both cinematic and musical for the next decade, her triumph was assured – but too late for her to enjoy. She died, aged forty-seven, of an overdose of barbiturates; the coroner ruled that it was not a suicide but the culmination of years of dependence. It seemed the shadow of that famous opening song still lingered:

> *I wanted to believe and I tried my damnedest to believe in the rainbow that I tried to get over and couldn't. So what? Lots of people can't. . . Behind every cloud is another cloud.*

Always be a first-rate version of yourself, instead of a second-rate version of somebody else.

*Every answer
you give should
bring up another
question*

KIM
NOVAK

Marilyn Pauline 'Kim' Novak
13 February 1933–

I never intended to be an actress. I never dreamed of it, never even thought about it.

If you're wanting glamorous or really beautiful or really sexy, well then, I wasn't really the one, but I could do all of that. You could just get really lost in that kind of image.

If you want to live on the edge of life, you need to be flexible.

I'm not like [Greta Garbo]. I don't ever want to be alone.

I loved acting, which was never about money, the fame. It was about a search for meaning. It was painful.

I tried so hard with movies like *Vertigo* and *Middle of the Night* and others. I felt those would show me that it's only a matter of time before I'd find the right one to reach out and touch people.

im Novak: pure-hearted embodiment of American beauty, or ambiguous icon of sexuality? In three years – from *Picnic* in 1955 to *Vertigo* in 1958 – she spanned both extremes, winning a BAFTA and a Golden Globe award along the way. Only later in her career would she reveal – or indeed discover – that her talent for complex, multifaceted characterization was a fundamental aspect of her off-screen personality.

Born Marilyn Pauline Novak to Czech parents in 1933 and raised in Illinois, she never aspired to a Hollywood life. She was a talented painter and won a scholarship to the prestigious Art Institute of Chicago, and while still at her local junior college she modelled for local papers to help pay her tuition fees. She soon won a job as 'Miss Deepfreeze', literally singing the praises of a brand of refrigerators with the jingle 'There's no business like Thor business'. Thankfully, she was soon to be offered more rewarding material to work with. During a summer break, she went on a national tour as Miss Deepfreeze; the trip ended on the West Coast and in Los Angeles she applied for a job as an extra in *The French Line* (1954), where she was immediately spotted by a talent agent who signed her to a contract with Columbia Pictures.

On her arrival at the studio, the legendary mogul Harry Cohn tried to persuade her to change her name to the more American Kit Marlowe, claiming: 'Nobody's gonna go see a girl with a Polack name!' Novak stood her ground: 'Well, I'm Czech. . . but Polish, Czech, no matter, it's my name.' They finally settled on 'Kim', but it would not be the last time she had to battle for her independence – or her dignity:

> *The head of publicity told me, 'You're a piece of meat, that's all'. It wasn't very nice but I had to take it. When I made my first screen test, the director explained to everyone, 'Don't listen to her, just look.'*

After a string of moderate successes, she took the part of Molly in the hugely popular *The Man with the Golden Arm* (1955) alongside Frank Sinatra; by 1957, promoted by the studio as 'a hot-blooded blonde', she had made the cover of *Time* magazine. In the accompanying interview she confessed: 'I'm worried because I didn't enjoy it on the way up, and now maybe I'm on the way down.' She was still only twenty-four, and her greatest successes still lay ahead of her.

> *Be yourself, and be honest. Don't try to act. Those were the wisest words ever told me, because any time I tried to 'act' it didn't come out*

right; it was phony. But let me tell you, that's hard to do when you go down to the make-up department and they start saying 'Let's see, let's put Joan Crawford's lips on you, let's put Marilyn Monroe's hair on you...' When you walk out of that make-up room you can't even recognize yourself. I felt like somebody else, not me.

Her real breakthrough in a true leading role came with *Picnic* (1955), the story of twenty-four hours in the life of a small Kansas town. It was directed by the notoriously driven and volatile Joshua Logan, noted for *Bus Stop* (1956), *Sayonara* (1957) and *South Pacific* (1958). Although the play on which the film was based was simply presented on the porches of two small-town houses, Logan re-staged the action on a broader canvas, insisting that 'It's gotta look like Kansas – and it will if I have to kill every last one of ya!' The shoot was hugely challenging – one location, Udall, was destroyed by a tornado shortly after shooting began – and yet the screen version radiates the prosperous tranquillity of the Eisenhower years with its well-tended front yards and courteous neighbours. Only when handsome drifter Hal Carter (William Holden) arrives looking for work and falls in love with Madge Owens (Novak), the local beauty queen, are the town's genteel manners profoundly challenged.

At first glance Novak's part is transparently simple: a modest young girl with modest ambitions who happens to fall in love with the wrong fellow. But 1954 had seen the release of Bill Haley's 'Rock Around the Clock', and the seismic effects of rock 'n' roll on youth culture were already trembling on the Richter scale. Neither Novak nor Logan can have known what was about to hit them – or the film industry – and the power of the story lies in what it reveals about a world on the cusp of transformation.

Novak's understated desires and determination deliver a far more powerful insight into – and indictment of – the values of 1950s America than Holden's macho bluster. The film portrays a remarkably diverse range of women of all ages in compelling roles, not least local schoolmistress Rosemary (played by Rosalind Russell, who refused to be nominated for an Academy Award because she felt her role worthy of the leading, not supporting, category). In some ways, Novak's performance seems reticent: she expresses a haughty indifference to those she disapproves of, yet we see a vulnerability beneath that archness. She radiates a profound humanity which becomes ever more vital as the characters surrounding her begin to crack, and she yearns for wider horizons:

                    MADGE
        Mom, you don't love someone because he's
        perfect.

Hal continues to charm and captivate the women he meets, but Madge remains aloof. The climax of the film (much of which had to be re-shot in a studio following more appalling Kansas weather) shows Madge winning the local beauty pageant. At the party afterwards – the eponymous night-time picnic – she sees Hal teaching her younger sister a racy new dance he learned while in L.A. Finally realizing the futility of her small-town fame, she cuts in and – to our amazement, as well as Hal's – instinctively picks up the steps, swirling and smouldering alongside him as the crowd watches. The transformation is shocking but absolutely believable, and the film made Novak Hollywood's most sought-after actress.

Although *Picnic* put her on the map, it is impossible to understand the power of her presence without also watching her in *Vertigo* (1958). Directed by Alfred Hitchcock, the story features a retired detective, 'Scottie' Ferguson (James Stewart), who is asked by an acquaintance to follow his wife Madeleine Ester (Novak). Scottie tails her to a church tower where she falls to her death in an apparent suicide. She subsequently reappears as a strange and seductive doppelgänger (Judy Barton, also played by Novak), forcing Stewart to question his own sanity – and his growing obsession with her. Critic David Thomson described Novak's role as 'one of the major female performances in the cinema' and Martin Scorsese said of it that it was 'extraordinary. . . brave and emotionally immediate'.

                    SCOTTIE
        I hope we will, too.

                    MADELEINE
        What?

                    SCOTTIE
        Meet again sometime.

                    MADELEINE
        We have.

On the face of it, the two films could not be more different: after the sunlit lawns and conservative emotions of *Picnic*, *Vertigo* explores a darker and more complex mystery. But what unites them is Novak herself, whose characters retain an ambiguity that provides the vital energy for both narratives. She shows no deliberation, none of the Method acting mannerisms that were just becoming fashionable – just an ineffable beauty and simplicity which draw us unquestioningly into her world.

In 1966, after a few respectable hits – *Middle of the Night* (1959), *Of Human Bondage* (1964), *Kiss Me, Stupid* (1964) – she retired from acting. Though she returned to the screen very occasionally after that, her reticence continued to puzzle her many fans until she revealed in a candid interview in 2013 that she had been diagnosed – many years earlier – with bipolar disorder.

> *I was very erratic. I did suffer from mental illness. I didn't know it at the time. At times I was focused. Other times, the press would come on the set and I'd feel the energy of people laughing at me or not approving of my style of acting. You could pick up those feelings. I was distracted. I couldn't perform as well.*

More poignantly still, she once confessed:

> *I don't feel I ever reached my potential as an actress.*

Sixty years of acclaim later, history has delivered a different verdict. A 2013 British Film Institute critics' ranking of the greatest movies of all time finally knocked *Citizen Kane* from the top spot – a position it had held since 1962. The film that took its place? *Vertigo*.

I had a lot of resentment for a while toward Kim Novak. But I don't mind her any more. She's okay.

*I leave before being
left. I decide*

BRIGITTE
BARDOT

Brigitte Anne-Marie Bardot
28 September 1934–

When you're thirty you're
old enough to know better,
but still young enough to
go ahead and do it.

I have always adored
beautiful young men. Just
because I grow older, my taste
doesn't change. So if I can still
have them, why not?

I don't think when I make
love.

I am really a cat transformed
into a woman. . . I purr.
I scratch. And sometimes
I bite.

It is better to be unfaithful
than faithful without wanting
to be.

Men are beasts and even
beasts don't behave as
they do.

Every age can be enchanting,
provided you live within it.

It is sad to grow old but nice
to ripen.

I gave my youth and beauty
to men. Now I'm giving my
wisdom and my experience,
the better part of me, to
animals.

t takes some kind of superstar to make a fan – no less than John Lennon – feel so nervous that he needs to drop acid before meeting her. Brigitte Bardot, the bombshell to end all bombshells after her appearance in *Et Dieu. . . créa la femme* (*And God Created Woman,* 1956), became so awe-inspiringly famous in her day that Charles de Gaulle summoned her to the Elysée Palace for an audience, and subsequently described her as a 'French export as important as Renault cars'. But not everyone approved of her explosion onto the scene: *Paris Match* ran an eight-page spread in which it consulted academics, psychiatrists and sociologists to evaluate the Bardot phenomenon and its verdict was that the world's hottest new face was 'immoral, from head to toe'.

In 1956 the world was still rebuilding itself after the war: Britain had only just abolished third-class rail travel, the first transatlantic telephone cable was laid, Morocco and Tunisia had declared independence from France, Elvis had his first chart hit with 'Heartbreak Hotel' and Norma Jean Mortenson changed her name legally to Marilyn Monroe. Audiences were flocking to see Cecil B. DeMille's *The Ten Commandments*, but while they were pondering Charlton Heston's pronouncements on morality, a young director named Roger Vadim was about to write a very different rule book – with Bardot as his muse.

Raised as a devout Catholic, Bardot trained as a ballet dancer at the Conservatoire de Paris and her precocious beauty caught the attention of *Elle* magazine, who featured her on their cover when she was still only fifteen. Vadim saw her pictures and was entranced; three years later, they were married. By then, Bardot had appeared in several movies, mostly with the same flirtatious agenda – *The Girl in the Bikini* (1952), *Naughty Girl* (1956) and *Nero's Mistress* (1956) – and Vadim, inspired by his wife's success, decided to create a vehicle for both of their talents. If God had created woman, Vadim would refashion her for the coming age of sports cars, jet planes and bikinis.

Et Dieu. . . créa la femme proved a landmark, if not a masterpiece. Vadim – who would later direct Jane Fonda in the equally controversial *Barbarella* (1968) – was a mercurial figure who admired the Young Turks of neo-realism and the *nouvelle vague* (De Sica, Godard and Truffaut) but lacked their stylistic and intellectual vigour. Bosley Crowther of *The New York Times* wrote: 'We can't recommend this little item as a sample of the best in Gallic films. It is clumsily put together and bizarrely played', but he admitted that its star lay at the heart of its impact:

It isn't what Mademoiselle Bardot does in bed but what she might do that drives the three principal male characters into an erotic frenzy. . . She is a thing of mobile contours – a phenomenon you have to see to believe.

Sadly many of those in America who wished to see the film were thwarted as the picture was condemned by the National Legion of Decency and police shut down several cinemas which screened it. One slogan in the conservative media became briefly popular: 'Ban Bardot'. It seems a harsh verdict for a woman whose happy, bourgeois childhood in Paris had revolved simply around dancing and her beloved pets. She felt no real drive to act, confessing shortly after the furore broke:

I am really not interested in the cinema. I loathed it when I started six years ago, and I don't enjoy it even now.

But the genie was out of the bottle. *Et Dieu. . . créa la femme* was set in St-Tropez, a picturesque fishing village on the French Riviera, untouched as yet by tourists, millionaires and developers – or, as Bardot would later describe them, 'mediocre, dirty, badly behaved, shameless invaders'. Juliette, a free-spirited orphan prone to naked sunbathing, dallies with three lovers, dances barefoot on tables and tears stuff up for the hell of it.

> ERIC
> Are you crazy?
>
> JULIETTE
> I'm shooting bottles.
>
> ERIC
> Where did you find this gun?
>
> JULIETTE
> In the drawer. I love to shoot. It's exciting.

Rich businessman Eric (Curd Jürgens) has intruded into her prelapsarian paradise, hoping to turn the town into a casino resort:

                    ERIC
    Ah! The Garden of Eden in St-Tropez!

                  JULIETTE
    Monsieur Carradine! And I suppose you are the
    Devil?

                    ERIC
    Perhaps so. I've brought the apple anyway.

Apple be damned: in this version of Genesis there can be no fall since there is no Adam worthy of Eve, and the film-makers cannot even seem to decide who is Satan. The breathy trailer begins with the words 'in the pagan paradise of the French Riviera swirls the fast-moving, fascinating story of a demon-driven temptress who thought the future was invented only to spoil the present!' As this sixpenny theology collapses under its own weight (or lack of it), Eric is left to lament:

                    ERIC
    That girl was made to destroy men.

Recent Oscar winners for Best Actress had included Grace Kelly, Vivien Leigh and Audrey Hepburn – but none of them would have been caught dead behaving like the insouciant Bardot, off screen or on. Everything about her performance is spontaneous: intense, and yet absolutely without agenda. She simply *is*, and the fabulous physique and the glorious abandon and the tousled hair all just seem by-products of her energy and innocence. If there is any lesson to be learned from the film, it is that God clearly did not rest on the seventh day.

While Bardot's formal skills remained tactfully undiscussed (she herself admitted 'I started out as a lousy actress and have remained one'), debate raged about what her performance meant. Was she challenging every norm society held good, or just liberating women at long last? Simone de Beauvoir was adamant it was the latter:

> *Bardot's naturalness seems more perverse than any kind of*
> *sophistication. To despise as she does jewels, make-up and high heels*
> *is to refuse to transform oneself into an idol. It is to assert oneself the*
> *equal of men. It is to recognize that between men and women, there is*

*only desire and mutual pleasure. This is precisely what made her
appear so dangerous in the eyes of society.*

Bardot became the darling of the Existentialists, which outraged the bourgeoisie
even further. But de Beauvoir's eulogy contained a paradox: Bardot *was* an idol
now, a term cinema had adopted in its earliest days to proclaim the power of its
anointed. Besides which, the chic French intellectuals were soon nonplussed by
Bardot's own admission that:

Women get more unhappy the more they try to liberate themselves.

The truth was simply that she had as little interest in the world of politics as she
did in the world of movies. One biographer recalled that 'she seemed to have
no ambition whatsoever, which made her a very curiously attractive creature
because she was never seeking any sort of approval'; the playwright Paul Fournel
noted that 'she was indifferent to the power she had. . . She didn't really want to
be an actress, a singer or a sex symbol but it just happened that way'.

Bardot continued to work until 1973 and then dropped out of the business
as casually as she had entered it, retiring to her beloved St-Tropez where she
continues to rail against the 'shameless invaders' and campaign for the rights of
animals. For all the barriers she broke – for actors, and for women everywhere –
it seemed she could never escape the pressures to conform to an image she had
conjured without even intending to:

*My soul is not my own any more. I cannot live like I want to. I am
going to give up films.*

I have been very
happy, very rich, very
beautiful, much
adulated, very famous
and very unhappy.

*I open doors to
intuition, because
rationality is really
death*

JEANNE MOREAU

Jeanne Moreau
23 January 1928–

Acting deals with very
delicate emotions. It is not
putting up a mask. Each time
an actor acts he does not
hide; he exposes himself.

I am a woman with absolutely
no sense of nostalgia.

I am open to what is
irrational.

We have so many words for
states of the mind, and so few
for states of the body.

Everything I have, I have
wanted.

I'm a passionate woman who
falls in love very easily.

If you don't give a damn, men
look at you.

Love is like soup: the first
spoonfuls are too hot, the last
ones too cold.

I was never interested in
existentialism, because of
[Jean-Paul Sartre's] famous
phrase, 'Hell is others'.
For me, this is a crazy idea.
For me, hell is one's self.

One should never say,
'When I was young. . .'

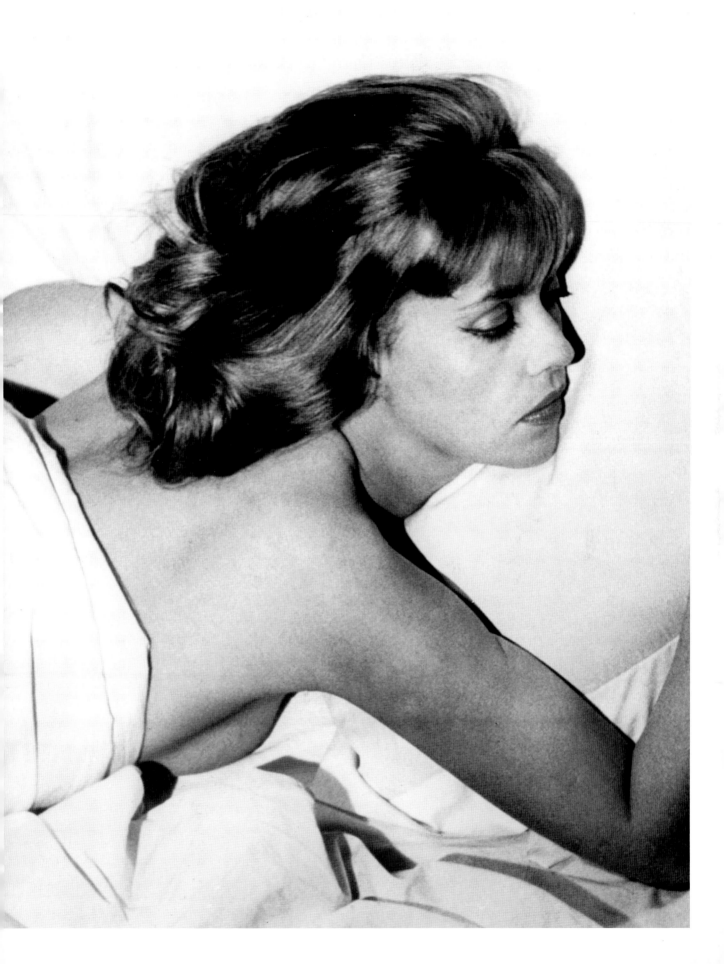

eanne Moreau, daughter of a French restaurateur and an English dancer at the Folies Bergère, became the youngest ever full-time member of the Comédie-Française, France's most prestigious theatre company, but even within that august environment her ambitions were iconoclastic:

> *At the beginning of my career I was seeking something traditional,*
> *strict; just to prove to my father that being an actress is not being*
> *a whore.*

By 1958, at the age of thirty, she had appeared in twenty-one films including *The Wages of Sin* (1956) and *Elevator to the Gallows* (1958), before being cast as Jeanne Tournier in Louis Malle's dazzling *Les Amants* (*The Lovers*, 1958). Jeanne is a young woman restless in her comfortable marriage but seeking genuine passion – a familiar predicament of yearning and adultery, yet one rarely told with such ravishing simplicity. As the film opens, Jeanne seems frozen, bound by convention, costume, and the company she keeps, turning ever inwards on herself. She instigates an affair with a dashing polo player, but even that comes to seem just another fragment in the mosaic of her isolation. Only when she meets the young archaeologist Bernard (Jean-Marc Bory) does she find herself brought alive again, as she reveals in her meditative third person narration:

> *Love can be born in a single glance. In an instant, Jeanne felt all*
> *shame and restraint fall away.*

The long shot of her lying shadowed against ice-white sheets, her immaculate pearls glittering like a halo around her throat, her hand opening and her arm falling aside as she abandons herself to Bernard, is one of the most perfect images of seduction in all cinema. Evoking Hedy Lamarr's orgasm in *Ecstasy* (1933), it makes many of the most iconic celluloid embraces look formal – and formulaic. What Jeanne experiences here is tenderly real yet utterly transcendent, and it captivated those who saw it.

Sadly, few did. Nico Jacobellis, a movie-theatre owner in Cleveland Heights, Ohio, was charged with showing an obscene film and was fined $2,500 [$20,000]. Bravely, since a European film with unknown actors released in a small Midwestern city was unlikely to turn a large profit, Jacobellis fought his case all the way to the Supreme Court. The First Amendment vigorously protects free speech with very few exceptions, one of them being hardcore pornography, but it is absurd to suggest that Malle's fine film was anything more than intelligently erotic. Justice Potter Stewart's verdict, vindicating Jacobellis and challenging the prudishness that had dogged American cinema for too long, famously noted: 'I know [obscenity] when I see it, and the motion picture involved in this case is not that.' It set a precedent that quickly liberated intelligent cinema from the idiocies of the Hays Code.

If Moreau did not reach the audience she deserved as Jeanne Tournier, she returned with redoubled radiance as Catherine in François Truffaut's *Jules et Jim* (1962). Shot with a hand-held camera, full of jump cuts and freeze-frames, with a kaleidoscopic soundtrack and a haphazard exuberance, it charts the complex three-way friendship between Catherine and her eponymous lovers. Moreau offers a whirlwind of moods and emotions, never letting herself – or us – settle into any moment of complacency. Beautiful as she is, she is unafraid to be ugly; where some act with their face, some with their body and some their voice, she comes closest to doing so with her soul. In a medium frequently shaped by producers and their desire to control and market their players as brands, she shattered the mould.

Happy to explore the fullest possible range of opportunities from historical drama to romantic comedy – she even had a small role in *Love Actually* (2003) – she continues to act to this day, with 145 film credits to her name. She has always preferred literary salons to glossy magazines, counting among her friends Jean Cocteau, Jean Genet, Henry Miller, Anaïs Nin and Marguerite Duras; the directors who have sought her out include Michelangelo Antonioni, Luis Buñuel, Elia Kazan, Rainer Werner Fassbinder, Wim Wenders and Orson Welles, who proclaimed her 'the greatest actress in the world'. Despite the august company she keeps, Moreau prides herself on not being a pure intellectual; for light relief, she used to sing with Frank Sinatra at Carnegie Hall. With this impressive range of talents, she inspired a generation of actresses to see their vocation in a wholly different way, as Catherine so winningly foretold in *Jules et Jim*:

```
                    CATHERINE
    I still like that girl. She wants to be free.
    She invents her own life.
```

Like every human being, I have everything in me – the best and the worst.

I have a great soul,
but so far nobody's
interested in it

MARILYN
MONROE

Norma Jeane Mortenson
1 June 1926–5 August 1962

I knew I belonged to the public and to the world not because I was talented or even beautiful, but because I never had belonged to anything or anyone else.

I am good, but not an angel. I do sin, but I'm not the devil. I'm just a small girl in a big world trying to find someone to love.

No one ever told me I was pretty when I was a little girl. All little girls should be told they're pretty, even if they aren't.

Dogs never bite me. Just humans.

I did what they said and all it got me was a lot of abuse. Everyone's just laughing at me. I hate it. Big breasts, big ass, big deal.

I don't mind living in a man's world as long as I can be a woman in it.

Suicide is a person's privilege. I don't believe it's a sin or a crime, it's your right if you do. Though it doesn't get you anywhere.

id Marilyn Monroe, the most famous movie star of all time, have a unique breakthrough role in her tragically short career? Before we knew it she was with us, and before we knew it she was gone. Christened Norma Jeane Mortenson, and raised principally in foster homes after her mother was committed to a psychiatric hospital, she was discovered in 1945 by army propaganda photographers at the factory where she was working. She signed with the Blue Book modelling agency where her first assignment paid $5 [$65] and she soon began to seek film work:

> *I want to be a big star more than anything. It's something precious.*

Her first leading role came in 1948 with the unremarkable *Ladies of the Chorus*, but none of the dozen or so films she made after that did much to boost or shape her career; ambitious but restless, she changed her professional name so frequently before she became known that when she gave her first autograph as Marilyn Monroe she had to ask a friend how to spell it.

During these first few fitful years as an actress she had to return regularly to modelling to support herself, but the 1949 photo shoot in which Tom Kelley first unveiled her naked form – with her arm languidly outstretched against a crimson drape – fired her into the public consciousness like a jolt of adrenaline. It required neither imagination nor conviction for directors to seek her out after that; nobody, least of all her audiences, cared where her talents lay so long as they could simply gaze at her. Everywhere she looked she saw herself reflected back from billboards, posters, the covers of *Life* and *Time* magazines and even the centrefold of *Playboy*, but this was not the fame she had dreamed of.

> *People had a habit of looking at me as if I were some kind of mirror instead of a person. They didn't see me, they saw their own lewd thoughts, then they white-masked themselves by calling me the lewd one.*

If she reluctantly accepted that her public persona was now beyond her control, she still yearned for more dignified acclaim:

> *My illusions didn't have anything to do with being a fine actress. I knew how third-rate I was. I could actually feel my lack of talent, as if it were cheap clothes I was wearing inside. But my God, how I wanted to learn, to change, to improve!*

How to Marry a Millionaire (1953), *The Seven Year Itch* (1955) and *Bus Stop* (1956) were all box-office hits, but even with the latter the press could only muster faint praise: 'Hold onto your chairs, everybody, and get set for a rattling surprise. Marilyn Monroe has finally proved herself an actress in *Bus Stop*.' She had been studying dramatic technique with Paula Strasberg, although her colleagues suspected her coach was more a confidante than a mentor: Laurence Olivier, who praised Monroe for her work alongside him in *The Prince and the Showgirl* (1957), believed Strasberg's only ability was to 'butter Marilyn up'. When Billy Wilder, who directed her as Sugar Kowalczyk in *Some Like it Hot* (1959), heard she was studying Method acting he was unimpressed, suggesting instead that 'she should have gone to a train-engineer's school. . . to learn something about arriving on schedule.'

> *I'm selfish, impatient, and a little insecure. I make mistakes, I'm out*
> *of control, and at times hard to handle. But if you can't handle me at*
> *my worst, then you sure as hell don't deserve me at my best.*

Her reputation for being unreliable on set was spreading, and Tony Curtis as Joe (Josephine) endured the agony (while wearing high heels in full-drag make-up) of performing a scene eighty-one times opposite his co-star before she correctly delivered her one simple line: 'Where's the Bourbon?' Wilder, to his credit – but only after he had recovered from making the film – later said of her that she had a 'certain indefinable magic' and an 'absolute genius as a comic actress'; she won a Golden Globe for her turn, and the film remains the defining legacy of her career.

Three years later, at the age of thirty-six, Monroe was discovered dead at her home after an overdose of barbiturates. Though she had been married three times – to policeman James Dougherty, baseball hero Joe DiMaggio and playwright Arthur Miller – she was in bed alone. Always charming and candid with the press, she remained hopeful to the last:

> *Please don't make me a joke. End the interview with what I believe. . .*
> *I want to be an artist, an actress with integrity. . . I want to grow and*
> *develop and play serious dramatic parts. My dramatic coach tells*
> *everybody that I have a great soul, but so far nobody's interested in it.*

Hollywood's a place where they'll pay you a thousand dollars for a kiss, and fifty cents for your soul.

THE
INDEPENDENTS

ANITA EKBERG

SOPHIA LOREN

URSULA ANDRESS

JULIE CHRISTIE

JULIE ANDREWS

CATHERINE DENEUVE

ANOUK AIMÉE

LIV ULLMANN

VANESSA REDGRAVE

FAYE DUNAWAY

BARBRA STREISAND

LIZA MINNELLI

JANE FONDA

CHARLOTTE RAMPLING

SISSY SPACEK

DIANE KEATON

HELEN MIRREN

MERYL STREEP

MICHELLE PFEIFFER

DEMI MOORE

UMA THURMAN

JULIETTE BINOCHE

NICOLE KIDMAN

*I'm very proud
of my breasts, as
every woman
should be*

ANITA
EKBERG

Kerstin Anita Marianne Ekberg
29 September 1931–11 January 2015

Now the name of Fellini
has become very great, mine
very little.

[Fellini] was the greatest
film director of all time but
I would not have looked at
him twice as a man.

I'm very much bigger than
I was, so what? It's not really
fatness, it's development.

I should be able to get work
myself on the strength of
my acting. I shouldn't have
to sleep with producers to
get parts.

I have a mirror. I would be
a hypocrite if I said I didn't
know I am beautiful.

[on the Trevi fountain scene
in *La Dolce Vita*] I was
freezing. They had to lift me
out of the water because I
could not feel my legs any
more.

n the red corner, feminist film theorist Laura Mulvey asserts: 'In their traditional exhibitionist role women are simultaneously looked at and displayed, with their appearance coded for strong visual and erotic impact.' In the blue corner, first lady Eleanor Roosevelt insists: 'No one can make you feel inferior without your consent.' Between them in the ring stands actress Anita Ekberg, protesting: 'I'm very proud of my breasts, as every woman should be.' The referee for the encounter is director Federico Fellini, who mesmerized audiences with *La Dolce Vita* (1960), a kaleidoscopic portrait of a post-war Rome conjuring decadence from poverty. The film was an unexpected hit worldwide and remains hugely influential to this day, provoking reverence and parody in equal measure.

Born the eldest girl and the sixth of eight children in Malmö, Sweden, Ekberg found work as a teenaged fashion model before winning the local, and then the national, beauty contest. Only one title remained to pursue: America's Miss Universe. She came sixth in the competition, but in those days film scouts routinely snapped up such potential talent and by 1951 she had been signed as a starlet at Universal Studios. She spoke little English and had no formal acting training, but she was in no doubt about her principal assets:

> It's not cellular obesity, it's womanliness.

Howard Hughes, designer of Jane Russell's famous underwired bra and no stranger to the glories of the female form, poached her for his RKO studio where he tried to persuade her to remodel her nose and teeth and even change her name, claiming it would be too hard for audiences to pronounce. Ekberg – to her credit – refused, arguing that if people noticed her they would learn it, and that if they didn't they wouldn't care.

Indignant, she returned to Universal where she was given roles in a number of unremarkable pictures, including *Abbott and Costello Go to Mars* (1953), *Blood Alley* (1955) and *Hollywood or Bust* (1956) – pun, presumably, intended. Offered drama lessons, but frequently ignoring them to go horse-riding in the Hollywood hills, Ekberg was well aware that her fame was not principally as a Method actress. Anticipating Janet Jackson's 'wardrobe malfunction' by several decades, she once arranged for her blouse to pop open at a strategic moment during an encounter with the paparazzi in London's Berkeley Hotel.

She continued to capture the public imagination, but the roles she was offered were largely inane. *Screaming Mimi* (1958), as here described on Wikipedia, would surely be a comedy today:

> *While Virginia is taking an outside beach shower, an escaped madman from the sanatorium shows up. He stabs her dog, Rusty, attacks her and is then shot to death by her stepbrother, Charlie. After the attack, Virginia is committed to a sanatorium. The psychiatrist falls in love with her. He fakes her death, and they go on the run. Virginia ends up dancing at the El Madhouse night club run by Gypsy Rose Lee. All the while Virginia is being stalked by a serial killer.*

Only her cabaret sequence, a shadowy turn in a silk bikini dress and Houdini-style chains, reminds us of Ekberg's true charisma as a performer: she is slinky, bold and irresistible.

Whether or not Ekberg hoped to transcend this B-movie fame is a moot point, but when Fellini cast her in *La Dolce Vita* she found herself in a very different league. Essentially playing herself as Sylvia, a Swedish film star on assignment in Rome, she is pursued by journalist Marcello Rubini (Marcello Mastroianni) as they flirt amid the city's most notable landmarks, ending up at the Trevi fountain. The script called for Ekberg to climb into the monument in all its sparkling glory before baptizing Marcello with drops from her elegantly curled fingertips. As so often happens while filming on location, reality intruded. The water was filthy and grey and, even though the film stock was monochrome, Fellini insisted it looked too gloomy for the shot. By some miracle of serendipity worthy of the script itself, one of the crew members also worked for the airline SAS and hurried to procure some dye marker used to call attention to aircraft that crash-landed at sea. Now tinted green, the fountain looked glorious but remained bitterly cold. Ekberg, in a sleeveless black cocktail dress, was irrepressible and waded around happily while Mastroianni chickened out. He refused to proceed until a full wet suit was found, only to face the challenge of disguising it beneath his trim jacket and trousers; by the time he had done so he had drunk an entire bottle of vodka.

Almost every review refers to Ekberg's exploits in the fountain as 'cavorting', and to the neckline of her dress as 'plunging'; Marcello, like the audience, is simply a voyeur to the voluptuous display, while Sylvia concentrates on how much of the cascade she can collect in her décolletage. Even so, he remains the focus of our emotional attention since Sylvia is merely an accessory to his desires, a projection of his (and our) sexual fantasies. One key definition of 'objectification' is that the process has everything to do with the act of looking at a person and nothing to do with responding to them as a unique human being. Yet here, in some strange way, Ekberg *is* unique: she is being herself in a way that nobody else could achieve. Try imagining the scene with Mae West – too knowing. With Grace Kelly? We would feel ashamed. With Lauren Bacall? She'd punch you.

Fellini later said of Ekberg:

> *She had the beauty of a young goddess. The luminous colour of her skin, her clear ice-blue eyes, golden hair and joie de vivre made her into a grandiose creature, extraterrestrial and at the same time moving and irresistible.*

It is a noble description, and one which Ekberg would cherish long after her other films had faded into obscurity, but even Fellini was to betray her two years later. In his episode of the portmanteau film *Boccaccio '70* (1962), he cast her as an over-endowed model who appears on a billboard for a milk marketing company. When a prudish onlooker complains about the image, she climbs down – a giantess, towering over her victim – and torments him by trapping him in her cleavage. There is nothing post-modern or ironic here; it suggests only semi-intellectual, adolescent fumblings. It hardly bears thinking about that Ekberg had turned down the role of Honey Ryder in *Dr. No* (1962) to appear in it.

Worse was yet to come. In 1963 Ekberg teamed up with actor and comedian Bob Hope in *Call Me Bwana*: 'Fake Africa expert Merriwether (Hope) is sent on a secret government mission with spy Luba (Ekberg) and a modest elephant.' The dialogue is hardly more edifying than the synopsis:

                    LUBA
        Matt, I can't breathe!

                  MERRIWETHER
        If *you* can't breathe, we're really in trouble.

The gags pile on relentlessly:

> LUBA
> After these few days in the jungle with you, my
> resistance has collapsed.

> MERRIWETHER
> Everything else seems to be holding up.

Cheesy dialogue is par for the course in cheesy movies, but Hope turned the experience of working with Ekberg into a whole shtick for his subsequent one-man shows.

> *Anita is a standout, even in Hollywood where beautiful girls [are] one of the leading crops. To put it mildly, Anita is spectacular by herself. Nature had certainly endowed her. When Anita walked on the stage, I'd say, 'Her parents got the Nobel prize for architecture'.*

By now, Ekberg was powerless to overturn the image she found herself complicit in creating. She clung to memories of her iconic turn as Sylvia:

> *When the film was presented in New York, the distributor reproduced the fountain scene on a billboard as high as a skyscraper. My name was in the middle in huge letters [and] Fellini's was at the bottom, very tiny.*

La Dolce Vita may not have offered Ekberg the scope to deliver a fully realized performance like that of Julia Roberts in *Pretty Woman* (1990) or Faye Dunaway in *Bonnie and Clyde* (1967) – so we will never know if she had been worthy of richer acclaim. Still, her defiance never left her: 'It was I who made Fellini famous, not the other way around.'

I don't know if paradise or hell exist but I'm sure hell is more groovy.

*Sex appeal is
50 per cent what
you've got and
50 per cent what
people think
you've got*

SOPHIA LOREN

Sofia Villani Scicolone
20 September 1934–

The two big advantages I had at birth were to have been born wise and to have been born in poverty.

Everything you see I owe to spaghetti.

A woman's dress should be like a barbed wire fence: serving its purpose without obstructing the view.

Many people think they want things, but they don't really have the strength, the discipline. They are weak. I believe that you get what you want if you want it badly enough.

Mistakes are a part of the dues one pays for a full life.

Hate is unfulfilled love.

I do not forget easily, but I do forgive.

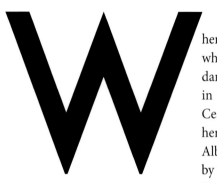

hen thou art at Rome, do as they do at Rome – or so Cervantes advised. But what do they do there? Anita Ekberg hurled herself into ancient fountains to dance, while Audrey Hepburn dodged chaperones to find herself (chastely) in the bed of a charming journalist. Sophia Loren's lot was grimmer: in 1944 Cesira, a young widow, flees a city under Allied bombardment to seek safety for herself and her twelve-year-old daughter. Based on the 1957 novel *La ciociara* by Alberto Moravia, *Two Women* (1960) tells the horrific true story of a mass rape by Moroccan auxiliary troops after the liberation of Monte Cassino. Vittorio De Sica's adaptation focuses almost exclusively on Cesira and Rosetta, who battle to find peace in a complex tale of war, politics, religion, treachery, greed and cowardice. It is a bleak journey with an even bleaker ending when Rosetta herself is raped, and the film-makers pull no punches: even the poster features just the mother and child averting their harrowed gazes from each other.

> CESIRA
> Do you know what your great soldiers have done in a holy church under the eyes of the Madonna?
>
> AMERICAN SOLDIER
> Peace, peace...
>
> CESIRA
> Yes, peace, beautiful peace! You ruined my little daughter forever! Now she's worse than dead. No, I'm not mad, I'm not mad! Look at her! And tell me if I am mad!

Loren brilliantly humanizes this almost unbearable portrait of a world in chaos, and her performance was in many ways autobiographical. Born in Rome to a mother who was a piano teacher and a father who worked as a construction engineer, despite his noble title (Loren, according to the family tree, was the Marchesa di Licata Scicolone Murillo), she began her career in show business singing to entertain the American troops who visited the modest bar in her grandmother's parlour. For the film, De Sica, a pioneer of the Italian neo-realist movement, favoured authentic locations and non-professional actors, and his star seems all the more beautiful amid barren landscapes and faces wearied by poverty and hunger. Exhausted by her struggles, but still full of fire, a dreamer while still remaining determinedly pragmatic, her bearing as compelling as her look, Loren towers over everything – and everyone – in the film.

Audiences across the Atlantic, who had experienced none of the carnage suffered by Europe during the war, were growing aware of the cinematic ripples spreading from France and Italy, but they were more interested in fresh and unusual talent than in aesthetic developments. Brigitte Bardot had wowed them in. . . *And God Created Woman* (1956), but her spectacular turn was capricious and ungrounded in any familiar reality; Anita Ekberg had delighted them in *La Dolce Vita* (1960) with visions of a hedonistic, bohemian life surrounded by culture and ennobling history, but she must have seemed just a magical confection, airy and transient. De Sica's almost painfully realistic vision – and Loren's incarnation of it – offered only bitter truths and disappointments, yet cinema-goers were captivated by its power. Loren was the first ever actress to win an Oscar in a leading role not spoken in English. She knocked Audrey Hepburn into second place with *Breakfast at Tiffany's* (1961) and her success prompted changes in the Academy that led to the permanent creation of a Best Foreign Film category.

Loren's career skyrocketed, and she soon became the biggest female star in the world, earning $1m [$7.5m] for her appearance as Lucilla in *The Fall of the Roman Empire* (1964). She went on to play opposite Gregory Peck (*Arabesque*, 1966), Marlon Brando (*A Countess from Hong Kong*, 1967) and Richard Burton (*The Voyage*, 1974), but she never allowed her head to be turned; apologizing for her decision not to attend the Academy Award ceremony at which she won Best Actress for *Two Women*, she simply said:

> *I decided that I could not bear the ordeal of sitting in plain view of millions of viewers while my fate was being judged. If I lost, I might faint for disappointment. If I won, I would also very likely faint with joy. I decided it would be better to faint at home.*

She remained married to Carlo Ponti, the producer of the film, from 1957 until the day he died fifty years later, declaring 'it would be impossible to love anyone else', and her one indulgence, she claimed, was that she loved to massage her feet with a rolling pin on the floor while she watched television. Even so, her glamour endures and she was photographed at the age of seventy-two for Pirelli's fiftieth anniversary calendar. Radiantly self-possessed and content, her mantra is simple enough:

> *Show business is what I do, not what I am.*

There is a Fountain of Youth: it is your mind, your talents, the creativity you bring to your life and the lives of the people you love.

*I don't use my body
to seduce, no, I just
stand there*

URSULA
ANDRESS

Ursula Andress
19 March 1936–

I never went to school.
I never went to acting school
because I was so scared.

I was scared because I didn't
know what [Paramount
Studios] expected me to be.
I had to go and study all the
Greta Garbo and Marlene
Dietrich films. I wasn't sure
I was able to deliver what
they asked me for.

To me, it's much more moral
to live with the man you love,
without signing a piece of
paper, than to live legally in
an atmosphere of boredom
which can eventually turn
to hate.

I have no problem with
nudity. I can look at myself.
I like walking around nude.
It doesn't bother me. I see all
the people walking around
nude; it doesn't bother me.

I mostly gave away what I had
from the James Bond movie.

**S**ome actresses are born to greatness, and others have swimwear thrust upon them; Ursula Andress's career, unlike her iconic bikini, was at best chequered. Although she went on to star in over forty films with co-stars as notable as Frank Sinatra, Marcello Mastroianni, Peter Sellers and Laurence Olivier, she never recaptured the fame of her first role as Honey Ryder in *Dr. No* (1962).

It seems for the first few years of her Hollywood career that her partners were more famous than any of her co-stars. She dated Marlon Brando (who helped her get a contract with Columbia); when he wrote his autobiography, he had to call her, somewhat unchivalrously, to check whether he had actually slept with her. At the same time she was seeing James Dean, and narrowly avoided accompanying him in his new Porsche the day he died in it. Their relationship was tempestuous; one gossip paper claimed Dean was learning German so the two could 'argue in another language'. Other lovers included Warren Beatty, Ryan O'Neal and Jean-Paul Belmondo, before she married director John Derek (*Bolero*, 1984). She described the ceremony as a farce 'in a small Las Vegas chapel with a cab driver as the best man and a ring that did not fit'.

But as far as the movie-going public is concerned, her most meaningful partnership remains her on-screen pairing with Sean Connery – in his first major role – and the scenes between them established the pattern for sexually suggestive names, double entendres, and the entire concept of the Bond girl as we know her. In Ian Fleming's original novel, Honeychile Rider has a well-drawn background as a white Jamaican and her story touches on controversial aspects of colonialism and sexual politics. She works as a diver, selling shells to American collectors in order to save up for plastic surgery on her nose, which was broken when she was raped as a teenager. Renamed Honey Ryder for the film, her revenge on the perpetrator remained vintage Fleming:

> RYDER
> I put a black widow spider underneath his
> mosquito net... a female, they're the worst.
> It took him a whole week to die.

Bond looks shocked.

> RYDER
> Did I do wrong?

                    BOND
Well, it wouldn't do to make a habit of it.

Andress's character here is less complex than in the book, but judging by the
popular reaction to her costume at the time, any further psychological depth
would have been wasted. She steps nonchalantly from the Caribbean and tosses
two large conch shells onto the beach before being startled by Bond, who is
watching her from the trees:

                    RYDER
Who's that?

                    BOND
It's all right — I'm not supposed to be here
either. I take it you're not? Are you alone?

                    RYDER
What are you doing here? Looking for shells?

                    BOND
No — I'm just looking.

                    RYDER
Stay where you are.

                    BOND
I promise you, I won't steal your shells.

                    RYDER
I promise you, you won't either.

Bond moves closer. Ryder pulls out her dagger.

                    RYDER
Stay where you are.

                    BOND
I can assure you, my intentions are strictly
honourable.

What seems to have captivated Commander Bond was not only Andress's extraordinary figure and European beauty, but the construction – and brevity – of her bikini. Two-piece bathing costumes had existed since Roman times, but advances in tailoring and tolerance had ensured that their coverage was becoming ever more concise. Nothing worn in previous decades by Ava Gardner or Rita Hayworth had exposed so much of the wearer's navel, nor had the garment even been properly named until 1946, when Louis Réard, a French engineer, jokingly likened its impact to that of a nuclear bomb which had recently been tested on Bikini Atoll in the Pacific.

The fallout from the fashion sensation, as Réard predicted, was immense, but it seems the design found its most perfect embodiment on Andress's lissom physique. The construction was of reasonably sturdy ivory cotton, which highlighted her bronzed skin, and the effect was both chic and shocking – especially when offset by tiny feminine bows and a decidedly masculine diving knife. For most viewers, the film *is* that scene and it remains one of the most memorable moments in cinema. With charming modesty, as if describing an old friend, Andress subsequently admitted:

> *This bikini made me into a success. As a result of starring in* Dr. No
> *as the first Bond girl, I was given the freedom to take my pick of*
> *future roles and to become financially independent.*

The Swiss-German Andress had enjoyed a cosmopolitan, jet-setting childhood, and as a result was unimpressed by the glamour of Hollywood – and even less so by its stiff morality. Her aloofness seemed to baffle directors and producers, and although she won a Golden Globe for Most Promising Newcomer as Honey Ryder, the parts she was subsequently offered showed that nobody really understood where her talents lay.

Most flatteringly, Pulitzer Prize-winning author William Styron had her in mind for Sophie Zawistowski in *Sophie's Choice* (1982), a part that eventually won Meryl Streep an Oscar. Sadly, few others saw her as an actress of such range; aside from a few modest successes with *What's New Pussycat?* (1965) and *The Blue Max* (1966), the roles she accepted included a handful surely destined to sabotage even the strongest reputation. In *The 10th Victim* (1965), opposite Marcello Mastroianni, she wears a bra that shoots bullets, and for *Loaded Guns* (*Colpo in canna,* 1975) the strapline carries the faint whiff of marketing desperation: 'An air hostess gets involved in Naples, against her will, in the in-fighting amongst rival gangs.' In 1967 she played another Bond girl, Vesper Lynd, in the independently produced spoof *Casino Royale*. Although intended as a comedy, it did little to confirm Andress's credentials as a heavyweight actress:

```
           SIR JAMES BOND
     The whole world believes that you were eaten by
     a shark, Miss Lynd.


           LYND
     That was no shark. That was my personal
     submarine. But enough of this polite
     conversation. What is the purpose of your
     visit?
```

Other titles in themselves – *The Sensuous Nurse* (1975), *The Mountain of the Cannibal God* (1978), *Tigers in Lipstick* (1979) – probably reveal all we care to know. Even so, she remained undaunted and still gloried in her uninhibited physical attributes: when asked why she had agreed to model nude for *Playboy* in 1965, she replied: 'Because I'm beautiful.'

Many stars, like one-hit wonders in the pop world, might be bitter that their reputation rests on a single, almost accidental, moment in movie history – as with Sharon Stone as Catherine Tramell in *Basic Instinct* (1992) – but Andress's moment was as iconic as they come. Everything about her appearance from the waves as a Swinging Sixties Venus heralded the style of that decade: insouciance, independence and an ineffable cool. More than fifty years after *Dr. No*'s release, the scene continues to be imitated in music videos, advertising campaigns by both Victoria's Secret and Marks and Spencer, and even in a subsequent Bond film, *Die Another Day* (2002), with Halle Berry as Jinx. In 2003, the UK's Channel 4 announced a poll of 100 Greatest Sexy Moments in films and Andress was still at number one: the epiphany endures.

Most of the films I made were not profound enough to really show myself.

'The most poetic of all actresses'

JULIE
CHRISTIE

Julie Frances Christie
14 April 1941–

I was born with a need to be the centre of attention, and, of course, you're the centre of the world when you're acting.

[in 1966] Being on top right now is a fluke.

All that concentrated adulation is terribly corroding.

I never really knew how to enjoy beauty, but it took the form of a subconscious arrogance, expecting things, all muddled up with celebrity.

There were some films I refused because the feminist aspect was a bit wonky.

In the 1970s I was amazed to be talked about as a 1960s sex symbol. I wasn't that person, as if I were a doll from the past. I had to learn to come to terms with that.

The rules were the same forty years ago as they are now. You can either choose your spotlight – or you can stay at home.

[on the media] It was difficult when I was a girl and they're not any kinder now. I just hate not being strong enough.

**J**ulie Christie – born on a tea plantation in India, but educated at a series of convent and boarding schools in England (one of which expelled her for telling a filthy joke) – studied acting at the Central School of Speech and Drama and made her professional stage debut in 1957 at the age of seventeen. A spell in the successful BBC science fiction series *A for Andromeda* (1961) brought her to the attention of film producers, although Cubby Broccoli reputedly turned her down for the role of Honey Ryder in *Dr. No* (1962) on the grounds that her breasts were too small.

In 1963, John Schlesinger cast her in his adaptation of Keith Waterhouse's 1959 hit novel *Billy Liar*. The story recounts the hapless adventures of William (Billy) Fisher (Tom Courtenay) as he fails to distinguish between his fantastic daydreams and his real life as clerk to a funeral director; set in a grimy Bradford, filled with characters obsessed by stability and respectability, the film portrays a post-war Britain on the cusp of a brave new world of liberty and technology. Liz (Christie) blazes into Billy's world as the epitome of style, beauty and adventure. Amazingly – like Hannibal Lecter in *The Silence of the Lambs* – she is only on the screen for a quarter of an hour, but she is incandescent, embodying everything about the King's Road chic that would characterize the 1960s.

> *It was incredible because I was terribly, terribly well-received, I mean, ridiculously well-received in that part. I see it now, and it's not very good, but still, something happened.*

She was right: something did happen, leading to *Life* magazine's declaration that 1965 was 'The Year of Julie Christie'. The world had just seen her as Diana Scott in Schlesinger's *Darling*, which won her an Oscar, and as Lara Antipova in *Doctor Zhivago*; David Lean's adaptation of Pasternak's epic Russian novel remains the eighth-highest-grossing movie since records began. She played both Linda Montag and Clarisse in *Fahrenheit 451* (1966), Bathsheba Everdene in Schlesinger's version of Thomas Hardy's *Far from the Madding Crowd* (1967) and Marian Maudsley in *The Go-Between* (1971), and yet some instinct held her back: between 1965 and 1975 she made only nine films. Many of them were critical and box-office successes – she won a second Oscar nomination as Constance Miller in Robert Altman's *McCabe & Mrs. Miller* (1971) – but she never seemed to settle into any one identity and she protected her privacy jealously. She wrestled with the star's perennial quandary about separating her professional from her private life and some say that she was so devoted to her lover Warren Beatty, whom she dated between 1967 and 1974, that she neglected everything but her passion for him. Beatty claimed she was 'the most beautiful and at the same time the most nervous person I had ever known', but after they split up they worked together on Hal Ashby's *Shampoo* (1975), a sexy and funny film which caught the spirit of that decade just as powerfully as *Billy Liar* had done for its own, more austere era.

By the time the 1970s rolled around, the industry had become more permissive and she delivered another memorable moment in Nic Roeg's *Don't Look Now* (1973), a psychological horror story in which a grieving couple pursues the spirit of their dead child through a chiaroscuro Venice. Christie's turn is heartbreaking and brilliantly brittle, but the film also contains one of the most explicit sex scenes filmed for general release to that date. Setting aside their grief for a rare moment, Christie and her husband (Donald Sutherland) make love in their hotel room. The encounter is starkly honest and intimate, although the *Daily Mail* tried to stir controversy by writing that 'one of the frankest love scenes ever to be filmed is likely to plunge lovely Julie Christie into the biggest censorship row since *Last Tango in Paris*'. The newspaper's principal concern was that the encounter showed cunnilingus, an activity with which their readers may have been unfamiliar, but the triumph of the performances (and of the kaleidoscopic editing) is more tender than anything else in Roeg's tragic depiction of love and loss.

Christie, naturally modest, must have hated the middlebrow media furore. Throughout the height of her fame, she remained charmingly self-deprecating:

> *Acting took me away from real life to a pretend life. I wanted that real life back. I'm not a dedicated actress, I'm afraid. I never have been.*

In one television interview, shot on the eve of the release of *Doctor Zhivago*, she seems to shy away from the camera, chain-smoking, forcing her radiant smile and making more effort to make the interviewers feel comfortable than herself. The footage is awkward but hugely endearing, and echoes a remark that John Schlesinger, a director she adored, once said about her: 'She's my incandescent, melancholy, strong, gold-hearted, sphinx-like, stainless steel little soldier.'

These contradictions were to remain at the heart of her career, but if it is true that one's peers are the best judges, she must have been delighted by Al Pacino's simple acknowledgement that she is 'the most poetic of all actresses.'

I think I've got something when I'm on screen, but that's nothing to do with acting or talent.

Sometimes I'm
so sweet even
I can't stand it

JULIE
ANDREWS

Julia Elizabeth Wells
1 October 1935–

Can I give them what they
think they're going to get
from me? That's always the
big question.

I had a very pure, white, thin
voice, a four-octave range –
dogs would come for miles
around.

All love shifts and changes.
I don't know if you can be
wholeheartedly in love
all the time.

Richard Burton rang me
up once and said, Do you
know you're my only leading
lady I've never slept with?
I said, Well, please don't tell
everybody, it's the worst
image.

If the director says you can
do better, particularly in a
love scene, then it is rather
embarrassing.

Some people regard discipline
as a chore. For me, it is a
kind of order that sets me
free to fly.

I have been called a nun with
a switchblade where my
privacy is concerned. I think
there's a point where one says,
'that's for family, that's for me.'

**D**oes the star make the movie, or does the movie make the star? Or, to borrow that glorious line from *The Sound of Music* (1965), how do you solve a problem like Julie Andrews? As the nuns at Maria's convent sing:

She is gentle! She is wild! She's a riddle! She's a child! She's a headache! She's an angel! She's a girl!

The problem in this case is not Andrews' Oscar-nominated performance, but that the role cemented the reputation she had earned the previous year in *Mary Poppins* as the epitome of prim perfection.

> MARY POPPINS
> Now the, the qualifications... item one: a cheery disposition. I am never cross. Item two: rosy cheeks... obviously. Item three: play games, all sorts. Well, I'm sure the children will find my games extremely diverting.
>
> MR BANKS
> Now this paper, where did you get it from? I — I thought I tore it up.
>
> MARY POPPINS
> Excuse me. Item four: you must be kind. I am kind, but extremely firm.

Toting an Academy Award for her turn as the eponymous, magical Edwardian nanny, Andrews returned to the screen as a more human but no less enchanting Austrian governess during its Nazi occupation; *The Sound of Music* remains, adjusted for inflation, the third-highest-grossing picture ever made. Industry insiders nicknamed it 'The Sound of Money'; its star Christopher Plummer thought it so mawkish that he referred to it as 'The Sound of Mucus'. Though the two roles share many key characteristics, Andrews articulates her humour, tenderness and strength in carefully distinctive ways – as Poppins through formality, and as Maria through compassion. Even so, both roles became conflated in the public imagination and it was a burden she found increasingly hard to shake off: 'I think of part of myself as a very passionate person, but I don't think that comes across. I don't know where it comes from, that reserve or veneer of British niceness. But it doesn't bother me if other people don't spot the passion. . . it's other people who have a problem with my image, not me.' Still, the contradiction lingered. When she received a BAFTA in 1989 for her 'outstanding contribution to world cinema', she acknowledged her success on home turf by declaring: 'I am first and always English, and I carry my country in my heart wherever I go.'

Andrews' post-*Poppins* years in Hollywood saw respectable successes with *Hawaii* (1966) and *Thoroughly Modern Millie* (1967), and a high-profile failure in *Star!* (1968). In 1969 she married Blake Edwards, director of *Breakfast at Tiffany's* (1961) and the long-running *Pink Panther* franchise; they remained together until his death in 2010, and he made several attempts to cast his new wife and leading lady in a fresh light. Although she had briefly appeared nude beside Paul Newman in Alfred Hitchcock's *Torn Curtain* (1966), Edwards was determined to invest her image with a more contemporary sexual energy.

In *Darling Lili* (1970), a modern riff on the story of the spy Mata Hari, Andrews performs a cabaret in which she tosses her corset aside just as she disappears off-stage; in the satirical comedy *S.O.B.* (1981), she plays a soft-porn actress who bares her breasts in a misguided attempt to resist the advances of a muscle-bound admirer. Her performance (largely clothed apart from this celebrated scene) is stylish and wryly self-mocking, but the movie was not a hit: it polarized critics and the public, garnering nominations for both the best (Writers Guild of America) and worst (Golden Raspberry Awards) screenplay of the year. As an attempt to escape the legacy of Maria von Trapp, it failed too: when Andrews appeared on the *Johnny Carson Show* to promote the picture, his ungallant introduction thanked her for 'showing us that the hills were still alive'.

Comfortable with herself, her family and her accolades now, it seems that Andrews has made her peace with the roles she was adored for. Mischievously, in an interview with *The New York Times* in 1982, she realized that if she could not change her public she could at least subvert the characters that they had so loved:

> *Does Mary Poppins have an orgasm? Does she go to the bathroom? I assure you, she does.*

A lot of my life happened in great, wonderful bursts of good fortune, and then I would race to be worthy of it.

*A star remains
pinned on a wall
in the public imagi-
nation*

CATHERINE DENEUVE

Catherine Fabienne Dorléac
22 October 1943–

A woman has to be
intelligent, have charm,
a sense of humour, and be
kind. It's the same qualities
I require from a man.

I was never a dangerous
woman. I'm not the prissy
blonde woman that could
take your husband away.

People who know me know
I'm strong, but I'm vulnerable.

I don't see any reason for
marriage when there is
divorce.

I am shocked when people
talk about me and sum me up
as: blonde, cold, and solemn.

Why should I go to the
States to do a film I wouldn't
consider in Europe, just
because it's English-speaking?

I'm not always the nicest
person to meet, because
I forget very easily that I'm
an actress when I'm not
working.

atherine Deneuve's life and career seem almost to caricature the image of a movie star who rose to fame in the 1960s. She dated director Roger Vadim, married photographer David Bailey, and subsequently lived with screen icon Marcello Mastroianni; she has made over a hundred pictures, including such milestones as Roman Polanski's *Repulsion* (1965), François Truffaut's *Le Dernier métro* (1980), Régis Wargnier's *Indochine* (1992) and Lars von Trier's *Dancer in the Dark* (2000). Born in Paris to actor parents, she won her first screen role at the age of thirteen, but it would take another seven years before collaboration with Jacques Demy would bring her before a global audience.

The Umbrellas of Cherbourg (*Les Parapluies de Cherbourg*, 1964) opens with one of the dullest images ever committed to celluloid – a wide shot of the city's bleak, windswept docks as a rain storm approaches – before exploding into a post-modern Technicolor musical with every last word set to a lush, exuberant soundtrack. No detail is too pedestrian to be sung:

> GENEVIÈVE
> Guy, I love you. You smell of gasoline.

> GUY
> It's just another perfume.

Tongue-in-cheek, the film challenges us to suspend our disbelief:

> GENEVIÈVE
> I can't live without him. I'll die.

> MADAME EMERY
> People only die of love in movies.

Geneviève (Deneuve) and Guy (Nino Castelnuovo) have fallen for each other and are now engaged. Guy is about to depart to fight in Algeria; they make love before he sails; Geneviève falls pregnant. Guy's passionate letters go astray; Geneviève loses hope, and marries another. Years later the two lovers meet by chance; they exchange a few diffident words before parting for the last time. What actress could make sense of this fragile world, a toy theatre of fairy-tale fragments? Deneuve moves like a dancer within the camera's swooping choreography, but her close-ups are like the timeless drawings in a child's picture book; her performance seems astonishingly natural within Demy's daring artifice. The film won the Palme D'Or at Cannes and critic Pauline Kael wrote: 'Deneuve, with her icy yet mysterious perfection, is the French Grace Kelly.' Wim Wenders, announcing her European Film Academy Lifetime Achievement Award in 2013, declared: 'You are the queen of European cinema and at the same time the most beautiful woman on earth.' (Deneuve rather grumpily told the press later: 'To achieve life is to mean that you are dead. It's not an award you give to someone who is still alive.') Germaine Greer also recognized Deneuve's impact, but with a caveat: 'Her effortless blankness allows her to take the imprint of her viewers' fantasies, and so she has achieved a reputation as one of the sexiest film actresses ever to grace the screen.'

Luis Buñuel's *Belle de jour* (1967) offers a fascinating counterpoint to *Les Parapluies,* and proved equally sensational. Deneuve plays Séverine, the stylish but reserved wife of the handsome, conventional Pierre; unable to enjoy their love-making, she retreats into a world of past fears and future sexual fantasies and seeks work in a high-class brothel in an attempt to confront her frustrations. Her adventures there, under the alias Belle de jour, eventually liberate her, and she embraces Pierre once again. Tellingly, as the couple grows closer, Séverine says to her husband:

SÉVERINE
Every day I think I understand you better.

But we realize it is herself she is growing to accept; as she stares into the mirror, so we gaze over her shoulder. The film was understandably controversial, not least because Séverine doesn't care what men want; the story is entirely her journey, and if she shows little on the outside, she lives it entirely on the inside. As Deneuve herself realized:

> *I think it is more interesting to give [the audience] a place where they can imagine things instead of knowing everything.*

I like being famous when it's convenient for me and completely anonymous when it's not.

It's so much better to desire than to have

ANOUK AIMÉE

Nicole Françoise Florence Dreyfus
27 April 1932–

Oh come on, it hasn't been an unimpressive career. If you look at the number of projects I've been involved in, the people I've worked with. . . But it's perhaps true that I haven't always made the right choices.

The moment of desire, when you know something is going to happen – that's the most exalting.

For a certain type of woman who risks losing her identity in a man, there are all those questions. . . until you get to the point and know that you really are living a love story.

You can only perceive real beauty in a person as they get older.

Art critic Jürgen Müller, writing about the great films of the 1960s, remarked that 'it's still hard for anyone to resist the melancholy aura of Anouk Aimée'. Hard, too, to argue with the $14m [$100m] in ticket sales generated in the US alone by Aimée's dazzling breakthrough in *Un Homme et une femme* (*A Man and a Woman*, 1966). Relentlessly French and exquisitely moving, the film is a paean to love; critic Pauline Kael described it as 'the most efficacious make-out movie of the 1960s'. But is enigmatic beauty enough to power a star?

The daughter of two actors, Aimée (née Nicole Dreyfus) made her first screen appearance aged fourteen as 'Anouk' in *La Maison sous la mer* (1946). She liked her character's name, and the French poet Jacques Prévert, who wrote *The Lovers of Verona* (1949) especially for her, suggested she adopt a new last name too: Aimée, meaning 'beloved'. By 1960 she had already taken a brief but vital role in Fellini's genre-bending, cosmopolitan portrait of post-war Rome, *La Dolce Vita*, playing a rich, world-weary young woman (Maddalena) who seeks sexual thrills to enliven her evenings; in one notable scene, she and the protagonist Marcello (Marcello Mastroianni) meet a prostitute, in whose seedy bedroom they make love together. The film, a worldwide hit, was a perfect showcase for Aimée's inscrutable beauty, and her hallmark sunglasses – making her seem like a cross between Audrey Hepburn and Catwoman – epitomized the growing glamour of European stars.

When Claude Lelouch offered Aimée the part of Anne Gauthier in *Un Homme et une femme* (*A Man and a Woman*) he distilled her elegant allure into another remarkable box-office success. As Aimée herself remarked in a later interview, this was pretty astonishing for a project which had a crew of only thirteen and was so low-budget that she was required to do her own make-up. The movie was seen to be daringly avant-garde in its visual styling as it mixed colour and black-and-white, although Lelouch cheerfully explained that the reason for this was simply that funds had limited him on occasion to purchasing monochrome film stock. Aimée recalled the experience proudly:

> It was the right time, the right way Claude directed, the way he photographed, the way we acted. . . there was a kind of magic to that film.

The widowed Anne and widower Jean-Louis Duroc (Jean-Louis Trintignant) meet while visiting their respective children at a boarding school in the fading seaside casino town of Deauville. Each parent has lost a spouse under tragic circumstances, and each remains so much in love with their former partner that they seem unable to escape the past – yet the connection between them is electric. Here, as Anne accepts a lift home with Jean-Louis, she has not told him that her husband is dead.

> ANNE
> I don't claim to be original. You meet someone, marry, have a baby. That sort of thing happens every day. But what is original is... the man you love.

> JEAN-LOUIS
> Your husband must be very original then.

> ANNE
> For me, he is. He's so fascinating, so exclusive. So real.

The film juxtaposes the couple's poignant memories against their mutual attraction as they battle propriety, dignity, love and lust in a portrait of fragile but intense passion. The film contains chauvinistic elements and fanciful scenarios in equal measure – Jean-Louis is a racing driver and Anne's previous husband was a famous stunt-man – but Lelouch gives Aimée enough space to create an emotionally credible mother and lover. Film historian Karel Tabery wrote of her performance that with her 'subtle portrayal of the heroine – self-protective, then succumbing to a new love – Aimée seemed to create a new kind of femme fatale'.

Married four times, including to fellow actor Albert Finney between 1970 and 1978, Aimée was no stranger to passion off screen. Dirk Bogarde, a long-time friend, said after her relationship with Omar Sharif collapsed: 'she is never so happy as when she is miserable between love affairs'. Even if this helps to explain the mysterious, restless energy of her portrayal of Anne Gauthier on those lonely beaches, it is still not the whole story. Like Garbo, Aimée compels us with her provocative yet introspective gaze; to watch her through the rain-swept windscreen of Jean-Louis's Mustang as they begin to explore the possibility of a life together is to understand what it means to be a man – and a woman – in love.

What helps me go forward is that I stay receptive, I feel that anything can happen.

*The human face is
the great subject of
the cinema*

LIV
ULLMANN

Liv Johanne Ullmann
16 December 1938–

Quick cuts and camera angles
– they think that's film. That
is not film. Film is to show
people and life, and to make
you know more about life
than when you went in. It's
not this cut, cut, cut, kill, kill,
kill, sex, sex, sex. . .

I sometimes try to avoid
conflict, so I agree instead of
saying no.

Sometimes it is less hard to
wake up feeling lonely when
you are alone than wake up
feeling lonely when you are
with someone.

Is [growth] not where life's
possibilities lie? Not
necessarily to arrive, but
always to be on the way, in
movement.

What I have always loved
most in men is imperfection.
I think it is sad that more
women don't take the chance
that maybe men will be
moved by seeing the chin a
little less firm than it used to
be, that a man will be more in
love with his wife because he
remembers who she was and
sees who she is and thinks,
God, isn't that lovely that
this happened to her.

ighty-four minutes; fourteen words. So gripping is Liv Ullmann's screen presence in Ingmar Bergman's *Persona* (1966) that we barely notice that her character, actress Elisabet Vogler, does not speak. Although perfectly sane and healthy, she has chosen – after an unexpected breakdown on stage – to remain silent for the rest of her life. Her psychiatrist tries to articulate the reasons for the decision:

```
DOCTOR
I understand, all right. The hopeless dream of
being — not seeming, but being. At every waking
moment, alert. The gulf between what you are
with others and what you are alone.
```

Ullmann, known best in her native Norway as a consummate stage actress, made nine films with Ingmar Bergman, and their relationship became so close that he fathered her only child, Linn Ullmann. *Persona* was the first of their professional collaborations and many, including Susan Sontag, consider it Bergman's masterpiece; critic Hubert Cohen cites it as 'one of this century's great works of art'. But is it an existentialist mystery, a love affair or a twisted psychological thriller? Certainly the soundtrack, even in moments of exquisite visual simplicity, makes it feel like a horror movie, but otherwise Bergman is scrupulously neutral in his unfolding of Elisabet's story. It seems she has rejected her dramatic career, abandoned her doting husband and forsaken her only son in order to retreat into (or away from) herself; she has nothing to say but everything to express – all from silence.

Her psychiatric nurse Alma (in an equally impressive turn by Bibi Andersson) acts as a foil to her patient, reflecting what she imagines Elisabet is experiencing – even if, ultimately, it is like holding a mirror up to another mirror. This metaphor is made explicit by the camera, which frequently superposes and dissolves one woman's face exactly onto that of her counterpart. To the very end Elisabet remains a svelte sphinx, making us feel finally that we are exhausted by our own questions. Perhaps this is the genius of Ullmann's performance: it forces the viewer to accept the unanswerable ambiguities Elisabet feels about her own life. The more we long to know, the more she makes us feel foolish and intrusive for hoping to understand her; yet she draws us inexorably towards her.

So how does Ullmann pull it off? It sounds like a poisoned chalice for any actress. If the film itself were not so great, it would seem almost a parody of downbeat

1960s black-and-white Swedish dramas, but Ullmann sidesteps the pitfalls adroitly. Even when she is crazy, she is calm; she never attempts to hoodwink or manipulate Alma (or us); she never suggests in any way that she is anything other than herself. The first close-up of her in the hospital bed, listening to Bach on the radio, is one of the most gripping in cinema. She lies on her side, absolutely motionless; at first we think the shot is a still photograph. Then the light fades and she rolls onto her back in silhouette, covering her face with her hands. Oliver Reed once said of his trademark glowering stare that, the trick with any portrait is never to blink while the lens is on you. Ingmar Bergman waxed more poetic:

The human face is the great subject of the cinema. Everything is there.

The film as a whole is alternately tranquil and shocking; it counterpoises nightmarish snippets of early cinema (skeletons, crucifixions, spiders, an erect penis) with jagged rips in the celluloid and blank frames against languid landscape shots of the women on the rugged Swedish coast. This turbulence – visual and emotional – forms the backdrop to Elisabet's own journey. The more Alma comes to depend on Elisabet and the more she reveals of her own past, the richer Ullmann's own performance becomes. She permeates the story like some striking monochrome deity, a repository for the fears and dreams of all who invoke her, who ultimately takes the shape of everyone who reaches out to her – Alma, her psychiatrist, her husband. For those who encounter her, she is both kaleidoscope and laser beam. Ullmann recalls clearly how she learned the secret of this power:

I thought I had to let the cigarette kind of shiver in my hand to show that I was getting upset or excited by [Alma's] story and put my other hand at one time to my chest. Ingmar told me: 'Stop it. Don't do things. Just listen.' So the cigarettes became quiet and the hand didn't go to the throat. It was just the face listening. And then things happened in the face that I as an actress wasn't even aware of.

The most shocking moment of the film is simply a slow, perfectly matched dissolve from Alma's face to Elisabet's; we can hardly tell which is which, or whether it is half of each, or simply both. If it is a truism to say that beauty contains mystery, Bergman and Ullmann show us that mystery also contains beauty.

The older one gets in this profession, the more people there are with whom one would never work again.

I am misrepresented very often, but so is everybody who has something to say

VANESSA REDGRAVE

Vanessa Redgrave
30 January 1937–

I choose all my roles very carefully so that when my career is finished I will have covered all our recent history of oppression.

I don't consider myself beautiful at all. I'm usually running around like a scruff.

Ask the right questions if you're to find the right answers.

How can we help the people in the audience – and ourselves – remove the cobwebs that prevent us all from being able to reach and touch things?

I have a tremendous use for passionate statement.

America is gangsterism for the private profit of the few.

[Speaking of her family] We are the sprigs of a great and beautiful tree.

One must never comment as an actor, never show that a character is shallow or vindictive, but let that be conveyed. I mean, none of us thinks of ourselves as being vindictive or shallow – perhaps we should.

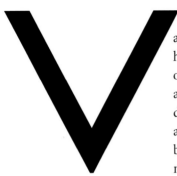anessa Redgrave comes from a British acting dynasty almost biblical in its reach: her parents, Michael Redgrave and Rachel Kempton, were as renowned as their offspring, Vanessa, Corin and Lynn Redgrave; Vanessa's own children – Natasha and Joely, by director Tony Richardson – became stars in their own right, as did Corin's daughter Jemma Redgrave. Vanessa, celebrated for her stage work as much as her screen appearances, has been nominated for an Oscar six times, but the role for which she won – as the eponymous *Julia* (1977) – brought her as much notoriety as it did fame.

There is a familiar Hollywood caution against mixing politics with show business: 'If you have a message, call Western Union'. So keenly does the industry fear preaching that the quote has been attributed to Harry Warner, Harry Cohn, Humphrey Bogart, Dorothy Parker, George S. Kaufman, Ernest Hemingway, Bernard Shaw, Samuel Goldwyn and even Marlon Brando. Brando is unlikely to have said it, since he famously sent Apache spokesman Sacheen Littlefeather to decline his Academy Award for *The Godfather* (1972) as a protest against the government's treatment of Native Americans. He had written a fifteen-page diatribe for her to deliver, but one of the broadcast's producers threatened that if she spoke for more than sixty seconds he would have her arrested. Littlefeather improvised her speech, but the statuette remained unclaimed; presenter Roger Moore just took it home with him. Eventually it was collected by an armed guard on behalf of the Academy.

Plenty of others have pledged their time and earnings to campaign for and support humanitarian causes: Elizabeth Taylor for AIDS, Jane Fonda for women's rights, and Angelina Jolie for refugees. But few have been so committed and outspoken as to threaten their own careers as Redgrave did in 1978 when she spoke in support of the rights of Palestinians. She had recently funded and narrated a film which appeared to condone the activities of the terrorist Palestinian Liberation Organization (PLO) and she had received death threats for her involvement; the Jewish Defence League burned effigies of her, and picketed the Academy Awards ceremony at which she had been nominated for her role in *Julia* – ironically, the story of a woman who is murdered for her resistance to Nazism. Redgrave won the Oscar, and in her acceptance speech praised the voters:

> I think you should be very proud that in the last few weeks you've
> stood firm, and you have refused to be intimidated by the threats of a
> small bunch of Zionist hoodlums whose behaviour is an insult to the

stature of Jews all over the world and their great and heroic record of struggle against fascism and oppression.

The controversy shadowed her for decades, but Redgrave did little to rein in her political passions; though she had nearly lost the role of Helen in *Yanks* (1979) as a result of her outspokenness, she still could not resist passing out Workers Revolutionary Party newspapers to the crew.

If her identity as a committed activist endures, her talents remain undisputed. She is the only performer, male or female, to have won an Oscar, an Emmy, a Tony, an Olivier, a Golden Globe, a Screen Actors Guild trophy and a Palme D'Or at Cannes; and two of the twentieth century's greatest playwrights, Arthur Miller and Tennessee Williams, hailed her as 'the greatest living actress of our times'. Her notable roles include *Isadora* (1968), *Mary, Queen of Scots* (1971), *The Bostonians* (1984), *Howards End* (1992) and *Atonement* (2007). But if such films suggest that she frequently played earnest characters, we would do well to recall that her breakthrough came with Karel Reisz's comedy *Morgan: A Suitable Case for Treatment* in 1966. Redgrave plays Leonie, a scatterbrained young heiress torn between the loves of Morgan (David Warner), a failed communist artist, and Charles (Robert Stephens), a rich, conservative gallery owner:

```
              LEONIE
If you want to come in with me you'll have to
fight him, won't you?

              CHARLES
Fight him?

              LEONIE
Yes, and the winner will drag me off and have
me!
```

Dazzlingly beautiful and vivacious, Redgrave seizes the comedy as she would do with all her subsequent work: with integrity, vivacity, rigour and truth. For her – then, as now – all roles are equally rich.

I give myself to my parts as to a lover.

I discovered a long time ago that the camera does lie, and thank God it does.

Any time people put you on a pedestal, you're doomed to disappoint

FAYE DUNAWAY

Dorothy Faye Dunaway
14 January 1941–

My mother's passion for something more, to write a different destiny for a dirt-poor farmer's daughter, was to shape my entire life.

I often say the last role I played that really touched me and where I was able to access what I really am was Bonnie, which is kind of sad when you think how early in my career that was.

I never liked parties, never felt comfortable. I was a little girl from the South and people were terribly judgmental. Oh, I had a hard time. I never felt good enough. I had large insecurities.

When you're younger they always try to get you to do every ninny role that's going.

What I realized long ago is that any time people put you on a pedestal, you're doomed to disappoint. I can't possibly be who they want me to be because, mainly, they want me to answer all their dreams. But we're just people with flaws, insecurities. Maybe more insecurities than anybody else.

T hose towering cheekbones, that piercing gaze, that smouldering voice: Faye Dunaway is like a Hepburn (Katharine – absolutely not Audrey) reinvented for the generation when a socially engaged, politically savvy independent Hollywood briefly flowered. But is she super-cool, or merely icy?

Dunaway, like many actors in a fickle business, has suffered a chequered career but five films stand out, and any one of them would have been enough to turn our heads: *Bonnie and Clyde* (1967), *The Thomas Crown Affair* (1968), *Chinatown* (1974), *Network* (1976) and *Eyes of Laura Mars* (1978). Each of them captured something very different about her magnetism on screen – and her detached but unmistakable beauty – and each, too, reflects something of the difficulties that dogged her from the start. Born in Bascom, Florida (current population 106), to a housewife and a non-commissioned army officer, Dunaway's childhood was by all accounts tough. Her blend of Southern elegance and unwavering resolution springs from those early days, but these qualities were also to inform her work – and her relationships with her peers.

After a spell with the American National Theater and Academy and then on Broadway, she began to get movie offers and in 1967 appeared in *Hurry Sundown*, directed by the legendarily dictatorial Otto Preminger (when Preminger appeared on *Desert Island Discs* in 1980 his musical selections were all taken from his films, the book he chose was his own autobiography, and his luxury was a mirror). The two fell out, with Dunaway claiming at the time that Preminger lacked the skills to work effectively with actors. Such contretemps, whether real or imagined, are a dime a dozen in a creative milieu filled with competing egos, but Dunaway was incensed. Most unusually for an actor on the verge of her first big break, she spoke candidly about the disagreement, adding: 'Once I've been crossed, I'm not very conciliatory.' If anyone doubted her seriousness, they soon changed their mind when Dunaway sued Preminger to escape from the five-picture deal she had signed with him. 'It cost me a lot of money to not work for Otto again. . . I regretted paying him [but] I thought he was awful.' Such resolve is rare – and, as we shall see, not always prudent in an industry with deep pockets and a long memory.

With a BAFTA Award for Best Newcomer and a Golden Globe nomination for Best New Star of the Year in *Hurry Sundown*, Dunaway soon came to the notice of Warren Beatty, who was about to start shooting – as both actor and producer – *Bonnie and Clyde*. The picture, based on the true story of two lovers who careened across America in the 1930s, fuelling their wild lifestyle with hold-ups, robberies and murder, was a huge success: a post-modern riff on gangster movies, it was filmed in a snappy contemporary style and with a disconcerting mixture of comedy and brutally explicit violence. But few were paying attention to director Arthur Penn's pioneering techniques when they had Beatty and Dunaway to engage them. The couple are incandescent: raw, compelling, guileless and perfectly matched both as lovers and as hapless partners in crime. Rumours abounded as to whether the relationship was as passionate off screen as on, although they both continue to deny it. Not that the movie needed gossip to fuel its reception; it returned its modest budget of $2.5m [$17.5m] twenty times over and garnered ten Oscar nominations, not least in the Leading Role category for both Beatty and Dunaway.

It would be true to say that playing Bonnie Parker transformed Dunaway's career, were it not for the fact that she barely had a career yet; it was only her third picture, made in her very first year as a screen actress. Few debuts can have been so persuasive, and the screenplay was almost magically matched to Dunaway's talents. In an early scene, when she spots Clyde trying to steal a car, she falls to talking – and soon flirting – with him, and the dynamic between them is perfect from the first word. Clyde flatters her, asking if she is a movie star (hardly likely, as she still lives with her mother in a Depression-hit one-horse town). When she denies it, secretly thrilled, he tries other gambits, each gradually less glamorous. Finally Bonnie asks him what he really thinks she does, and without missing a beat he replies: 'a waitress'. Her whole body seems to recoil as she turns away, speechless with disappointment that he has seen through her all along – and that the barrier between her dreams and her reality is so easily smashed. The sudden fall from pride and delight is wordless, and when we watch Dunaway in that moment, we realize there is not another actress in the world who could have captured it so exactly.

> I was a southern girl and so was Bonnie. We share the frustrations of living in that small, limited environment – dying to get out and move forward in the world. That was part of my make-up as a girl.

Towards the end of the picture, Bonnie and Clyde kill a man, and are seen doing so. Clyde has a criminal record and fears he will be recognized, but Bonnie is unknown and he tries to persuade her to leave him and return home before trouble starts. When she demurs, he tries to explain himself:

                    CLYDE
     Now it's going to get rough. I can't get out,
     but right now you still can. I want you to say
     the word to me and I'll put you on that bus
     back to your mama... because you mean a lot to
     me, and I ain't gonna make you run with me.

                    BONNIE
     No.

                    CLYDE
     Look, I ain't a rich man. You could get a rich
     man if you tried.

                    BONNIE
     I don't want no rich man.

     The camera stays on Bonnie's face. She is adamant
     she will stay with him.

                    CLYDE
     You ain't going to have a minute's peace.

                    BONNIE
     You promise?

The childlike excitement with which she seizes the chance to embrace love, mayhem and most likely death comes purely from her look – another flash of pure Dunaway. And yet, in retrospect, just as we fear for Bonnie's safety in the story, we look back on a performance capable of such uncompromising passion, and we wonder: can Dunaway herself survive, or will she too crash and burn?

Well, survive she did – and in grand style – for another decade. *The Thomas Crown Affair* (1968) showed her as a canny, self-knowing and staggeringly seductive investigator, playing opposite Steve McQueen; *Chinatown* (1974), starring Jack Nicholson, gave us Evelyn Mulwray, a heartbreaking paradox of chilly vulnerability; *Network* (1976) won her an Oscar as a driven, brilliant but philistine TV news boss; and *Eyes of Laura Mars* (1978) took her right to the edge as a fashion photographer who has visions of murders that have yet to take place. But then the perfect roles began to dry up. An Oscar for *Network* should have made her a red-hot property, but she no longer seemed to be getting the kind of scripts she deserved. Perhaps her reputation as headstrong and outspoken – or 'temperamental', as she prefers to put it herself – was beginning to catch up with her. Roman Polanski, after directing her in *Chinatown*, described her as 'unhinged' and 'a gigantic pain in the ass'.

She appeared in *Mommie Dearest* (1981), *Barfly* (1987), *The Handmaid's Tale* (1990) and *Don Juan DeMarco* (1994), and had a minor role in the 1999 remake of *The Thomas Crown Affair*, but it seems she never really learned to handle slights and setbacks with the grace other stars managed. In 2008, years after her success in *Bonnie and Clyde*, she gave a speech – bizarrely, in rhyme – honouring Warren Beatty at the American Film Institute. The camera lingers on a distinctly uncomfortable Beatty as she recites:

> *I say this with pride, he was perfect as Clyde / But for Bonnie, no one could tell. / He saw stars left and right, all day and all night / He just couldn't find the right girl. / Till he said to me, it's just a small fee / But I'd love you to give Bonnie a whirl.*

> *Bonnie and Clyde finally did open; the critics went wild from the start. / It became a sensation across this great nation / For it had romance, and violence, and heart. / So Warren. . . was now a producer, and much richer, thanks to his fee. / His deal was so bold, he brought home the gold – I just wish he could have shared more with me.*

Polite (or canned) laughter from the audience notwithstanding, the episode is unsettling, being not entirely funny, sweet or self-deprecating. From the looks on the faces of the guests, it seems the speech confirmed Hollywood's fears about a woman who was undeniably a star, but who positioned herself so far outside the normal firmament that they just couldn't handle her. But if we demand grace in our heroes, we have plenty of others to choose from: Kelly, Bergman, Binoche, Ullmann. If we want fire, Dunaway blazes across the screen.

For a long time, I tried to live up to something that was in people's minds. I don't know what it is they want, nor do they, but movie stars fulfil some lack in people's lives.

Why am I so fa-
mous? What
am I doing right?
What are the others
doing wrong?

BARBRA STREISAND

Barbara Joan Streisand
24 April 1942–

I knew that with a mouth like mine, I just had to be a star or something. . . I [only] became a singer because I could never get work as an actress.

I arrived in Hollywood without having my nose fixed, my teeth capped, or my name changed. That is very gratifying to me.

It's work to be a star. I don't enjoy the stardom part. I only enjoy the creative process.

To have ego means to believe in your own strength. . .
So, yes, my ego is big, but it's also very small in some areas. My ego is responsible for my doing what I do – bad or good.

Now when I look at *Funny Girl* I think I was gorgeous. I was too beautiful to play Fanny Brice.

The audience is the barometer of the truth.

When I sing, people shut up.

I never sing in the shower.

Oh God, don't envy me, I have my own pains.

Three-time Oscar-winning director William Wyler was once asked whether it had been tough having Barbra Streisand star in his 1968 version of *Funny Girl*. He sighed: 'No, not too hard, considering it was the first movie she ever directed.' Vilmos Zsigmond, cameraman on *Close Encounters of the Third Kind* (1977), *The Deer Hunter* (1978) and *Heaven's Gate* (1980), was fired after three days because he refused to follow Streisand's strict instructions to film only the more flattering side of her face.

To say that Barbra Streisand exists as much as a tightly controlled brand as she does as an actress is not to disparage her success; her career has grown unstoppably as a result of both raw talent and canny self-management to the extent that her screen persona is virtually indistinguishable from her real self. The talent has been acclaimed with two Oscars, eight Grammys, five Emmys, four Golden Globes, a special Tony, and even a Peabody Award for 'distinguished and meritorious public service' in the media; a quarter of a billion album sales across fifty years easily make her the industry's top-ranked female recording artist. But if there is one performance that celebrates and embodies everything about what – and who – Streisand is, it is *Funny Girl*.

                    FANNY
    I'm a bagel on a plate full of onion rolls!

Unsurprisingly, Streisand's show-business ambitions were apparent from the start. Born and brought up in Brooklyn, New York, where her father was a teacher and her mother a singer, she was taking parts in community plays from the age of seven, singing and recording demos throughout high school, and working as a nightclub singer before she was out of her teens. A series of increasingly prestigious engagements eventually brought her to the notice of the variety talk programme *PM East/PM West*, where she famously said to her co-presenter Mike Wallace, 'I like the fact that you are provoking. But don't provoke me.' Future collaborators would do well to pay heed.

Streisand took her first Broadway role in *I Can Get It for You Wholesale* (1962), but two years later she played Fanny Brice in *Funny Girl*, an overnight hit which ran for nearly two years and put Streisand fully in the limelight – and on the cover of *Time* magazine. Four years later she would reprise the role on celluloid to even greater acclaim, but the story of the stage musical and the movie are essentially one: the creation of Streisand herself.

Fanny Brice was a hugely popular Jazz age singer and comedian. Hollywood producer Ray Stark, her son-in-law, had a long-standing ambition to make a film musical about her life. He first conceived of the idea in 1951, seventeen years before it eventually hit our screens, and the struggles he faced along the way would make a fine movie in themselves. Broadway and Hollywood luminaries were hired and fired ceaselessly; the cast of contributors (whether casualties or survivors) comprises composers Jule Styne and Stephen Sondheim, lyricist Bob Merrill, director Garson Kanin, choreographer Carol Haney, impresario David Merrick, eleven screenwriters (including Ben Hecht), and a slew of A-list directors, including Bob Fosse, John Patrick Shanley, Jerome Robbins and Sidney Lumet. Despite the relentless chaos, Stark's determination to bring Brice's story to his audience was matched by his smart instincts about how to nurture his creation: he made the extraordinary decision to stage it as a theatre musical before he filmed it.

This book celebrates screen stars, not stage actresses, but in this unique instance the Broadway production was the film. Director William Wyler certainly added a Hollywood grandeur that liberated the key scenes from the confines of the proscenium arch, but otherwise all the ingredients were already in place – not least Streisand herself, who was compelling on stage but still more incandescent in front of the lens. Part of the script's charm was that it allowed the star to be self-deprecating about her unconventional looks:

> NICK
> I'd be happy to wait while you change.

> FANNY
> I'd have to change too much — nobody could wait
> that long.

It was classic Jewish shtick, which made it all the more astonishing that, less than a year after the Six Day War of June 1967 between Israel and Egypt, the film's dashing love interest Nick Arnstein was played by an Egyptian, Omar Sharif:

> FANNY
> Where I come from, when two people... well,
> sort of love each other... oh, never mind.

                    NICK
Well? What do they do when they 'sort of love
each other'?

                    FANNY
Well, one of them says, 'Why don't we get
married?'

                    NICK
Really?

                    FANNY
Yeah, and sometimes it's even the man.

The film version was a smash with the public, if not universally acclaimed
by the critics – although Streisand's performance surely was. As Roger Ebert
said when he reviewed the film for a second time in 2004, 'She has the best
timing since Mae West, and is more fun to watch than anyone since the young
Katharine Hepburn. She doesn't actually sing a song at all; she acts it. . . It is
impossible to praise [her] too highly; hard to find much to praise about the rest
of the film.'

                    NICK
I like to feel free.

                    FANNY
You could get lonesome being that free.

                    NICK
You could get lonesome being that busy.

                    FANNY
Now who'd think to look at us that we got the
same problem!

                    NICK
Fanny, you're an enchanting girl. I wish I
could get to know you better.

```
            FANNY
    So give me six good reasons why not?
```

The movie confirmed her as an absolute star, and hits followed relentlessly with *Hello, Dolly!* (1969), *What's Up, Doc?* (1972), *The Way We Were* (1973) and *A Star is Born* (1976). But not everybody on set adored her as they had Carole Lombard or Grace Kelly; along with fame came controversy, not least because she was confirming a reputation for being egotistical and controlling. Between the success of the Broadway run and the studio production, her power had become evident to everyone involved, and one producer's diary later revealed that she had ruthlessly exploited the frequent disputes between the creative team to bolster her own position. One crew member, interviewed on the set of the shoot, was asked why everything seemed to be taking so long. Tactfully, he replied: 'Barbra's a perfectionist. She knows all about the lights and cameras.' When pressed to reveal whether this meant Streisand was being a diva, he simply repeated 'Barbra's a perfectionist' like a captured soldier ordered to reveal no more than his name, rank and serial number.

A heavy PR campaign delivered ambiguous coverage, with *Vogue* magazine deliberately running a picture of the actress in profile to highlight her infamous nose above the caption: 'The gorgeous singing exuberance of Barbra Streisand and her long, lean, homely good looks (which may yet touch off a trend).' It touched off more than a trend; Streisand's wattage has never dimmed, and what she achieved was surely earned. Ray Stark gained his success, too, after his seventeen-year journey. When Streisand was recording one of the show's most memorable numbers, she sang the line:

```
            FANNY
    It cost me a lot, but there's one thing I've
    got: my man.
```

When the take was finished, Stark walked over to his leading lady and murmured with a smile: 'It cost me a lot, but there's one thing I've got. . .'

I am simple, complex, generous, selfish, unattractive, beautiful, lazy and driven.

I believe all drunks go to heaven, because they've been through hell on earth

LIZA MINNELLI

Liza May Minnelli
12 March 1946–

I've got a good life, and I don't think anything can rock that any more.

Reality is something you rise above.

My mother gave me my drive but my father gave me my dreams.

I remember playing in the Beverly Hills park with Mia Farrow, Candice Bergen and Tisha Sterling and while we sat in the sandbox we could hear our nannies talking about picture deals and costume direction and whose employer was going to win the Academy Award.

[on *Cabaret*] Fosse caught a total performance that could have been nothing, but he found these pieces and put them together to make it the one thing that I don't really have, which is a film of what I really do. I'm an animal of the stage. I was bred to be that.

My biggest talent is I know who is more talented than I am. I find them and I go to them, and I learn.

[on her mother, Judy Garland] She was a friend of mine, a trying friend, but a friend.

T here are countless show-business dynasties: Douglas Fairbanks, Sr and Jr, Charlie and Geraldine Chapman, Ingrid Bergman and Isabella Rossellini, the Fondas, Francis Ford and Sofia Coppola, three generations of Hustons, the Curtis-Leigh clan, and too many Redgraves to mention. But few actors have a career whose trajectory matches so closely that of their forebears.

> *My family's been in show business since the 1700s. I traced them. I'm bred to this. Like a racehorse. A thoroughbred. Look at my parents, my God.*

Liza Minnelli was born in 1946 to Vincente Minnelli and Judy Garland. Her father was described by lyricist Alan Jay Lerner as 'the greatest director of motion picture musicals the screen has ever seen'; her mother will need no introduction for readers of this book. Both her parents had won Oscars, Minnelli for *Gigi* (1959) and Garland (a Juvenile Award) for *The Wizard of Oz* (1939) and *Babes in Arms* (1939). They would not have to wait long for their daughter to claim a statuette of her own.

Minnelli grew up in Hollywood amid a glittering crowd of house guests; her godparents were Ira Gershwin and renowned singer and actress Kay Thompson. But as the centre of a gaggle of step- and half-siblings, she found herself frequently looking after her family, including her mother who was fighting battles with depression, alcoholism and barbiturate addiction.

> *It was no great tragedy being Judy Garland's daughter. I had tremendously interesting childhood years – except they had little to do with being a child.*

Minnelli put a brave face on it for the press, but echoes of her mother's own youth must have been ever-present in the household. Garland herself had once told an interviewer:

> *I was born at the age of twelve on a Metro-Goldwyn-Mayer lot. . . I started to feel like a wind-up toy.*

At sixteen, having attended fourteen schools, Minnelli told her parents she was moving to New York – alone – to try her luck on stage. Her parents agreed, but warned her she should expect no financial support from them; Frank Sinatra sent her $500, which she returned, preferring to sleep rough or slip out of hotels before dawn to save money. By the time she was nineteen she had won a Tony Award for her lead role in *Flora the Red Menace* (1965), an accolade her mother had earned only at the age of thirty for *Vaudeville* (1952). A year previously, the two had appeared together on stage in London, and Minnelli recalls realizing for the first time that she had a voice of her own, with its own power and magnetism – but she was aware of its dangers, too.

> *It was like Mama suddenly realized I was good, that she didn't have to apologize for me. It was the strangest feeling. One minute I was on stage with my mother, the next moment I was on stage with Judy Garland. One minute she smiled at me, and the next minute she was like the lioness that owned the stage and suddenly found somebody invading her territory. The killer instinct of a performer had come out in her.*

Perhaps the competitive streak ran both ways; Minnelli signed on to voice Dorothy in an animated version of her mother's greatest hit movie, *Journey Back to Oz* (1974).

Luckily, director Alan J. Pakula saw in her a talent that was unique when he cast her as Pookie in *The Sterile Cuckoo* (1969). Pookie is a disoriented dreamer from a disinterested family who starts college longing to find friendship – and love – with someone who shares her unconventional view of life. She lies to nuns to get better seats on buses, gives presents of rare bugs and refers to anyone who is not as eccentric as herself as a 'weirdo'. When she falls for Jerry (Wendell Burton), a buttoned-up freshman, she seduces him with a precocious brazenness:

Pookie stands beside the bed, arms outspread.

                    POOKIE
     So, would you like to peel a tomato?

Jerry looks non-plussed.

                    JERRY
     What?

<pre>
                    POOKIE
        Do you want to strip me?
</pre>

The scene is both tender and funny, a combination Minnelli balances sweetly until the bitter ending.

<pre>
                    JERRY
        What's the matter?

                    POOKIE
        Nothing... It's just that everything's a
        little bit perfect and I... somehow or other
        when everything's perfect I just get a little
        bit nervous. I mean, it just can't last.

                    JERRY
        I love you, Pookie. I love you.
</pre>

Eventually Pookie's desire to be loved frightens Jerry – he is a good, kind boy, but utterly unequipped to deal with her passionate individuality and iconoclasm. They part, leaving Pookie bereft and more alone than before. Minnelli is spectacularly persuasive in the role and it won her an Oscar nomination, but the ripples of that need to be adored would darken the surface of her radiant career.

Cabaret (1972) cemented Minnelli's fame as an actress and a singer. The producers had originally hoped to cast Barbra Streisand, who was at the peak of her success, but was trying to shift her work away from musicals – but such was the triumph of Minnelli's interpretation that it is impossible now to imagine how Streisand could have made the role her own. Sally Bowles is a carefree, libertine nightclub singer in Berlin in the years leading up to the Second World War, who befriends a reticent English academic, Brian (Michael York):

<pre>
                    SALLY
        I suppose you're wondering what I'm doing,
        working at a place like the Kit Kat Club.

                    BRIAN
        Well, it is a rather unusual place.
</pre>

SALLY
That's me, darling. Unusual places, unusual
love affairs. I am a most strange and
extraordinary person.

Minnelli is electrifying on stage and mesmerizing in the rest of the drama, hurling the rule book aside so forcefully that we are swept away by her chaotic charm. Bob Fosse's direction, styling and choreography coalesce effortlessly to create the milieu for such an extraordinary performance and the film won eight Oscars – including one for Minnelli.

SALLY
I'm going to be a great film star! That is, if
booze and sex don't get me first.

Minnelli was twenty-six; at exactly the same age, her mother was suspended from her contract with MGM for alcohol and morphine abuse. An entry in Andy Warhol's diary from 1978 records Minnelli arriving at a party with the words 'Give me every drug you've got'. Cocaine, marijuana, Valium and Quaaludes were duly supplied, and the battles Minnelli fought with addiction became a staple of press reports thereafter. She had further screen successes with *New York, New York* (1977) and *Arthur* (1981), and continued to win awards for her stage work, but there was a feeling that she had already reached her peak. Like her mother, she made repeated comebacks as a singer, but in 1997 Ben Brantley of *The New York Times* wrote: 'her every stage appearance is perceived as a victory of show-business stamina over psychic frailty. She asks for love so nakedly and earnestly, it seems downright vicious not to respond'. Not for the last time, we are reminded of Garland's own confession:

In the silence of night I have often wished for just a few words of love from one man, rather than the applause of thousands of people.

I'm not a very good singer. I just know how to present a song, and honey, I think I've been through enough to do it right.

*Working in Holly-
wood does give one
a certain expertise
in the field of pros-
titution*

JANE
FONDA

Lady Jayne Seymour Fonda
21 December 1937–

People think actresses find
public speaking easy, and it's
not easy at all; we're used to
hiding behind masks.

I would have given up acting
in a minute. I didn't like how
it set me apart from other
people.

When I left the West Coast I
was a liberal. When I landed
in New York I was a
revolutionary.

It's always great to rehearse
on a plane because people
think you're mad.

Emotionality is really easy for
me. My father always said
that Fondas can cry at a good
steak.

All my life I had believed that
unless I was perfect I would
not be loved.

T he best insight into the life, ambitions and screen presence of Jane Fonda is a story that is almost certainly untrue. At Vassar, the prestigious American college she attended, the students (all women at that time) were required to wear white gloves and pearls if they attended the daily tea party in the Rose Parlor. When Fonda was turned away for being improperly dressed, legend has it that she returned in the gloves and pearls – but nothing else. This iconoclasm would remain a key aspect of her film career and many other strands of her public life.

Daughter of actor Henry Fonda and Frances Ford Seymour, a Canadian socialite, Jane was not initially enamoured of the acting world. Despite making a brief stage appearance aged seventeen alongside her father, she pursued her academic career; after leaving Vassar prematurely, she travelled to Paris for two years where she studied painting. But few students are likely to have supplemented their income as Fonda did. Before she had made even her professional stage debut, she appeared on the cover of *Vogue* – twice. Clearly she enjoyed the limelight, although she later confessed that she suffered from bulimia from the age of seventeen for twenty years, living largely on a diet of 'cigarettes, coffee, speed, and strawberry yogurt'. When she returned from Europe to New York in 1958, a chance meeting with Method-acting guru Lee Strasberg was to prove a revelation:

> *I went to the Actors Studio and Lee told me I had talent. Real talent.*
> *It was the first time that anyone, except my father – who had to say so*
> *– told me I was good. At anything. It was a turning point in my life. I*
> *went to bed thinking about acting. I woke up thinking about acting. It*
> *was like the roof had come off my life.*

By 1960 – aged twenty-three – she had made her bow on Broadway in *There Was a Little Girl* and earned her first Tony Award nomination. The rest, as they say, is history – except there was much more to come besides the acting.

> *The kind of parts that I think are the most exciting to play and are the*
> *most viable in terms of communication are characters that are*
> *complex; that is, characters that are full of contradictions that can be*
> *shown, that are in motion, that are trying to deal with problems that*
> *are real to people.*

Many stars have espoused social or activist causes, using their public status to promote charities or noble enterprises, but Fonda made politics the very backbone of her career with films such as *They Shoot Horses, Don't They?* (1969), *The China Syndrome* (1979) and *Nine to Five* (1980), a comedy about office and gender warfare. Judy, a newly hired secretary, fantasizes about hunting down and shooting her boss Franklin Hart (Dabney Coleman):

          HART
Judy? Judy, you've got to help me - that mob
out there is crazy - they're trying to kill me!

          JUDY
Now, why would they want to do a nasty little
thing like that?

          HART
I don't know! I'm not such a bad guy!

          JUDY
You're a sexist, egotistical, lying,
hypocritical bigot.

          HART
So I have a few faults; who doesn't? Is that
any reason to kill me?

          JUDY
You're foul, Hart. A wart on the nose of
humanity, and I'm going to blast it off.

She raises her shotgun.

          HART
Judy... Judy... Judy...

          JUDY
Goodbye boss man. It's quittin' time!

Her outspoken beliefs brought her notoriety as well as fame; even after winning her first Oscar as a feisty call girl in *Klute* in 1971, she was best known to the

American public as a result of her tour to Vietnam where she was photographed sitting with Vietcong troops on an anti-aircraft gun, apparently supporting them in their fight against 'capitalist imperialism'. 'Hanoi Jane', as she became known to many patriots, seemed to be undermining the value of the lives of the tens of thousands of US troops who had died in the war.

> *It hurt so many soldiers. It galvanized such hostility. It was the most horrible thing I could possibly have done. It was just thoughtless.*

She subsequently published many apologies about her lapse of judgement, declaring that her actions were humanitarian rather than partisan, but her controversial views have remained provocative – and occasionally inconsistent. In 1970 she urged students at the University of Michigan that 'If you understood what Communism was. . . you would pray on your knees that one day we would become Communist,' yet in 1991 she married billionaire media mogul Ted Turner. With equal irony, having appeared on the cover of countless glossy magazines, she said of her role in *Klute*: '[In] it I expose a great deal of the oppression of women in this country – the system which makes women sell themselves for possessions.'

In the film she plays Bree Daniels, a high-class escort who is unwittingly caught up in a murder investigation. The film is a superbly stylish dissection of cultural, social and sexual mores at a time when America's whole identity was in upheaval, and Fonda distils the energy and the uncertainty of that era in an intense and charismatic performance.

>   BREE
> And for an hour... for an hour, I'm the best
> actress in the world, and the best fuck in the
> world. Men would pay $200 for me, and here you
> are turning down a freebie. You could get a
> perfectly good dishwasher for that.

Sassy, spiky and funny, she is also wonderfully human:

>   BREE
> Don't feel bad about losing your virtue. I sort
> of knew you would. Everybody always does.

But paradox had always been part of her persona. Fonda had enjoyed a growing reputation from her earliest screen appearances and was hailed by *Newsweek* in 1963 as 'the loveliest and most gifted of all our new young actresses'. She was noted for being careful in her choice of scripts; she had turned down lead roles in *Bonnie and Clyde* (1967) and *Rosemary's Baby* (1968), so it was all the more astonishing when she agreed to play Barbarella in Roger Vadim's camp, sexy sci-fi extravaganza of the same name (1968). The story, intentionally trashy, recounts her adventures in space while trying to capture Dr Durand Durand, inventor of a lethal Positronic Ray which threatens the safety of the earth. As the original trailer declares:

```
         VOICE-OVER
Meet the most beautiful creature of the future.
Barbarella is a five-star double-rated astro-
navigatrix earth girl whose speciality is
love... See Barbarella do her thing in the wild
excessive machine, in the biting bird cage,
in the chamber of dreams, in the labyrinth of
love, in the deadly doll's house, in the palace
of pleasure.
```

Barbarella's own lines, delivered deadpan, include 'A good many dramatic situations begin with screaming' and 'Could you. . . hand me a garment?' Clearly this is not Hanoi Jane speaking. But Fonda's verve is so irresistible (as are her outrageous costumes, and frequent lack of them) that the movie works – if we surrender to it. In a way, her performance is the flip-side of *Klute*'s shadowy exploration of the female persona; here, sex is not a transaction but an exuberant celebration, an integral aspect of every human (and alien) interaction.

Fonda continued to grasp life with both hands. She adopted the daughter of two activist Black Panthers, created a bestselling exercise regime, campaigned for Native American rights and against the war in Iraq, founded the Women's Media Center and married three times. Amid all this, she won a second Oscar for *Coming Home* (1978) and earned a further five nominations. Despite the stardom, the controversy and the acclaim, Fonda remains eminently grounded. As she puts it simply:

To be a revolutionary you have to be a human being.

When I start down a path that I know is the right path, I go with all of me.

*If everyone's going
one way, I will go
the other*

CHARLOTTE RAMPLING

Tessa Charlotte Rampling
5 February 1946–

I was incredibly fatalistic. I just thought, 'If it works, it works'. But I've always been like that. I've never been easily impressed, and I've never thought I didn't deserve something. If I got it, then I deserved it.

Doing cinema is not about watching yourself.

One of the reasons I don't see eye to eye with Women's Lib is that women have it all on a plate if only they knew it. They don't have to be pretty either.

Women in their fifties are confident people now. They are allowed to exist as they want, which means they have great power and they want to show that power, because they have been suppressed for a very long time.

Filming is quite difficult, very uncomfortable. . . People think the industry is such fun, and I say it is because people hate to hear you say it's not.

Many actresses trade on their looks, great scripts and lucky breaks; a pretty face and good timing are enough to swing the spotlight their way. Others navigate a tougher route, seeking out projects that challenge as much as they divert. Even so, entertainment was the springboard for Charlotte Rampling's career. Born in Essex, but brought up and educated in France as well as England, she used to perform *chansons* with her sister; when she suggested to her father that they might take up an offer to perform in a nightclub, she was packed off to secretarial college instead. Ironically, while there, she was spotted by a talent agent and cast in a commercial for a chocolate bar. Soon after, she was given an uncredited part as a water-skier in Richard Lester's *The Knack. . . and How to Get It* (1965), a picture which epitomized the Swinging Sixties.

Rampling's professional modelling shots from that time confirm how perfect a look she had for that era: alluring, casual, intelligent and absolutely comfortable with her sexuality. She embraced the spirit of rebellion:

> *Ever since I was a small child, I've had this feeling – it's in my nature,*
> *and so it's not even pretentious – that if everyone's going one way,*
> *I will go the other, just by some kind of spirit of defiance.*

She first made her mark in two intensely dark and challenging films: Luchino Visconti's *The Damned* (1969) and Liliana Cavani's *The Night Porter* (1974). In both narratives Rampling plays an inmate of a concentration camp; in the latter film, her character, Lucia Atherton, survives only to re-encounter her former Nazi SS guard (Dirk Bogarde, in a pitch-perfect role). She resumes a complex and controversial relationship with her captor, who had been both her tormentor and protector; the film explores violence, submission and emotional co-dependence with a rigorous honesty but a profound degree of tenderness.

```
                LUCIA
     I'm here of my own free will. This chain is so
     none of you can take me away.
```

Where many lesser actors would have exploited the horror of her memories, Rampling maintains a lucidity and calm throughout: her performance is almost unwatchably moving.

> *I generally don't make films to entertain people. I choose the parts*

that challenge me to break through my own barriers. A need to
devour, punish, humiliate or surrender seems to be a primal part of
human nature, and it's certainly a big part of sex. To discover what
normal means, you have to surf a tide of weirdness.

This intellectual and emotional curiosity has resulted in a vastly diverse run of films across Rampling's fifty-year career. The best known include *Farewell, My Lovely* (1975), *Stardust Memories* (1980), *The Verdict* (1982), *The Wings of the Dove* (1997), *Spy Game* (2001), *Swimming Pool* (2003) and *Melancholia* (2011), but the majority of projects have been away from Hollywood:

European films were what it was about for me – the sensations I
needed, the depth, the storytelling, the characters, the directors, and
the freedom that you can't really find in American films. . . I could
have been a superstar in America – I was certainly taken out there.
But I said, 'No way, José, I'm not staying here in this madhouse'.

Formerly married to musician Jean-Michel Jarre, she keeps homes both in England and France, where she is known as 'La Légende'; on this side of the Channel, critic and television host Barry Norman coined the term 'to rample', meaning 'an ability to reduce a man to helplessness through a chilly sensuality'. Her fame is certainly different from that of her peers. Since she never played their game, we no longer quite know how to read her rule book, which means her presence is as fresh as it was when she first hit our screens. Nor does she shy away from any form of performance as a challenge: in 2000, photographer Jürgen Teller – whom she had once kicked off a shoot because she disliked the way he made her look – invited her to pose naked alongside the *Mona Lisa*. Her first reaction was 'who wants to see an old woman naked?' but she could not resist the opportunity and said afterwards it gave her 'a very spiritual feeling. You feel you are part of hundreds of years of art'. The results were as spectacular as any shots of her in a Mary Quant dress in the super-hip King's Road four decades earlier. As befits someone who has always remained true to her vision of herself, age has only confirmed Rampling's looks: although enduringly beautiful, she has never been just a pretty face.

It's sort of fun. If someone's eyeballing you, it makes you feel good.

*We did everything
for the love of art*

SISSY
SPACEK

Mary Elizabeth Spacek
25 December 1949–

When I started out in
independent films in the early
'70s, we did everything for
the love of art. It wasn't about
money and stardom. That
was what we were reacting
against. You'd die before
you'd be bought.

I've always been a people-
watcher, and as an actor,
later, I just mined all those
little details.

It's so amazing how many
different things an individual
can project and what
different things different
people can see in different
ways. I love that.

My cousin, Rip Torn,
persuaded me not to change
my name. You shouldn't
change what you are in the
search for success.

There's a real danger in trying
to stay king of the mountain.
You stop taking risks, you
stop being as creative,
because you're trying to
maintain a position. Apart
from anything else that really
takes the fun out of it.

I've not had a mean life.

ome stars are knowingly worldly – Marlene Dietrich, Ava Gardner, Angelina Jolie – while others are ethereally otherwordly: Greta Garbo, Anouk Aimée, Liv Ullmann. Sissy Spacek, with her Pre-Raphaelite face and limpid blue eyes, might seem almost ghostly if her sheer presence were not so fierce. Born in Texas to parents of Czech and German ancestry, she later moved to New York where – thanks to her cousin, actor Rip Torn – she swung into the orbit of Andy Warhol's Factory crowd, and signed up for classes at Lee Strasberg's Actors Studio.

She has played a huge range of roles over the years in movies as diverse as *Coal Miner's Daughter* (1980), *Missing* (1982), *JFK* (1991), *The Straight Story* (1999), *In the Bedroom* (2001) and *The Help* (2011), but her two most enduring early films – *Badlands* (1973) and *Carrie* (1976) – share remarkable similarities. Her opening voice-over as Holly Sargis in Terrence Malick's *Badlands* marks her out at once as an outsider:

> HOLLY
> My mother died of pneumonia when I was just a kid. My father kept their wedding cake in the freezer for ten whole years. After the funeral he gave it to the yard man. He tried to act cheerful, but he could never be consoled by the little stranger he found in his house.

Kit, a local ne'er-do-well, played by Martin Sheen in the spirit of James Dean, sweeps Holly off her feet and murders her disapproving father. The couple flees into the remote woods where they pursue a life of innocence and paranoia in equal measure. As the story swings between pastoral beauty and brutal violence, Holly's dislocated narration hypnotizes us; Spacek is unfathomable and yet absolutely sympathetic. The production transformed her vision of what a film could offer: 'After working with Terry Malick, I was like, "The artist rules. Nothing else matters". My career would have been very different if I hadn't had that experience.'

Where *Badlands* was elegiac, *Carrie* – a twisted supernatural high school anti-romance – is visceral. Spacek plays Carrie White, a teenager whose deranged religious mother (Piper Laurie) has failed to equip her for the upheavals of school life and her burgeoning sexuality. To her own surprise, she develops telekinetic powers, presented by the film-makers as the desperate manifestation of a young woman's longing to be normal in a world of adolescent barbarism and oppressive guilt:

> CARRIE
> I'm funny. I mean, the kids think I'm funny. I
> don't want to be. I want to try and be a whole
> person before it's too late.

When she is invited to the prom by a handsome jock, Carrie – who does not know she is being set up by a rival pupil – shows her mother her dress and corsage:

> CARRIE
> Look what Tommy gave me, Mama. Aren't they
> beautiful?

> MOTHER
> I can see your dirty pillows. Everyone will.

> CARRIE
> Breasts, Mama. They're called breasts, and
> every woman has them.

Spacek understood that she would have to remove herself from daily life in order to maintain Carrie's eerie intensity. For the screen test she rubbed Vaseline in her hair, left her face unwashed and wore a sailor dress her mother had made for her schooldays; during the shoot she hid away in a dressing room filled with religious icons and read a Bible illustrated by Gustave Doré. She studied the body language of the macabre engravings and tried to incorporate those postures into each scene. Nothing about Carrie's life is conventional, and any actress would need to operate at the edge of her capabilities to portray these extremes of fear, anger, longing and innocence: Spacek unifies every aspect of her character in a performance as moving as it is terrifying. It won her that year's Oscar, and not until *The Silence of the Lambs* (1991) would audiences surrender themselves again to such unsettling powers.

Fame sweeps you away. I had to go home every six months to remember who I am.

*Oh, screw it, just go
out there and do it*

DIANE
KEATON

Diane Hall
5 January 1946–

I think that people who
are famous tend to be
underdeveloped in their
humanity skills.

I build a wall around myself.
I'm hard to get to know. Any
trait you have, it gets worse as
you go along.

I'm limited, so, I kind of
know where I fit as an actress.
I kind of get it now, finally,
after all of these years of
trying to be a dramatic
actress. I kind of think that
I'd like to continue dealing
with these things in a funny,
lighter vein, but also truthful
and honest.

When I was younger I had
these enormous vanities
about what I expected from
myself. I'm glad to have a
comfortable and fascinating
life, but now I see it for what
it is, so I can be braver and
more spontaneous.

I just have to keep going back
to the core and think that
we're all afraid of it and when
we're afraid of it, you run to
something much easier,
something that looks like
candy.

f it's hard to imagine Diane Keaton without thinking of Woody Allen, it's time to watch *The Godfather* trilogy again – or, better still, *Looking for Mr. Goodbar* (1977); for although Allen credited his on- and off-screen partner with being his muse, most famously for the Oscar-winning *Annie Hall* (1977), Keaton remains an extraordinary actor whose early triumphs are easily overlooked.

Greta Garbo in *Mata Hari* (1931), Ava Gardner in *The Killers* (1946), Faye Dunaway in *Bonnie and Clyde* (1967): we have seen many an actress hold her own in a world of menace and machismo, but Diane Keaton's confrontation with her husband Michael Corleone (Al Pacino) in *The Godfather: Part II* (1974) is one of the most astonishing moments in Francis Ford Coppola's saga.

```
                    KAY
    Oh, Michael. Michael, you're blind! It wasn't a
    miscarriage. It was an abortion. An abortion,
    Michael. Just like our marriage is an abortion.
    Something that's unholy and evil. I didn't want
    your son, Michael! I wouldn't bring another
    one of your sons into this world! It was an
    abortion, Michael! It was a son, Michael! A
    son! And I had it killed because this must
    all end!
```

After studying acting with Sanford Meisner in New York, Keaton quickly came to prominence as Kay Adams in *The Godfather: Part I* (1972); unafraid to defy the Corleones, the greatest dynasty in movie history, she puts paid to the myth that women cannot exist as fully fleshed characters in such a male milieu. Amid the complex family politics played out by Brando, Duvall, Caan and Pacino, she shines as a still point in a turbulent world: she does not emphasize gender differences but simply expresses herself as an individual, casting the family's story in stark relief as we share her journey of discovery and shock at their actions. Her performance seems all the more extraordinary when we remember it was only her second big-screen appearance.

The same year she appeared opposite Woody Allen in *Play It Again, Sam* (1972), the first of four films with him. In all of them, she is smart, funny, sexy, challenging and charming, but the highlight of their collaboration is surely *Annie Hall* (1977). Subtitled 'a nervous romance', it chronicles the gradual decline of the relationship between Alvy and Annie with a bitter but irresistible humour. One famous scene shows a split-screen of the two with their respective shrinks; the dialogue is simultaneous.

>   ALVY'S THERAPIST
> How often do you sleep together?

>   ANNIE'S THERAPIST
> Do you have sex often?

>   ALVY
> Hardly ever. Maybe three times a week.

>   ANNIE
> Constantly. I'd say three times a week.

Few actors could handle playing straight man (or woman) to Allen's sardonic one-liners, but Keaton held her own better than anyone who ever starred – or sparred – with him.

>   ANNIE
> Yeah, but you wanted to keep the relationship
> flexible. Remember, it's your phrase.

>   ALVY
> Oh stop it, you're having an affair with your
> college professor, that jerk that teaches that
> incredible crap course, Contemporary Crisis in
> Western Man.

>   ANNIE
> Existential Motifs in Russian Literature.
> You're really close.

>   ALVY
> What's the difference? It's all mental
> masturbation.

<pre>
                    ANNIE
      Oh, well, now we're finally getting to a subject
      you know something about.
</pre>

Sparkling as they are, these roles turn her inwards, narrowing her range into territory circumscribed by Allen's own preoccupations. As Keaton herself said later, 'When I first got to know Woody and I was going out with him, I noticed that people never wanted to hear anything that I had to say at all. They just wanted to be in the shadow of his light and I remember really having a hard time with that.'

After four pictures with Allen in five years, it must have been a relief for Keaton when Richard Brooks cast her as Theresa in *Looking for Mr. Goodbar* (1977). Theresa is a bright, compassionate teacher of deaf children who finds herself stifled by the constraints of her family, her work and her culture. Simultaneously inspired and daunted by the libertine exploits of her self-destructive sister Katherine (Tuesday Weld), she seeks escape through the men she finds in the singles bars of New York. The story shows her as a sensitive, determined individual who seeks honesty and self-fulfilment and yet whose loneliness is also a vital part of her character; it celebrates the feminist optimism of the 1970s while recognizing – with its shocking denouement, when she is murdered by a lover – that for many women equality was a hollow promise. What sets it apart from any other movie Keaton had yet starred in was that it is her story throughout. It offers a minute examination of her every mood, and she carries it with an extraordinary confidence. Her dialogue is as poignant as it is hard-boiled:

<pre>
                  THERESA
      Most guys first time out they try to score, they
      expect it. And some of them get pretty nasty if
      they don't get it. So by the second time it's
      either fuck or forget it.
</pre>

When she asks her local bartender why he never accepts the drinks she offers to buy him, he confesses his addiction:

<pre>
                  BARTENDER
      Confidentially, with me... one's too many and a
      million's not enough.
</pre>

>   THERESA
>   I got the same problem with men.

She spans the entire spectrum of emotion from anxiety and frustration to exuberance and eroticism effortlessly, forcing us – as she does – to live in the moment:

>   THERESA
>   Don't stop, don't stop...

>   TONY
>   What do you want?

>   THERESA
>   Everything... Everything.

The strength of the film – and of Keaton's performance – is that it suggests there are no easy answers, no single way of being that can reflect all the facets of her character. For an actor to fascinate us through her very ambiguity is an astonishing challenge, and in this case Keaton's vulnerability – the very opposite of what Allen demands of her – is what makes her outstanding. There is no glamour to Theresa's lifestyle, yet in director Brooks's hands she finds a wholly new kind of beauty. Where Allen makes her skittish and gives her free rein with her gamine, almost androgynous style, in *Looking for Mr. Goodbar* she is freer and far more sensual, despite her formal schoolteacher façade. She is not afraid to be a woman in a man's world – and she captivates us just as she does her unthinking lovers.

Hits followed with *Reds* (1981), *Shoot the Moon* (1982), *Father of the Bride* (1991), and *Something's Gotta Give* (2003), although Keaton's output in other areas is equally impressive: she works as a producer, writer, photographer, property developer and campaigner for architectural restoration, and she brings the same acuity to all these activities as she does to her film work. In 2011 she published her first memoir, *Then Again*, in which she quotes a remark her mother once made:

> *Diane is a mystery. . . At times, she's so basic, at others so wise it frightens me.*

Don't give up on yourself. So you make a mistake here and there; you do too much or you do too little. Just have fun. Smile. And keep putting on lipstick.

HELEN MIRREN

I'm a would-be rebel

Ilyena Lydia Vasilievna Mironoff
26 July 1945–

[About herself] Being famous for being cool about not being gorgeous.

Actors are rogues and vagabonds. Or they ought to be. I can't stand it when they behave like solicitors.

All you have to do is to look like crap on film and everyone thinks you're a brilliant actress. Actually, all you've done is look like crap.

Theatre is more tiring, demanding, more frightening, everything. Film, you have to get up early in the morning, and I hate that.

My success grew slowly but constantly. I've been working every year since I started acting and I got many awards before I won the Oscar for *The Queen*. Maybe it's because I've never been interested in big Hollywood flicks and I've only been in a few recently.

There's nothing sexy about doing a nude scene. It's rather uncomfortable. I like dressing up rather than dressing down. . .

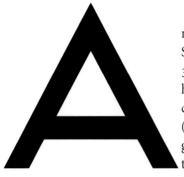

nd the Oscar goes to. . . Cedric Gibbons, Emilio 'El Indio' Fernández, George Stanley and eighteenth-century chemist James Vickers. Oscar himself stands 34cm (13.5 inches) tall and weighs in at a hefty 3.85kg (8.5 lb) – 240 times heavier than a DVD disc. The body of the statuette, a knight standing on a film can while holding a resting sword, is cast from Vickers's invention, britannium (92 per cent tin, 6 per cent antimony and 2 per cent copper), and plated with gold. Originally sketched by art director Gibbons, the award's sleek physique was that of Mexican actor Fernández, and it was sculpted by Stanley. Each trophy takes a month to manufacture, and the design has remained unchanged since 1928 – quite a process, considering that one of its fêted recipients, Helen Mirren, described the entire Academy Awards ceremony (on being nominated for her role as Queen Charlotte in *The Madness of King George* (1994)) as 'the crème de la crème of bullshit'.

Plenty of movie folk have expressed dismay that any artistic production or performance should be so formally ranked – especially since the halo of success surrounding each win is so disproportionately great. As film producer Dean Cavanagh put it, 'Our minds are big enough to contemplate the cosmos but small enough to care about who wins an Oscar'. Halle Berry, who won for *Monster's Ball* (2001), voiced a less metaphysical objection: 'People win Oscars, and then it seems like they fall off the planet. And that's partly because a huge expectation walks in the room and sits right down on top of your head.' James Cameron had no such reservations after *Titanic* (1997) won in eleven categories, crowing 'I'm king of the world!' But Meryl Streep, a three-time winner, demurred: 'When they called my name, I had this feeling I could hear half of America going, "Oh no. Come on. . . Her, again?" You know. But, whatever.'

Helen Mirren, born Ilyena Lydia Vasilievna Mironoff, of Anglo-Russian descent, grew up in Essex and as a young woman worked at a local amusement park as a 'blagger', encouraging punters to go on the rides. But her street savvy was soon overtaken by fiercer ambitions: when she was thirteen, her parents took her to see an amateur production of *Hamlet*.

> *I was blown away by all this over-the-top drama. We grew up without TV and never went to the cinema, so after* Hamlet *all I wanted to do was get back into that world where all those fabulous things were possible.*

By the age of eighteen she had joined the National Youth Theatre, and after an impressive spell there was hired by the Royal Shakespeare Company; her many stage successes remain a key aspect of her talent as her reputation flourished internationally. Even starring in Hollywood hits like *National Treasure* (2007) and *RED* (2010), her classical training is unmistakable. This ability to captivate us on the big screen had been fully evident in her theatre appearances. Trevor Nunn's RSC production of *Macbeth* in 1974 attracted furious discussion among critics for Mirren's overt eroticism: it was as if audiences had never realized that Shakespeare could write roles for red-blooded, fully realized women.

From the mid-1960s, Mirren had been appearing in movies and television for renowned directors such as Ken Russell, Lindsay Anderson and Michael Powell, but despite her growing popularity she had not yet hit the world stage. Aptly, the film that would first deliver that revelation overtly references her *Macbeth*, restaged in a vicious, bitterly humorous London underworld setting: *The Long Good Friday* (1980). Starring opposite Bob Hoskins as gang boss Harold Shand – also in a breakthrough role – Mirren plays Victoria, Harold's lover.

At first she seems the classic gangster's moll – sexy, pouty, tough as nails. Harold is relying on her to entertain potential Mafia investors in a huge property scheme, and he insists her duties are simply to flirt, pour drinks and show off her classy pedigree. We suspect Victoria's background is less grand than she claims, a fact echoed in a confession by Mirren herself:

> *My poshed-over voice was learned and assimilated. I was an*
> *Essex girl.*

But even from the opening scenes it is clear she's nobody's fool – and nobody's moll – and that she intends to play a long game. Throughout the story, this disparity between her surface charm and her deeper intelligence remains a driving force every bit as powerful as Harold's ambition and aggression. The more furious Harold becomes at the violent threats to his empire, the calmer Victoria becomes – she has a feline instinct for the strengths and vulnerabilities of the men around her, and an icy calm under pressure.

Her role is all the more extraordinary because she plays almost the only woman in a masculine world. Like Diane Keaton amid the Corleone family in *The Godfather*, she is not impressed by machismo, thus offering a more revealing perspective on the figures around her. She loves Harold but she is not in thrall to him; she shares his vision, but in a tougher, wiser way. Comparisons to Lady Macbeth are fully justified (and Hoskins himself has some memorably Shakespearean East End monologues), though Mirren startles us by adding a deeper layer of humanity when she reveals a chink in her elegant armour. After Victoria confesses she has been forced to reveal one of Harold's secrets to their Mafia investors, Harold lashes out at her. She remains utterly unafraid:

> VICTORIA
> I had to tell them everything or the deal would have been finished. Harold, your problem is you just don't understand their psychology.
>
> HAROLD
> Bollocks, you smart-arsed prat!
>
> VICTORIA
> I can't talk to you. I'm going to bed. Goodnight.
>
> HAROLD
> Oi, come 'ere. I'm talking to you —
>
> VICTORIA
> Don't treat me like one of your thugs.

She turns away and Harold restrains himself – until he sees she is crying. As he takes her in his arms, she says:

> VICTORIA
> I'm so scared Harold — I don't want to die. Don't let them kill us!

Her tears are somehow as shocking as any of the car bombs or crucifixions in the rest of the story's mayhem, and the fact that her fear explodes so unexpectedly makes it doubly powerful. This ability to seize a role and then subvert it, as the character or the script demands, remains a hallmark of Mirren's work. In *RED*, as Victoria, she plays a trained assassin:

                    VICTORIA
I was in love with an agent once.

                    SARAH
What happened?

                    VICTORIA
Well, I was with MI6, and the relationship
wasn't... sanctioned. So when it came to light,
my loyalty was questioned, and I was ordered to
kill him. It was a test.

                    SARAH
What did you do?

                    VICTORIA
I put three bullets in his chest.

Her riposte, though perfect, is not quite as wonderful as the scene in Stephen
Frears's *The Queen* (2006) in which, as the monarch herself, she drives her car
into a ditch on the estate at Balmoral. Few actors could so vividly portray an
almost unknowably remote figure and bring her alive with three simple words:

                    THE QUEEN
Oh, bugger it.

I can't say no to an
interesting role. I
always tell my
husband, 'That's it, I
quit, I've done all I
wanted', and he's just
like, 'Yeah, yeah. Sure'.

*You can't get
spoiled if you do
your own ironing*

MERYL
STREEP

Mary Louise 'Meryl' Streep
22 June 1949–

I mean, come on; when you have [critics] writing these things, that you're the greatest thing that ever ate scenery, you're dead. You're fucking dead. How can you even presume to begin a new character? It's a killer.

Sometimes under-preparation is very good, because it instils fear and fear is galvanizing. It makes you break out of yourself. If you're prepared, then you think you're ready, and if you think you're ready, then you're not ready.

In my own experience of male and female directors, people have a much, much harder time taking a direct command from a woman. It's somehow very difficult for people.

It's hard to negotiate the present landscape with a brain and a female body.

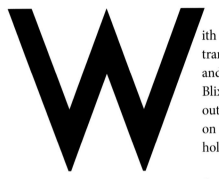

ith a delicious irony, Meryl Streep – an actress celebrated for her ability to transform herself and inhabit roles invisibly – is frequently lampooned by satirists and impersonators. John Sessions gently mocked her performance as Karen Blixen in *Out of Africa* (1985), when Robert Redford appears at the flower bed outside her window, by intoning in a Danish drawl: 'Oh noooo! You're treading on my aaah-ccents – and they were just ready for Oscaring!' But his sketch is like holding a mirror up to a mirror; what can he really hope to ridicule?

Streep – her core fans are known as Streepers – is *the* actor's actor, unafraid of any technical challenge, disdainful of fame and just about as unaffected by her nineteen Oscar nominations and three statuettes as any true star could be. Born in New Jersey, she was a keen participant in school and college plays before she enrolled at the Yale School of Drama; in 1975 she moved to New York, where she appeared in six productions in the first year before deciding she wanted to audition for movies too. Not all of her meetings were encouraging: when she was auditioned by the gruff Dino De Laurentiis for the lead female role in *King Kong* (1976), the mogul turned and berated his son in Italian: 'She's ugly. Why did you bring me this thing?' Streep's reply, in the same language, salved her pride but did not win her the role, which went instead to Jessica Lange. Even so, the coming years were to establish her as a distinctive new face with a string of hits that followed unstoppably one after another, including *Julia* (1977), *The Deer Hunter* (1978), *Manhattan* (1979), *Kramer vs. Kramer* (1979) and *The French Lieutenant's Woman* (1981). These five alone (which yielded four Academy Award nominations and a win for *Kramer vs. Kramer*) would have been quite enough to place her in the pantheon of screen greats, but five years into her cinema career, at the age of thirty-three, she played the role which still haunts every viewer's memory: Zofia Zawistowski in *Sophie's Choice* (1982).

The 1979 book by William Styron had been a bestseller, controversial for its unsparing portrayal of the horrors of a Nazi concentration camp:

> SOPHIE
> My children were sent with me to Auschwitz.
> When the train arrived at Auschwitz the Germans
> made the selection. Who would live, and who
> would die. Jan, my little boy... Jan, my little
> boy, was sent to the Kinderlager, which was the
> children's camp. And my little girl, Eva, was

```
sent to crematorium II. She was exterminated.
```

The terrifying truth Sophie reveals only at the end is that she has been forced to choose which of her children should live – and which will be sent for summary execution. In withholding – and then delivering – this crucial fact, Streep's command of emotional pace is compelling. As Roger Ebert wrote in his review at the time: 'There is hardly an emotion that Streep doesn't touch in this movie, and yet we're never aware of her straining. This is one of the most astonishing and yet one of the most unaffected and natural performances I can imagine'. A well-crafted novel glides smoothly between layers of narrative and emotion, but this is a balance harder to achieve in film. On screen everything seems more literal, and we attend to the nuances of an actor's performance with a less forgiving ear than we allow an author's prose. Speaking in Polish and German and with perfectly pitched accents when she switches to English, Streep's technical mastery is unmatched. Her grief is so understated that it dignifies every frame of the film – all the more amazing because it is told in flashbacks, but the shadow of what is yet to be revealed to us inflects every scene that leads up to it.

Not every script an actress is sent can offer the moral and emotional profundity of *Sophie's Choice*, but in subsequent films Streep has continued to realize the fullest potential of her material, regardless of its subject. Nominated again and again for films as diverse as *Silkwood* (1983), *Out of Africa* (1985), *Ironweed* (1987), *The Bridges of Madison County* (1995), *Adaptation* (2002) and *The Devil Wears Prada* (2006), she won her third Oscar for her acclaimed performance as British prime minister Margaret Thatcher in *The Iron Lady* (2011), thirty-two years after her first. Even so, few who have followed her journey will easily forget the calm, radiant beauty of her close-up as she confesses the truth of her inhuman choice: a face by Watteau in a landscape by Dante.

Happily married since 1978 to sculptor Don Gummer, by whom she has four children, Streep is noted for her modest lifestyle. Perhaps the battles her memorable characters have fought on screen have allowed room for a more contented and contemplative way of being than most stars have managed:

> *In love and hope and optimism – you know, the magic things that*
> *seem inexplicable. . . I do have a sense of trying to make things better.*

Listening is everything. Listening is the whole deal. That's what I think. And I mean that in terms of before you work, after you work, in between work, with your children, with your husband, with your friends. It's everything. And it's where you learn everything.

I act for free, but I demand a huge salary as compensation for all the annoyance of being a public person-ality

MICHELLE PFEIFFER

Michelle Marie Pfeiffer
29 April 1958–

I have the thing that people say Swedes have – of looking like they're keeping a secret.

Acting's an odd profession for a young person; it's so extreme. You work, and the conditions are tough and the process is so immersive, and then it stops, and then there's nothing.

You know, I look like a duck. I just do. And I'm not the only person who thinks that. It's the way my mouth sort of curls up or my nose tilts up.

I do think that, at one time, being an actress was the equivalent almost of being a prostitute. It garnered roughly the same respect. That's changed a lot, thank goodness.

Just standing around looking beautiful is so boring.

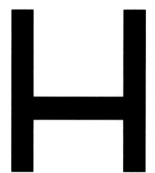ollywood is a strange place if you're in trouble. Everybody thinks it's contagious.' So said Judy Garland, whose career spanned more highs and lows than most. In a business where everyone dreams of overnight success, overnight death is just as common. Geena Davis hit the big time with *Thelma & Louise* (1991), but sank without trace after *Cutthroat Island* (1995); Mike Myers was a huge box-office draw with the *Austin Powers* series, but virtually disappeared after *The Love Guru* (2008), and Brandon Routh won the coveted lead role in *Superman Returns* (2006) only to remain unemployably earthbound thereafter.

Michelle Pfeiffer almost suffered the same fate with *Grease 2* (1982), not so much a sequel as a re-fry of 1978's smash musical. *EFilmCritic*'s Carina Hoskisson wrote: 'The absence of talent, heart, script, motive or sense has never gotten in the way of a producer hell bent on remake territory, and so one of the most blasé, unaffecting and boring sequels in film history is green-lit.' Only Janet Maslin of *The New York Times* stepped in with a reprieve: 'The one improvement is Michelle Pfeiffer, who can't sing as prettily as Olivia Newton-John but who can certainly outdo her in every other department.' Pfeiffer did her best, looking bubble-gum-poppingly gorgeous as Stephanie Zinone opposite Maxwell Caulfield as Michael, delivering her small handful of good lines with zest:

> MICHAEL
> I wanted to ask you if you're free after school
> today.
>
> STEPHANIE
> Yeah, I'm free every day. It's in the
> Constitution.

But the film bombed and even her agent admitted that 'she couldn't get any jobs. Nobody wanted to hire her'. After leaving Fountain Valley High School in California, Pfeiffer had trained as a stenographer until deciding she wanted a career in movies. After winning the Miss Orange County beauty pageant in 1978, she was offered a few minor roles, but was struggling to get herself taken seriously: 'I needed to learn how to act. . . In the meantime, I was playing bimbos and cashing in on my looks'.Brian De Palma, who was about to make *Scarface* (1983), was pursuing Glenn Close for the female lead Elvira and refused even to audition a virtual unknown until his producer overruled him, warning that Melanie Griffith, Kim Basinger, Kathleen Turner and Jodie Foster had already turned down the role. Al Pacino didn't want her either. Pfeiffer was still having to support herself by bagging groceries and was called to audition so repeatedly for the reluctant director that she lost hope. Out of the blue, the producers invited her for an actual screen test with Pacino. 'I was petrified. I vomited before I went out on the set.' The scene called for the two leads to stage a fight: 'I was so keyed up my arms went flying and I broke a glass and cut Al. There was blood all over the place. I was sure I'd lost my chance. . . This is the guy who already hates me. But I actually think it's when he began to like me. And I got the job'.

Scarface is a fictionalized account of the drug wars in 1980s Miami, and the story's cynicism, profanity and violence convinced censors it could not be widely released in its original form. De Palma largely ignored their suggested list of changes; if anything, his uncompromising depiction of the vicious gangland feuds proved more compelling than disconcerting, and the picture was a hit with critics and viewers alike. Elvira, who is first approached by the predatory Tony (Al Pacino) in a nightclub, seizes her audience just as quickly as she grabs her admirer's balls:

```
               ELVIRA
    Hey, José. Who, why, when, and how I fuck is
    none of your business, okay?
```

Like a cocaine-fuelled Lauren Bacall, she insinuates herself into Tony's heart, and then his wild life, but as their narcotics empire begins to unravel, not even drugs can mask the truth. Tearful and furious but still radiant, Elvira abandons everything:

```
               ELVIRA
    Can't you see what we're becoming, Tony? We're
    losers. We're not winners, we're losers.
```

Suddenly, nobody could get enough of her. Vincent Canby praised her as 'a beautiful young actress without a bad – or even an awkward – camera angle to her entire body', while Pauline Kael was more succinct, writing that she was 'paradisically beautiful'. Offers flooded in, and hits soon followed: *The Witches of Eastwick* (1987), *Dangerous Liaisons* (1988), *The Fabulous Baker Boys* (1989), *Batman Returns* (1992) and *The Age of Innocence* (1993). If nobody now cares to remember Stephanie or *Grease 2*, the world knows exactly who we mean when we say 'the blonde in *Scarface*'.

I don't like talking about the characters I do in film, ever. There's no deep, dark meaning. It's just an idea.

There's this idea
that if you take
your clothes off,
somehow you must
have loose morals

DEMI
MOORE

Demi Guynes
11 November 1962–

I think of myself as still being about five.

I want things to be the best they can be. I want greatness.

When you feel sexy or sensuous, you naturally want to open up and give, and I think that comes from being able to receive love and desire.

Once you've tasted a bit of success, it's more challenging. We have to continue to be willing to take a risk so that we don't get too safe.

I'm sure there are a lot of people who think I'm a bitch.

I think we all want the same things. We all want to feel loved, and feel part of something, but we all have self-doubt no matter where we come from.

n 1981, aged nineteen, Demi Moore appeared fully nude in *Oui* magazine. Within fifteen years she was the world's highest paid actress, earning $12.5m [$18.5m] to star in *Striptease* (1996). Movies in which she appears naked or semi-naked include *Indecent Proposal* (1993), *Disclosure* (1994) and *The Scarlet Letter* (1995); she has also appeared nude on the front cover of *Vanity Fair* – twice. Satirical interviewer Dennis Pennis (aka Paul Kaye, English comedian and actor) once asked her: 'Are there any circumstances, if it wasn't gratuitous and it was tastefully done, [in which] you would consider keeping your clothes *on* in a movie?' But if Moore wasn't breaking taboos, she was breaking boundaries of a different kind.

The first example of undressed women – and men – on celluloid was photographer Eadweard Muybridge's *The Human Figure in Motion* (1884). As many a film would later claim, its intent in getting its subjects to shed their clothes was artistic (and scientific: it was a genuine study in physiology). In 1896, the first ever striptease on film was privately shown; by 1908 *À L'Écu d'Or, ou la Bonne Auberge* had established the genre of hardcore pornography for the rich and salacious. None of these depictions had anything to do with mainstream cinema, but by the time Moore came to bare her assets the movie-going public had grown accustomed to full-screen nudity in a context that was patently not X-rated.

> *There's this idea that if you take your clothes off, somehow you must have loose morals. There's still a negative attitude in our society towards women who use a strength that's inherent – their femininity – in any way that might be considered seductive.*

Moore's battle was not with morality so much as with equality. She was the first actress to demand the same salary and benefits as her male counterparts, including equal billing on a movie's credits. In a business notorious for sexism – and for being hypocritical about the value of its female stars – she made more impact flaunting her conscience than her body.

Born Demi Guynes in Roswell, New Mexico, Moore moved to California with her family when she was a teenager, but dropped out of school early to sign with the prestigious Elite Modeling Agency. She spent a good deal of time in Europe, where her neighbour, actress Nastassja Kinski, inspired her to enrol in a drama class; by the time she was eighteen she had returned to Los Angeles, where she married rock singer Freddy Moore, and began to pursue film work in earnest.

After increasingly noticeable appearances in unremarkable films, she was cast in the ensemble hit *St. Elmo's Fire* (1985).

The following year she took the lead in *About Last Night. . .*, an adaptation of David Mamet's 1974 stage play, *Sexual Perversity in Chicago* (1986) (and yes, she does take her clothes off). The story features Debbie (Moore) and Danny (Rob Lowe) as a young couple negotiating the highs and lows of their relationship. Moore, who had barely had a chance thus far to demonstrate her talents, seemed instantly born to celluloid. Beautiful in a guileless and natural way, she falls in love with a rush of palpable joy and falls out of it with mesmerizing anguish. Many actresses are noted for their exuberance and others for melancholy, but Moore rides the roller-coaster with perfect assurance and steals the movie from her co-star. When she breaks up with one lover Steve (Robin Thomas), she plays it ice-cool:

```
        STEVE
I thought we had something kind of special.


        DEBBIE
No, it was kind of sleazy. And now... it's
kind of over.
```

But when she breaks up with Danny, she burns:

```
        DANNY
Hey, know one thing — I never screwed around on
you.


        DEBBIE
Oh, well, let's just give the boy a medal!
I didn't realize it was such a sacrifice.
```

The *Chicago Sun Times* review was everything a nascent star could dream of: 'There isn't a romantic note she isn't required to play in this movie, and she plays them all flawlessly'. More flattering still was the word *The New York Times* subsequently coined to describe the slew of tactfully nude celebrity portraits she inspired: 'Demi-clad.'

Don't let your wounds make you become someone you're not.

Desperation is the perfume of the young actor

UMA THURMAN

Uma Karuna Thurman
29 April 1970–

I spent the first fourteen years of my life convinced that my looks were hideous. Adolescence is painful for everyone, I know, but mine was plain weird.

I was an escapee of childhood. I always wanted to grow up.

Most films these days are men's stories. Women are for add-on romance. That's very hard.

Desperation is the perfume of the young actor. It's so satisfying to have gotten rid of it.

And also I think particularly as a female, you're taught to be defensive your whole life. You're taught not to be aggressive.

It's better to have a relationship with someone who cheats on you than with someone who doesn't flush the toilet.

Nothing about Uma Thurman's upbringing, ambition or even her physicality seemed likely to make her a mainstream star who now commands $14m a picture and works with the hippest directors in the business. Raised in New England as the daughter of a Buddhist professor and a psychotherapist, she endured her school years feeling introverted and acutely self-conscious about her height, gawky limbs and outsized feet.

> *I was not particularly bright, I wasn't very athletic, I was a little too*
> *tall, odd, funny looking. I was just really weird as a kid.*

Even after she had become one of the most admired actresses in the world, she described herself as 'tall, sandy blonde, with sort of blue eyes, skinny in places, fat in others. An average gal.' An average gal? Mia Wallace in Quentin Tarantino's *Pulp Fiction* (1994), dancing the Twist with her minder before overdosing on heroin? Blanche in Woody Allen's *Sweet and Lowdown* (1999), a dead ringer for the sexually ambiguous Marlene Dietrich? The Bride in *Kill Bill: Vol.1* (2003), a vengeful assassin with a custom-made Samurai sword? Dig a little deeper into her background, however, and you sense her family raised a child who was never going to be content to take life at face value. As she later said:

> *I think we all exude essential truths about ourselves, and then, as an*
> *actress, there's what you do with it. There's your wit and your*
> *imagination, and what you can cook up from your experience and*
> *understanding of what makes a human being tick.*

Thurman's grandfather Baron Karl von Schlebrügge was jailed by the Nazis for defending his Jewish business partners, and her grandmother Birgit Holmquist was such a noted beauty that a nude statue of her still stands in her home town of Trelleborg, Sweden. Karl and Birgit moved to Mexico, and their daughter Nena was discovered as a photographic model by Norman Parkinson; the pictures from her subsequent career bear a startling resemblance to Uma, not least in the cool, intelligent gaze that holds the lens. But it was not merely looks that made the family so extraordinary. Nena made a wide circle of friends and, shortly after she was introduced to LSD guru Timothy Leary by the surrealist painter Salvador Dalí, they decided to get married – on camera, in the documentary *You're Nobody Till Somebody Loves You* (1964). The film-makers were the Maysles brothers, the cameraman D. A. Pennebaker and the music was by Miles Davis – all legendary creative figures of the 1960s.

Despite the memorable ceremony, Nena left Leary after only two years for Robert Thurman, a Buddhist academic who had been expelled from Phillips Exeter Academy – America's grandest private school – for trying to join Castro's revolutionary party. The couple were married in 1967, and Uma was born into this heady mix of political and artistic influences in 1970. Leary was invited to be her godfather, but his counter-cultural leanings were amply balanced by another key figure in their household: the Dalai Lama, who taught Robert for almost three decades and was a regular visitor to the family.

Against this extraordinary history, Thurman's first taste of dramatic exposure was charmingly pedestrian. Aged fourteen, she appeared as Abigail in a local production of Arthur Miller's *The Crucible* and was spotted by a talent scout who suggested she might have a promising career as an actress. She dropped out of school and signed to the Click Models agency, and within two years had made it onto the cover of British *Vogue*. Small screen roles began to come her way, but it would be 1988 before she appeared in the two films which marked the beginning of her unstoppable rise: *The Adventures of Baron Munchausen* (Terry Gilliam) and *Dangerous Liaisons* (Stephen Frears).

> *Even today, when people tell me I'm beautiful, I don't believe a word of it.*

Although Gilliam's original trailer for his film cheekily captions Thurman as 'seafood', she plays Botticelli's Venus – or, rather, *is* Venus incarnate, rising wordlessly naked and radiant from a life-sized scallop shell, before having her modesty saved by two nymphs who weave her a diaphanous dress as if by magic. Even if Thurman's role here is as flimsy as her costume, her beauty is captivating. She is far too confident to let the fact she is mere submarine soft porn demean her; one can only imagine that Birgit, her grandmother, would have approved heartily. She only has a matter of minutes on screen (including the wonderful line: 'I am a goddess! I can do what I like!'), but the producers featured her name and face prominently on the subsequent DVD releases, a sure sign they understood a new star had been born.

It was Stephen Frears's lavish adaptation of Christopher Hampton's 1985 play, itself based on the eighteenth-century epistolary novel by Choderlos de Laclos, which persuaded the public Thurman had more than enough talent to back up her extraordinary looks. As the teenaged Cécile de Volanges, in a succession of dresses and nightgowns that leave precisely the right amount to the imagination before being cast aside, she plays a vulnerable pawn in the sexual intrigues between the Marquise de Merteuil (Glenn Close) and Vicomte de Valmont (John Malkovich). Within the complex story Cécile is given little space to establish herself as a rounded character, but in her handful of scenes she perfectly balances both ravishing sexuality and heartbreaking innocence. This combination, frequently exploited by Hollywood for cheap thrills, can easily leave audiences feeling as squeamish as they are titillated, but here – as Valmont first seduces her against her will and then coaches her as a lover – Thurman seizes the initiative with such earnestness that our prurience is shamed. This is not merely being sexual but being alive, and Cécile wants to embrace it utterly.

Thurman noted in an interview at the time that her character was 'bursting with life. . . and eager to experience. It has a lot to do with feminism and it has a lot to do with women being denied the opportunity to have a life'. If this was to become a mantra for her later work, she established it in a single telling scene:

                    MARQUISE DE MERTEUIL
          Tell me... you resisted him, did you?

                         CÉCILE
          Of course I did... as much as I could.

                    MARQUISE DE MERTEUIL
          But he forced you?

                         CÉCILE
          No... not exactly. But I found it almost
          impossible to defend myself.

                    MARQUISE DE MERTEUIL
          Why was that? Did he tie you up?

                         CÉCILE
          No, he just has a way of putting things.

                    MARQUISE DE MERTEUIL
          You can't think of an answer. Not even 'no'?

                    CÉCILE
I kept on saying no all the time. But somehow,
that wasn't what I was doing...

She looks away.

                    CÉCILE
I'm so ashamed.

            MARQUISE DE MERTEUIL
You'll find the shame is like the pain - you
only feel it once. Do you really want my
advice?

                    CÉCILE
Please.

            MARQUISE DE MERTEUIL
Allow Monsieur de Valmont to continue your
instruction.

The sense of paradox Thurman conveys throughout her swift evolution is exquisite, flashing every facet of doubt, hunger, fear, pride and ambition. Her story is a mere sketch, yet all the more perfect for its small scale; glimpsed amid the tortured emotions and duplicities of the world around her, Cécile remains uniquely clear-eyed and self-aware. These qualities would remain a hallmark of her subsequent work, through *Henry & June* (1990), *Batman & Robin* (1997), *Gattaca* (1997), *The Producers* (2005) and *Bel Ami* (2012), and she shows no sign of slowing down:

> *In this business a lot of people go nuts, go eccentric, even end up dead from it. Not my plan.*

I'm very happy at home. I love to just hang out with my daughter, I love to work in my garden. I'm not a gaping hole of need.

You can look ugly in a film but the beauty still comes out of your perfor-mance

JULIETTE BINOCHE

Juliette Binoche
9 March 1964–

Movies are open doors, and at every door, I change character and life. . . I live for the present always. I accept this risk. I don't deny the past, but it's a page to turn.

I want to make films that are political and social. Films with a message or an idea. Films that dare to ask.

My earliest memory is loneliness. That's a hard thing to live with.

The only way for me to stay young is to let go of youth. You cannot hang on to the past.

But I think it's a little different in Europe, because forty is really the best age for a woman. That's when we hit our peak and become this ripe fruit.

If you're a film actress, your career is from twenty to forty-five, but you can still dream.

Oh, I'll be forgotten too, don't worry.

ome stars burst into being in a single scene: Bette Davis in *Of Human Bondage* (1934) or Lauren Bacall in *To Have and Have Not* (1944). Others require the full span of a movie to unfold their radiance: Vivien Leigh in *Gone with the Wind* (1939) or Liv Ullmann in *Persona* (1966). Juliette Binoche – 'La Binoche' to her adoring French fans – preferred a slow burn, and Philip Kaufman's *The Unbearable Lightness of Being* (1988), based on the novel by Milan Kundera, offered the perfect place for her to flicker into our consciousness.

Binoche plays Tereza, a young idealist working in a rural spa where little has changed since the nineteenth century. She reads Tolstoy and longs for love, and her daydreams of being an artist are undisturbed by Communist apparatchiks in the distant capital. She meets Tomas (Daniel Day-Lewis), a handsome doctor, and welcomes his flirtatious advances – not realizing that he is considerably freer with his affections than she wishes to be.

```
                    TEREZA
      I don't understand how someone can make love
      without being in love.
```

She moves to Prague to be with him, and tries to accept the fact that he has other lovers. They marry, but the shadows of the women in Tomas's world remain. When Soviet tanks roll into the city to quell the spread of liberalism, Tereza finds a new voice as a photographer documenting the invasion – and a new way of being herself.

Binoche was born in Paris into an artistic family and had already had considerable success in films by Jean-Luc Godard, André Téchiné and Leos Carax, but when Kaufman cast her as Tereza, she could barely speak English and had to work from a translation. There is something about this dissociation which intensifies the feeling that she is experiencing every moment as if it is entirely uncoloured by her past and heedless of her future; Binoche is absorbed in herself and yet absolutely connected to the people around her. When she sits next to Tomas's mistress Sabina at a dance, her body language is stilted, as if she is crushed by her bohemian company. With Tomas, she is surprised, delighted and frustrated. When a party official confiscates the pictures she has taken of civilians obstructing the Russian tanks, her eyes burn with disgust and fury. The polarities of her character, as much conveyed by her physicality as by her words, constantly expand – threatening to tear her apart.

TEREZA
I know I'm supposed to help you, but I can't.
Instead of being your support I'm your weight.
Life is very heavy to me, but it is so light
to you. I can't bear this lightness, this
freedom... I'm not strong enough.

'Acting is like peeling an onion,' she insists. 'You have to strip away each layer to reveal another.' A familiar metaphor, but we feel Binoche is readier to shed tears than most. Despite her success as Tereza, she was determined to remain close to her roots, avoiding America and refusing offers of roles in Steven Spielberg's *Jurassic Park* (1993) and Brian De Palma's *Mission: Impossible* (1996). Hollywood, though, was happy to meet her on her own terms and the whole of *The English Patient* (1996) was shot in Italy and Tunisia. Binoche plays Hana, a wartime nurse devoted to her convalescent in an abandoned monastery; barely aware of the encroaching conflict, she and her charge live in a world constructed of memories and daydreams.

HANA
I'm not in love with him. I'm in love with
ghosts. So is he, he's in love with ghosts.

Many of the reviews described Binoche's presence as 'ethereal', yet it is grounded in a meticulously detailed reality. She changes the bandages on her patient's burns every day, suggesting that by these innumerable small gestures larger truths can be apprehended.

I try to see my films just once. It's like a dream you've been through when it's been intense, and you just have to go through it once more just to make sure you've had it.

With other acclaimed appearances in Krzysztof Kieślowski's *Three Colours* trilogy (1993–4), *Chocolat* (2000) and *Camille Claudel 1915* (2013), her talent is hardly in doubt, but in 2010, Gérard Depardieu savaged her: 'Tell me, what is Juliette Binoche's secret? I wonder why she has been so respected for so many years. She has nothing. Absolutely nothing.' The attack was unprovoked and widely derided. Bemused, Binoche said simply: 'The secret is that we all have a secret and we have to find it'.

I think being an actor is not very far from being a journalist. Because you investigate, you try to understand, you're asking questions, you're interested in the other.

*I don't really cel-
ebrate fame be-
cause I get enough
attention*

NICOLE
KIDMAN

Nicole Mary Kidman
20 June 1967–

I can't believe I made it. It
feels like a long haul to get
here. I'm so fine with it.
People want you to have
some sort of breakdown, but
I'm relieved to be forty years
old, and I've lived a life.

I want to be in places I've
never been before.

It was very natural for me to
want to disappear into dark
theatre; I'm really very shy.

I think love is the core
emotion. Without that, and
I've certainly existed without
that, it's a very empty life.

Once I start putting all my
little insecurities in my mind,
I'm not actually acting. Then
it's about me – and it should
never be about me. It should
be about the character.

You don't have to be naked
to be sexy.

These different people that
I play become the loves of
my life.

s it ever possible for a huge star to recapitulate the mystery of her earliest films, when public persona is not yet conflated with acting talent? Nicole Kidman, whose films to date have racked up an adjusted gross of $1.6bn in ticket sales, balances *Vogue* cover shoots and commercials for Chanel with global trips to promote women's rights, while still remaining red-hot at the box office. Roger Ebert, that unusually perceptive critic of both commercial and independent films, said of her:

> *She seems to be two people: the glamorous star of* Moulin Rouge
> *(2001) and* Nine *(2009), and the risky, daring actress in* Birth
> *(2004),* The Hours *(2002) and* Eyes Wide Shut *(1999). . . Celebrity
> has clouded her image; if she were less glamorous, she would be
> more praised.*

Not since Grace Kelly has there been an icon who has lived so publicly both on and off screen. Even so, her ambition seems charmingly direct: she is, quite simply, an actor who likes to take on projects of every kind:

> *Always choose a film by its director. You're never certain how
> the movie will turn out, but you're always guaranteed an
> interesting experience.*

Kidman was born in Hawaii to Australian parents, but the family returned to Sydney when she was three. She pursued ballet and acting from an early age, and by the time she was twenty-one had already won her first Australian Film Institute Award nomination as Helen McCord in the screen adaptation of David Williamson's hit play *Emerald City* (1988). By the time Phillip Noyce cast her, aged twenty-one, in *Dead Calm* (1989), she was already well known in her home country, but the rest of the world remained unconquered territory.

The film, which proved a huge international success, is a Hitchcockian thriller set aboard two yachts adrift on the ocean; it shares the intense claustrophobia of *Lifeboat* (1944) with the enigmatic narrative and characterization of *Vertigo* (1958). Kidman, as Rae Ingram, takes a long holiday retreat with her husband John (Sam Neill) to heal their relationship after their young son's death. Alone on their yacht, they pick up Hughie (Billy Zane), a fugitive stranger from another boat whose shipmates have all died under mysterious circumstances. Rae, alone in her grief while John explores Hughie's deserted yacht, finds that Hughie intends to abandon John and set sail with Rae as his captive – and, he hopes, his lover.

At the start of the story, Kidman seems so wrapped up in her grief and exhaustion that she herself is adrift and becalmed. The camera lingers on her uneasily, allowing us to read into her emotions whatever we ourselves imagine about her predicament. Desperation – for John's life, and for her own safety – soon brings her alive again, and once the story is fully under way, she quickly becomes its driving force; shifting from raw fear to a more determined self-control as she remains trapped alone with a killer, she draws on every facet of her character's strength to control and defeat her opponent.

Rae tries to reach John on the ship's radio.

> RAE
> John, can you hear me? Saracen to black
> schooner. Come in, please. Come in, please.
> John. John, it's me. I got the key up onto the
> deck, but he... What's wrong? Are you hurt? Is
> it the boat? John, is it sinking?

In the scene where Hughie rapes her, she pretends to acquiesce, but the intense close-ups become increasingly gripping: even in the moment of her surrender, we sense that she remains unbroken and ready for revenge. While the story itself is simultaneously simplified and intensified by its restricted location – a handful of cabins, the deck, the desolate ocean – Kidman's performance transcends its setting. She proves vulnerable, invulnerable, wily, guileless, desperate and ice-cold by turn – and each of these moods is absolutely central to her character's presence. 'Being an actor is about adapting – physically and emotionally. If that means you have to look great for it and they can make you look great, then thank you. And if you have to have everything washed away, then I'm willing to do that too.'

Because Kidman the actress was as unknown to us as Rae the protagonist, there was no template on which to base our expectations. Everything she does here seems fresh and gripping, and there is no path down which the story can lead us where she cannot make the narrative her own. It feels almost as if the entire movie was created as a world for her to explore, and she is riveting: persuasive, honest and powerful. She continues to be celebrated for her current work – *The Golden Compass* (2007), *Australia* (2008) and *Rabbit Hole* (2010) – but this, her breakthrough performance, remains unforgettable.

I would describe myself as emotional and highly strung. If something upsets me, it really upsets me. If something makes me angry, I get really angry. But it's all very upfront. I can't hide it.

THE
MODERNS

JULIA ROBERTS

JODIE FOSTER

PENÉLOPE CRUZ

EMMA THOMPSON

TILDA SWINTON

SANDRA BULLOCK

JULIANNE MOORE

KATE WINSLET

CATE BLANCHETT

GWYNETH PALTROW

ANGELINA JOLIE

CATHERINE ZETA-JONES

JENNIFER CONNELLY

SCARLETT JOHANSSON

NATALIE PORTMAN

AMY ADAMS

KEIRA KNIGHTLEY

MARION COTILLARD

JENNIFER LAWRENCE

I get dressed up like
a doll, a nice man
puts lipstick on
my lips and I say
words – it's deeply
satisfying

JULIA
ROBERTS

Julia Fiona Roberts
28 October 1967–

You know I'm like a total geek, right? I sit on the set and knit. It's a very social hobby – I can chat with people and still be fully engaged.

The first time I felt I was famous was when I went to the movies with my mom. I had gone to the loo, and someone in the bathroom said in a very loud voice, 'Girl in stall No. 1, were you in *Mystic Pizza*?' I paused and I said, 'Yeah, that was me'.

I wouldn't do nudity in films. To act with my clothes on is a performance. To act with my clothes off is a documentary. . . I just don't feel that my algebra teacher should ever know what my butt looks like.

I've never had to pretend to be having sex with somebody. I'm like the queen of the foreplay dissolve.

Fame is just a summer breeze that comes and goes.

I'm tall and smart. If you're aggressive and energetic it can be intimidating for people who aren't very smart themselves.

I believe that the way you feel about your life will eventually show up on your face.

P*retty Woman* (1990), billed as a romantic comedy, explores the burgeoning love between Vivian (Julia Roberts), a Hollywood Boulevard streetwalker, and Edward (Richard Gere), her rapacious corporate raider client. Although the story was originally intended as a darker socio-political parable about money, power and sex, producer Laura Ziskin and then-Disney president Jeffrey Katzenberg saw the broader commercial potential of the movie and removed its more controversial elements, including Vivian's addiction to cocaine. For the financiers, this was a smart move: the project grossed $484m [$866m] against a budget of $14m [$25m]. It also brought Roberts her second Oscar nomination – astonishing, since it was only her third significant role.

Roberts was born in Smyrna, Georgia, to parents who had been actors and writers before founding a local drama school; Martin Luther King and his wife Coretta enrolled their daughter Yolanda there, and paid the Roberts's hospital bill as a gesture of gratitude when Julia was born. Nineteen years later, in 1986, Roberts moved to New York where she signed with Click Models and began taking acting lessons herself. It would take only a further three years for her to earn her first Academy Award nomination, playing Shelby in *Steel Magnolias* (1989). The film was a hit, but nothing could prepare the young actress for the tide of fame that would break over her following her next major release.

Pretty Woman presents a tightly constructed fable with wonderful dialogue – evocative of the hard-boiled repartee of the great 1950s noir classics – and remains a memorable evocation of the 1980s with all its bullish excesses and fashion horrors. But at its heart it offers a delightful, energetic portrait of Vivian's struggle to find love without compromising her integrity. Gere, although playing a classic male lead, generously reins in his performance to allow Roberts the space she needs to win us over. (Director Garry Marshall understood this was essentially Roberts's movie, as he reportedly toned down Gere's early scenes: 'No, no, no. Richard. In this movie, one of you moves and one of you does not. Guess which one you are?')

Beautifully scripted and crafted, the story offers any number of scenes to highlight Roberts's star qualities. When Edward haggles with Vivian over her fee, they both sound like smooth operators:

EDWARD
Give me a ballpark figure. How much?

>   VIVIAN
> Six full nights. Days too. Four thousand.

>   EDWARD
> Six nights at three hundred is eighteen
> hundred.

>   VIVIAN
> You want days too.

>   EDWARD
> Two thousand.

>   VIVIAN
> Three thousand.

>   EDWARD
> Done.

>   VIVIAN
> I would have stayed for two thousand.

>   EDWARD
> I would have paid four.

Their nimble switch from mutual triumph to disappointment – and then to pride – is a sparkling example of two actors working in perfect partnership. We relish it again in this exchange, worthy of Billy Wilder:

>   VIVIAN
> You're late.

>   EDWARD
> You're stunning.

>   VIVIAN
> You're forgiven.

Gradually the dynamic changes from professional relationship to friendship, and this part of the journey proves the most fruitful for Roberts as it allows her to display a more nuanced emotional evolution. Her natural feisty wit, used as a kind of self-defence against the mercenary trade of sex for money, is here in abundance – yet the need to deal with her growing affection for Edward allows us to glimpse a more moving uncertainty behind her million-dollar smile. As their love for each other develops, the story edges dangerously close to the Cinderella myth. Cleverly, screenwriter J. F. Lawton confronts the theme head-on, allowing Vivian to maintain a disarming scepticism when Edward offers to set her up as his mistress:

```
                    VIVIAN
When I was a little girl, my mama used to
lock me in the attic when I was bad, which was
pretty often. And I would — I would pretend
I was a princess... trapped in a tower by a
wicked queen. And then suddenly this knight...
on a white horse with these colors flying would
come charging up and draw his sword. And I
would wave. And he would climb up the tower and
rescue me. But never in all the time... that I
had this dream did the knight say to me, 'Come
on, baby, I'll put you up in a great condo'.
```

Although the story reprises the Cinderella element when Edward finally returns to woo Vivian in earnest (in a white limo, testing the film's triumph of content over style to its limit), we forgive the foregone conclusion because we actually believe in every step of Vivian's struggle. With a lesser talent, the film's climax might have collapsed under the weight of its own sugar-coating, but Roberts has shown us such a charming, convincing and rounded Vivian that no amount of Hollywood schmaltz can undercut it.

Roberts's had a string of hits with *Sleeping with the Enemy* (1991), *The Pelican Brief* (1993) and *My Best Friend's Wedding* (1997). Not all of her characters reprised the piquancy of Vivian, however:

```
                  WILLIAM
I live in Notting Hill. You live in Beverly
```

Hills. Everyone in the world knows who you are;
my mother has trouble remembering my name.

           ANNA
I'm also just a girl, standing in front of a
boy, asking him to love her.

In *Erin Brockovich* (2000) she plays a gutsy lawyer demanding compensation from a corporation that has been letting chemical run-off poison local water supplies:

           ERIN
Then you take out your calculator and you
multiply that number by a hundred. Anything
less than that is a waste of our time.

One of the defence team picks up a glass of water.

           ERIN
By the way, we had that water brought in
specially for you folks.

Sharp, funny and uncompromising, the performance won her an Oscar; it seems directors had discovered that Roberts played best with her rough edges intact. And she seems to like it that way too:

*I'm too tall to be a girl, I never had enough dresses to be a lady,
I wouldn't call myself a woman. I'd say I'm somewhere between a
chick and a broad.*

You can be true to the character all you want, but you've got to go home with yourself.

*I'm nervous every
day on a film set*

JODIE
FOSTER

Alicia Christian 'Jodie' Foster
19 November 1962–

It's not my personality to be extroverted emotionally, so acting has been helpful to me.

It's an interesting combination: having a great fear of being alone, and having a desperate need for solitude and the solitary experience. That's always been a tug of war.

I'm lucky that people do leave me alone. I'm not Madonna. The red carpet is work. I work from 9-to-5 and when I get home, I don't want to go back to work by going to an industry event. For me, putting on make-up and a fancy dress is work.

Acting, for me, is exhausting. I'm always more energized by directing. It's more intense to direct. I can pop in and express myself, then pop out again. It's a huge passion for me.

I've reached that point where I don't want to act very much anymore. I am much more interested in holding off on acting, after 45 years as an actor. It's a long period of time to do the same thing.

Being understood is not the most essential thing in life.

If I fail, at least I will have failed my way.

odie Foster's career has been so diverse that trying to identify the single film that secured her fame is like hunting for a strand of straw in a stack of needles.

I burn out periodically. Maybe I've lasted because I've had a weird career, doing so many different things.

She got a head start on her peers by modelling as the Coppertone baby at the age of three; most of her contemporaries were still auditioning for high school productions when she won leading roles in *Freaky Friday* and *Bugsy Malone*, both released in 1976. But her performance that same year as teenage prostitute Iris opposite Robert De Niro's Travis Bickle in *Taxi Driver* remains one of the most memorable scenes of that decade:

```
                IRIS
Why do you want me to go back to my parents?
I mean, they hate me. Why do you think I split
in the first place? There ain't nothin' there.


                TRAVIS
But you can't live like this. It's a hell.
A girl should live at home.


                IRIS
Didn't you ever hear of women's lib?


                TRAVIS
What do you mean, women's lib? You're a young
girl. You should be home now. You should be
dressed up, going out with boys, going to
school.


                IRIS
God, are you square.


                TRAVIS
You're the one that's square, man. I don't
screw and fuck with a bunch of killers and
junkies the way you do. You call that being
```

hip? What world you from?

                    IRIS
Who's a killer?

                    TRAVIS
Sport's a killer, that's who.

                    IRIS
Sport never killed nobody.

                    TRAVIS
He killed somebody.

                    IRIS
He's a Libra.

                    TRAVIS
He's a what?

                    IRIS
I'm a Libra, too. That's why we get along so
well.

                    TRAVIS
He looks like a killer to me.

                    IRIS
I think that Cancers make the best lovers...
but, God, my whole family are earth signs.
(Pause) Sport never treated me bad. He didn't
beat me up once.

Iris has street smarts and emotional savvy in spades, and her tough insouciance brings out a tenderness in Travis that provides a vital counterpart to his anger and loneliness. Foster was nominated for an Academy Award for her performance, but returned to the Lycée Français in Los Angeles to pursue her studies before being accepted at Yale:

*[I wanted to] get as far away from home as I could. . . far away from
the film business and. . . just to go to a completely different
atmosphere that was really academic.*

Her graduation in 1985 was dramatically delayed after stalker John Hinckley, Jr
tried to assassinate President Ronald Reagan in a bid to bring himself to Foster's
notice, but she returned to acting and soon won her first Oscar playing Sarah
Tobias in *The Accused* (1988). Sarah struggles to reclaim her strength and sanity
after being gang-raped in a small town bar and she tries to rebuild her life with –
or without – the help of those who try to defend her in court. As with Iris in *Taxi
Driver*, she plays a controversial character who confronts deeply discomfiting
issues about our culture and its sexism.

The film focuses on the harrowing scene of her attack, but the profundity of the
performance lies in the smaller, incidental details of her everyday life – the grim
relentlessness of her waitress job, her fragile friendships, and the heartbreaking
call she makes to her mother after the event. These fleeting emotions do not
diminish the impact of her story: they humanize it in a way that makes it possible
for us to fully grasp her situation.

Was Foster a star by now? A meteor shower for sure, if not yet a supernova.
The wide range of films she had appeared in by 1988 make it hard for us to
assess the qualities we now perceive in her: a cool truthfulness and a restless
determination to reach the heart of her story and her character. But with *The
Silence of the Lambs* (1991) came the opportunity – the script, the director, the
cast – to showcase everything she does best.

*I think all of us – director Jonathan Demme, Anthony Hopkins and I
– still feel like it's the best work we've ever done. We were scared that
we'll never do anything that good again.*

Clarice Starling (Foster) and Hannibal 'the cannibal' Lecter (Hopkins)
proved, with a perverse but compelling magic, one of the all-time great movie
partnerships: with a desperate, grudging respect they engage each other with the
real-life poise of Astaire and Rogers and the fictional zest of Holmes and Watson.
Foster plays both the toughest, best-trained FBI agent and the most intense,
emotionally articulate detective of recent times.

HANNIBAL
You know how quickly the boys found you...
all those tedious sticky fumblings in the back
seats of cars... while you could only dream of
getting out... getting anywhere... getting all
the way to the FBI.

CLARICE
You see a lot, Doctor. But are you strong
enough to point that high-powered perception at
yourself? What about it? Why don't you — why
don't you look at yourself and write down what
you see? Or maybe you're afraid to.

Everything we have known about Foster from her previous work – the intensity, the quietly articulate details, the search for simplicity in each role – is perfected in this performance, which won her a second Academy Award. Ten years later, Lecter returned to the screen in *Hannibal* (2001). Hopkins reprised the role but Foster and director Demme declined; audiences were devastated, although Julianne Moore and Ridley Scott proved creditable replacements. Producer Dino de Laurentiis spread rumours that Foster had demanded an unheard-of $20m [$28m], plus 15 per cent of the gross profits, even to read the script, while Foster claimed she was unavailable because she was directing a film of her own. After the furore died down, she admitted she felt that in the sequel Starling had 'negative attributes' and 'betrayed' the original character: 'Clarice meant so much to Jonathan and me, she really did, and I know it sounds kind of strange to say but there was no way that either of us could really trample on her.'

As with Starling, so with Foster – a disarming honesty. There are countless ways to become a star, and talent, beauty, notoriety and luck are just a few. For every Garbo there is a Mae West, for every Bardot a Jane Fonda. It is no indictment of Foster's acting achievements to say that we remember her most powerfully when she seems wholly herself.

I really need to love the director. I need him to be a good parent. And then I will lie down on the train tracks and go to the ends of the earth for him.

*They would share
all their secrets*

PENÉLOPE
CRUZ

Penélope Cruz Sánchez
28 April 1974–

Ego is like a lion that we have to keep under control.

I was eleven when I first said I wanted to become an actress, and everyone looked at me as if I had said I wanted to go to the moon.

I like roles that people don't recognise me in.

In terms of the work, it always seems like it's a first date. I mean, every time I go to the movie set and start a project, I feel the same feeling – the butterflies in the stomach, not having control over it – because acting is like that.

One thing that I'm proud of: I'm really capable of laughing at myself.

You cannot live your life looking at yourself from someone else's point of view.

Love is a rebellious bird that no one can tame.

There's so much more I want to do. I refuse to get to fifty and wait at home for the phone to ring.

For Penélope Cruz, there was no Big Bang: her journey to A-list status was beset by misunderstanding, miscasting and a spectacular run of expensive flops. Not that this deterred her, or the directors who flocked to work with her. Long before she won her first Academy Award, she had collaborated with Stephen Frears, Billy Bob Thornton, Ted Demme, John Madden and Cameron Crowe, but not even these luminaries could prevent the startling embarrassment of 2001 when Cruz was nominated for three simultaneous Golden Raspberries for worst actress. The culprits were all high-budget, high-profile Hollywood productions: *Blow* (2001, opposite Johnny Depp), *Captain Corelli's Mandolin* (2001, with Nicolas Cage) and *Vanilla Sky* (also 2001, alongside Tom Cruise), in which Cruz has to deliver the excruciating line:

```
              DAVID
    I like your life.


              SOFIA
    Well, it's mine and you can't have it!
```

Cruz was born and raised in the suburbs of Madrid, where her mother ran a hair salon:

> It was my first acting school. I would pretend to be doing my homework, but I was really observing the women. I found their behaviour mesmerizing – what they were hiding, how they left feeling a little different after they'd been helped to become a little more like whom they wanted to look like. They treated the place a little bit like a psychologist's office. They would share all their secrets.

If curiosity was to prove the engine of her ambition, it was reinforced by a natural exuberance and a fierce determination. Aged fifteen, she won a talent contest and decided she needed representation, little realizing how precocious she must have seemed. Katrina Bayonas, a leading agent, turned her away (and for a second time when Cruz returned a week later), saying she was too young. The third week, Bayonas signed her – and remains her agent to this day. True to her fighting spirit, Cruz had to lie about her age to win her first role as the teenaged Silvia in Bigas Luna's *Jamón Jamón* (1992) – and then lie again to her parents about what the role entailed in order to gain their permission to play it. But play it she did, in spades.

In hindsight it seems impossible to miss the power and honesty of her interpretation, but the film itself is so eccentric, and Cruz's energy so unheralded, that critics might forgive themselves for not having paid closer attention at the time. The story centres on a series of thwarted love affairs but its tone veers giddily from that of *Oedipus Rex* to *La cage aux folles*, and the mixture of farce with tragedy is frequently unsettling. The metaphors – naked bullfighting, seduction by imitating a parrot, cascading pearls from broken necklaces and a duel to the death using cured hams as clubs – are almost as bizarre as the relationships themselves. The direction is heartfelt but utterly camp, and the handling of emotion and sexuality so raw but so ludicrous that we hardly know where to look. Luna, however, was clearly looking at Cruz, whom he treats as a kind of icon from her very first scene.

Early in the film, Silvia's boyfriend José Luis (Jordi Mollà) begins to kiss her breasts:

> SILVIA
> What do they taste like?

> JOSÉ LUIS
> I don't know.

> SILVIA
> You're sure they don't taste like a potato tortilla?

> JOSÉ LUIS
> That would be fantastic. One would taste like a tortilla... and the other, like ham.

> SILVIA
> José Luis...

He stops licking her.

> JOSÉ LUIS
> Yes?

SILVIA
When we have a house... can I have a closet
just to keep shoes?

Whether she is hiding from her drunken father behind frosted glass, fainting in slow motion as she suffers pregnancy sickness, kissing the red-hot Javier Bardem or running in tears through a rain storm, she is riveting. Her tenderness and passion are dignified and credible in every frame; it seems extraordinary that she was only a teenager when the cameras rolled, and yet her performance is as mature as anything she has portrayed since. Success, however, came at a price. *The Guardian* later wrote: 'A hypersexual hit in her native Spain, [*Jamón Jamón*] transformed her into a national fantasy – a tousled, naked, writhing minx. She was seventeen, suddenly a star, and she was scared.' Cruz herself admitted to the interviewer:

> *There was some strong energy around me, and I didn't know how to handle it. . . I had a strong rejection of anything sexual or sensual for a while. I cut my hair very, very short. I didn't do any love scenes, not even kisses, for many years. I was told by everyone, 'You are risking your career.' But I followed my heart, and I never regret that.*

She paid her dues in Spanish films, shooting a further seventeen in the following six years alone before being offered her first Hollywood role; she admits with a disarming modesty that 'when I did my first movie in America, I already had my return ticket to Spain'.

> *I came to Los Angeles for the first time in 1994. I spoke no English. I only knew how to say two sentences: 'How are you?' and 'I want to work with Johnny Depp'.*

The industry saw her as a European beauty with a Mediterranean fire, but nothing in the scripts she accepted remotely recaptured the qualities she had shown in *Jamón Jamón*. It seems the world had been tempted to take her – all too literally – at face value:

> *The most difficult thing in the world is to start a career known only for your looks, and then to try to become a serious actress. No one will take you seriously once you are known as the pretty woman.*

It would take Pedro Almodóvar, who had already directed her in *Live Flesh* (1997) and *All About My Mother* (1999), to remind us what she could truly deliver:

> *Penélope was born to be an actress. She is someone who is extremely emotional, and if she was not an actress it could be a problem for her. It's luck she has chosen a profession that allows her to express something that would be too much for a normal person. Otherwise she would suffer a lot. And even now maybe she suffers too much.*

The director enticed Cruz home to Spain to shoot *Volver* (2006) and the film brought her a mantelpiece full of awards and an Oscar nomination. It echoes the surrealism and complexity of *Jamón Jamón*, featuring murders, false identities and ghosts, and it returned Cruz to her roots and reawakened interest from directors who finally understood how to cast her.

Volver was followed swiftly by Woody Allen's *Vicky Cristina Barcelona* (2008), which won her an Academy Award; the following year Rob Marshall's *Nine* (2009), a kaleidoscopic celebration of the chaos of the creative life, earned another Oscar nomination. In the film, Carla, the mistress of fictional film director Guido (Daniel Day-Lewis), tries to entice her lover away from his work:

```
                    CARLA
     I'll be waiting for you, with my legs open.
```

It seems Cruz had finally shed her fear of love scenes; Europe had reclaimed her, and her radiance was redoubled. As Allen himself admitted:

> *I don't like to look at Penélope directly. It's too overwhelming.*

The most important lesson I've learned in this business is how to say no. I've said no to a lot of temptations, and I'm glad I did.

Where are all the stories?

EMMA THOMPSON

Emma Thompson
15 April 1959–

I don't think it is liberating to get your tits out. I don't hold with that. But I am much more comfortable with being a woman now than I was in my twenties.

I am who I am and there is nothing I can do about that.

When I lose my temper, I find it difficult to forgive myself. . . My worst quality is impatience.

I mind having to look pretty, that's what I mind, because it is so much more of an effort.

If you get an Oscar for your film, then the revenue for your film goes up. They mean a great deal. I can't deny it.

I would rather have a root canal treatment for a year than go on Twitter or Facebook. The irony of Facebook is [that you speak out but] don't say it to anybody's face. It revolts me, repels me.

Gone are the days of studio contracts where players would be assigned films just to keep them busy; nowadays, for an actor to decide whether or not to accept any of the endless scripts they are offered can be tricky, and motives vary according to circumstance. Should one choose according to the screenplay, the director, the fee, the rest of the cast or even the location? Nicole Kidman suggested 'always choose a film by its director. You're never certain how the movie will turn out, but you're always guaranteed an interesting experience.' Hitchcock insisted the three most important things about a film were 'the script, the script and the script' – but he also said: 'When an actor comes to me and wants to discuss his character, I say, "It's in the script". If he says, "But what's my motivation?"' I say, "Your salary".' One interviewer asked Robert Mitchum what he looked for in a project and he replied simply: 'Days off'.

Emma Thompson has long found the written word to be a key inspiration for her work. Her mother, Phyllida Law, is an actress, as was her father Eric Thompson, best known for narrating the children's TV series *The Magic Roundabout*; her first husband, Kenneth Branagh, is a noted actor, director and writer. Thompson studied English literature at Cambridge, where she was a prominent member of the Footlights Dramatic Club, before establishing a successful career in television comedy, creating much of the material she performed. A leading role as Harriet Pringle in the acclaimed BBC series *Fortunes of War* (1987) led to film offers, and with only her fourth part – as Margaret Schlegel, in E. M. Forster's *Howards End* (1992) – she won an Academy Award. The moving and intelligent screenplay was by Ruth Prawer Jhabvala, to date the only novelist ever to have won the Booker Prize for fiction as well as an Oscar for her script. Margaret is a clever and passionate woman who struggles to balance her progressive views against the strict proprieties of Edwardian society. Bookish, beautiful and as exuberant as her corsets and manners permit, she expresses as much in her dignified silences as in her rare outbursts and the most remarkable aspect of her performance is that this restraint does nothing to disguise the fire in her soul.

```
             HENRY
I shall do what I can, but I can't treat your
sister as if nothing has happened. I should be
false to my position in society if I did.


           MARGARET
Tomorrow she will go to Germany, and trouble
```

```
society no longer. Tonight she asks to sleep
in your empty house. May she? Will you give my
sister leave? Will you forgive her... as you,
yourself, have been forgiven?
```

The following year Thompson was nominated for two Oscars simultaneously, one as housekeeper Miss Kenton opposite Anthony Hopkins (Mr Stevens, the butler) in *The Remains of the Day* (1993), adapted by Jhabvala from the novel by Kazuo Ishiguro; and one as a campaigning lawyer in Jim Sheridan's drama *In the Name of the Father* (1993). But her next win would be as a writer for her adaptation of Jane Austen's *Sense and Sensibility* (1995), in which she also appears as the 'sensible' sister Elinor Dashwood. Thompson remains the only artist ever to have been recognized at the Academy Awards for a screenplay as well as for a performance, and she continues both to write (*Nanny McPhee*, 2005 and *Effie Gray*, 2014) and to act (*Love Actually*, 2003, the *Harry Potter* series from 2004 to 2011, and *Saving Mr. Banks*, 2013).

> *I've found over the years – and this was a surprise to me – that I can get the same kind of creative satisfaction from writing as I have heretofore gotten out of acting.*

Actor Christian Bale confessed that 'I only sound intelligent when there's a good scriptwriter around', confirming both Hitchcock's and Thompson's view that everything starts with the words. Guy Pearce affirms: 'I feel I do my best work when it's all there on the page, [when] the character is very vivid and I'm not having to create stuff and trying to cobble together something.' Thompson offers proof that an actor who engages with a screenplay and draws out its every nuance with respect and truthfulness will win hearts and acclaim in equal measure. As her success with contemporary audiences has shown, there is nothing remotely old-fashioned about her beliefs, but she does offer a caution about the importance of the craft of writing:

> *I sometimes think that the young must get very bored with the parts that they are required to play. It's not as though there are that many complex, interesting roles for anyone. The guys are now required to stand around looking beautiful and be superheroes. And I'm very, very bored. They must be bored too. Where are all the dramas we used to love? Where are all the stories?*

I can't stand this new culture of the instant disposable celebrity. It's all so vulgar.

I am probably a woman

TILDA SWINTON

Katherine Mathilda Swinton
5 November 1960–

It's a real comfort zone for me to feel alien.

I wouldn't know how to approach a character if I tried. People will ask about choosing a role; I don't choose roles. People will talk to me about preparation. Aside from putting together a disguise, I'm not aware of any preparation at all.

I've been on the other side of the table many times, trying to get people to be sympathetic to projects, and I've been the victim of that kind of intense kindness masking extreme stupidity.

Upsetting people is never a reason for not doing something, is it?

[on the Oscar statuette] I have an American agent who is the spitting image of this. Really truly, the same shape head and, it has to be said, the buttocks.

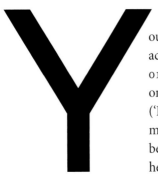

You know you will be stepping into unknown territory when an Oscar-winning actress has her email set to auto-reply with the greeting: 'Hello, I am away until 01/01/2070 and am unable to read your message'. Tilda Swinton insists that the only preparation she makes for a role is 'putting on a disguise', eschews theatre ('I don't love it – I'm just not one of them'), and has played men in three of her movies. Agelessly beautiful and frequently described as androgynous, she has been the face of Chanel as well as muse to countless designers, yet still finds herself addressed as 'sir' by strangers.

Swinton paid her dues as a member of the Royal Shakespeare Company but soon left to pursue less conventional work. Her years with the visionary and iconoclastic Derek Jarman brought us *Caravaggio* (1986), *The Last of England* (1988) and *Edward II* (1991), but the role that established her quirky brilliance was Orlando in Sally Potter's 1992 adaptation of Virginia Woolf's novel by that name. She plays a young man who lives, eternally youthful, from the time of Elizabeth I to the present – and who by the end becomes a woman.

> ORLANDO
> Same person. No difference at all... just a
> different sex.

The film is a visually opulent and humorous meditation on identity, with Orlando as the still point in a kaleidoscopic series of episodes exploring love, politics, age and geography. He/she seems occasionally bewildered by the journey itself and his/her asides to camera offer a modern twist on the soliloquy, stepping outside the production's stylized reality to create a further layer of artificiality. Clearly, there is nothing of the Method school here; there is barely any acting at all in the traditional sense of the word, and yet with this anti-performance Swinton engages us just as powerfully as might a Leigh, a Loren or a Jolie.

> ORLANDO
> But you are mine!

> PRINCESS SASHA
> But why?

> ORLANDO
> Because... I adore you.

In *Possible Worlds* (2000) she plays Joyce, the lover of a man who exists in multiple universes: she is the only thing that connects his disparate identities. *The Guardian* celebrated her 'devastatingly charismatic screen presence, and. . . beautifully calibrated, differentiated performances'. All of her films elicit such praise, with the *Chicago Sun Times* noting 'a directness so forceful you want to look away' and *Time Out* warning that 'she doesn't craft a performance so much as turn into Hurricane Tilda, obliterating everything in her path'.

She pursues only opportunities that intrigue her and largely ignores the lure of Hollywood, although some of America's more distinguished directors – Wes Anderson, Spike Jonze, David Fincher, Jim Jarmusch and the Coen brothers – have persuaded her to cross the Atlantic. Perhaps her most conventional appearance was as remorseless corporate lawyer Karen Crowder in Tony Gilroy's *Michael Clayton* (2007), which she described mischievously as the 'strangest role' she has ever taken; it won her an Oscar, which she promptly gave to her agent on the grounds that it resembled him, notably his sculpted buttocks.

Swinton lives in a remote Scottish village away from the hubbub of London and Los Angeles, where she cherishes an absolute artistic freedom encompassing the mundane – she runs the Ballerina Ballroom Cinema of Dreams in Nairn, with an entrance fee of £3 or a tray of home-baked cakes – as well as the magical: in 2013 she spent eight hours a day for a week sleeping in a glass case in the lobby of New York's Museum of Modern Art. The plaque beside the installation simply read:

> *Tilda Swinton. Scottish, born 1960. The Maybe, 1995/2013. Living
> artist, glass, steel, mattress, pillow, linen, water and spectacles.*

She draws no distinction between these outlets for her creativity, although that does not mean she is not passionate about the projects she commits to: on several occasions she has nurtured ideas with directors over a decade or more before even a penny of funding has been raised. At the opposite end of the spectrum, she plays the White Witch in *The Chronicles of Narnia* series; *The Lion, the Witch and the Wardrobe* (2005) earned $745m worldwide. Somehow, without vanity or egotism, she maintains it is all part of a vital continuum:

> *You're always playing yourself. It's all autobiography, whatever you're
> doing. It's using [the roles] as a kind of prism through which to throw
> something real about yourself.*

I don't really look like people in films; I look like people in paintings.

I was always long-ing to do, emotion-ally and physically, what my male counterparts got to do

SANDRA BULLOCK

Sandra Annette Bullock
26 July 1964–

I've learned that success comes in a very prickly package. Whether you choose to accept it or not is up to you.

Nobody can make me cry in public. I'll punch them first before they make my mascara smear.

Fame means when your computer modem is broken, the repair guy comes out to your house a little faster.

I have no desire to maintain a lifestyle. I am a horrible celebrity. If I am out in public, I dress like a pig.

Everyone told me to pass on *Speed* because it was a 'bus movie'.

I was a Brownie for a day. My mom made me stop. She didn't want me to conform.

Movie sex scenes are never romantic, and you're never swept off your feet. It's always very technical. I'm counting the beats: Okay, we're supposed to kiss for two beats, then I say my line, then they want another kiss for four beats.

I don't understand why there needs to be a love interest to make women go see a film.

**S**peed (1994) is a high-octane fairy tale with a heart of gold, and also a rare boy's movie where a girl, Sandra Bullock as Annie Porter, steals the show. Her noble stallion is a beaten-up public transit bus, her knight in Kevlar body armour the scrupulously well-mannered cop Jack Traven (Keanu Reeves), and their nemesis a bomb-maker (Dennis Hopper) with an old-fashioned bottle of Coke and nicotine-burnished cackle. The happy ending, as it should be, is a kiss that takes place aboard a runaway subway carriage as it screeches to a halt on a Los Angeles boulevard:

                    ANNIE
          You didn't leave me. I can't believe it...
          You didn't leave me.

                    JACK
          Didn't have anywhere to be just then.

They kiss.

                    JACK
          I have to warn you, I've heard relationships
          based on intense experiences never work.

                    ANNIE
          OK. We'll have to base it on sex then.

                    JACK
          Whatever you say, ma'am.

Almost every single name actress in Hollywood had turned the script down, from Meg Ryan to Sigourney Weaver. Bullock, who had only played one notable role in *Demolition Man* (1993), was cast just two weeks before production started, and the shooting proved so complex that the project ran out of money before the final scenes had been completed. The audience test screenings had to be shown with animated story-boards sketched in, and studio executives were in a cold sweat. Only when one marketing chief noticed that viewers were so gripped by the action that when they took a bathroom break they walked backwards to keep their eyes on the screen did he realize they had a sure-fire winner on their hands. The film is a masterpiece of switchback plotting and its characters are all the more compelling because they evoke archetypes found in any timeless story. But Bullock, who finds herself driving a bus which has been booby-trapped to explode if she lets the speed drop below fifty miles an hour on busy public roads, is our everywoman. Scared but sassy, wholesome but cute in her pale blue cardigan, she is the perfect screwball heroine, subverting a *Die Hard* formula; sixty years earlier, Frank Capra would have killed for a leading lady like her.

```
            ANNIE
I should probably tell you that I'm taking the
bus because I had my driver's license revoked.

            JACK
What for?

            ANNIE
Speeding.
```

The movie made a fortune and established Bullock as an actress who could play tough and sexy without seeming aloof. She can do kookiness with dignity, she can do elegance without being arch; she makes her roles accessible without being mundane. She capitalized on these qualities in a range of acclaimed hits, including *Crash* (2004), *The Blind Side* (2009) and *The Proposal* (2009), and in 2013 she got to play a part which would take her to the outer limits of any actor's skills – a project with no props but a space suit, and for which the only Method-style preparation would be endless rides aboard NASA's training aircraft, the Vomit Comet.

Gravity is an existential science-fiction adventure that follows a couple of astronauts, Ryan Stone (Bullock) and Matt Kowalski (George Clooney), who are seeking a way back to earth after their space shuttle has been destroyed in a hailstorm of satellite debris. At the end, alone and battling panic as she races to find a way to save herself from freezing, asphyxiating or plummeting to her death, Ryan realizes the only things she can rely on now are her technical skills and her humanity. With no co-stars surviving, but myriad galaxies reflected in the visor of her helmet, she draws us ineluctably into her diminishing world. Not since Kubrick's *2001: A Space Odyssey* (1968) have we seen the human soul confront the cosmos so movingly; not since Deborah Kerr's Sister Clodagh in *Black Narcissus* (1947) have we seen such emotion conveyed in a face alone.

Always be the student. Once you find yourself to be the teacher, you've lost it.

The audience don't come to see you, they come to see themselves

JULIANNE MOORE

Julie Anne Smith
3 December 1960–

The great disappointment is that when you're acting, you've literally become a different person in your head, [but] when you see it you go, Oh! It's the same face!

I do remember when I was starting acting, going from one set to the next, with not much else going on in my life. And at the end of the day, you get back to your hotel room and just feel this awful loneliness, because the cameras have stopped rolling.

You never have sex the way people do in the movies. You don't do it on the floor, you don't do it standing up, you don't always have all your clothes off, you don't happen to have on all the sexy lingerie. You know, if anybody ever ripped my clothes, I'd kill them.

I was always on the lookout for clues. And there are a lot of clues in how people dress.

I always say that to be fearless you actually have to be afraid.

When I go to a movie and can't figure it out, I'm just thrilled.

**P**ower games abound in the production of any movie. In the old days, as legend has it, a starlet would drop her knickers for a juicy role; today, she is more likely to drop her price to win one. An appearance in a blockbuster may bring a fat pay cheque, but greater acclaim is often to be found in independent productions less hamstrung by marketing and budget constraints. At the 2010 Oscars, the highest-earning movie was *Avatar* [$2.8bn], while the Best Picture award went to *The Hurt Locker*; the following year *Toy Story 3* made $1.1bn but *The King's Speech* collected the top four prizes. Jonah Hill, nominated for his role in *The Wolf of Wall Street* (2013), agreed to work for the minimum union wage of $60,000 against his co-star Leonardo DiCaprio's $10m, while Lindsay Lohan accepted $100 a day to work on Paul Schrader's *The Canyons* (2013). It seems the smart stars want kudos as well as cash, and few are smarter than Julianne Moore.

> *You have to remember that Hollywood is in the business of making movies that they can sell tickets to – they're not in the business of finding great roles for actors.*

Moore's father was a paratrooper in the US army, and the family travelled constantly. Moore had originally dreamed of becoming a doctor, but while she was attending the Frankfurt American High School she was inspired by an English teacher to pursue her acting talents; in 1979 she enrolled at Boston University to study theatre.

> *When you move around a lot, you learn that behavior is mutable. I would change, depending on where I was. . . It teaches you to watch, to reinvent, that character can change.*

Shortly after settling in New York in 1983 she won the dual roles of Frannie and Sabrina Hughes in the daytime soap *As the World Turns*, and after five years on the show she earned her first Emmy Award. Movie offers followed, but her ambition was tempered by integrity; for four years from 1990 she worked periodically with director Andre Gregory in performance workshops of Chekhov's *Uncle Vanya*, which culminated in Louis Malle's film *Vanya on 42nd Street* (1994). Moore cited the time as 'one of the most fundamentally important acting experiences I ever had'. Robert Altman saw the eventual production and cast her in *Short Cuts* (1993), where she was a virtual unknown among an ensemble that included Robert Downey Jr, Tim Robbins, Frances McDormand and Jack Lemmon. She plays Marian, a painter whose husband Ralph (Matthew Modine) suspects her of infidelity, but whose airy refusal to discuss the matter infuriates him:

```
                RALPH
He's the kind of guy women find attractive,
isn't he? The outdoorsman type.


                MARIAN
I don't know a lot about them. I hope they like
something other than chamber music.


                RALPH
Isn't it wonderful, Marian, how we can skate
around an issue, always playing our little
game?


                MARIAN
That's a good idea, a game. Might help break
the ice.
```

An argument ensues in which Marian spills her wine and is forced to deliver a furious monologue about her drunken fling while she tries, naked from the waist down, to blow-dry her skirt before guests arrive for supper. The scene is funny, frightening and irresistible all at once, and led to an offer for Todd Haynes's *Safe* (1995), Moore's first lead role. The film is a kind of existential thriller about Carol, a well-to-do homemaker whose health begins to decline in steps that lead from allergies to nosebleeds to seizures. These illnesses seem to be caused by nothing – or, indeed, by everything: simply life itself. David Thomson subsequently praised the picture as 'one of the most arresting, original and accomplished films of the 1990s', while *Empire* magazine wrote that it 'established [Moore's] credentials as perhaps the finest actress of her generation'.

But the best was yet to come. Steven Spielberg admired her brief appearance in *The Fugitive* (1993) so much that he offered her the role of Sarah Harding in *Jurassic Park: The Lost World* (1997) without even an audition. Moore accepted, but she was careful to balance the blockbuster with independent productions. Paul Thomas Anderson, a young auteur director, approached her to play the part of porn star Amber Waves in *Boogie Nights* (1997), a rambling and exuberant portrait of the 1980s sex movie industry. She found the script 'exhilarating' and signed on, and the decision led to her first Academy Award nomination. When Amber shoots a cheesy sex scene with newcomer Dirk Diggler (Mark Wahlberg), she has already fallen for him, and her determination to protect him from the brutalities of the industry feels oddly maternal:

>   AMBER
>   Do you want to practice your lines with me?
>
>   DIRK
>   I know them.
>
>   AMBER
>   You look great, honey.
>
>   DIRK
>   Does he want me to keep going until I come?
>
>   AMBER
>   Yeah. You just come when you're ready...
>
>   DIRK
>   Where should I come?
>
>   AMBER
>   Where do you want?

It was her breakthrough international role, with the *Los Angeles Times* hailing the film's 'sureness of touch, its ability to be empathetic, nonjudgmental and gently satirical, to understand what is going on beneath the surface of this raunchy universe and to deftly relate it to our own.' Moore hurls herself into this free-wheeling narrative, and her performance balances its humorous excesses with the bleakness that shadows its hedonism. Here, Amber calls her estranged husband:

Amber does a quick line of coke. She takes a valium, lights a cigarette, then dials the phone.

>   AMBER
>   Tom... hi... yeah. I know it's late, but... Is Andy

there? Is he... ? I'd like to say hello, I'd like
to say hello to my son and that's all. (Pauses.)

                    AMBER
Lemme tell you something, Tom. Lemme tell you
something you don't know; I know a lawyer, you
understand? You might think I don't but I do,
and I'll take you to court...

She is begging now.

                    AMBER
No... please don't, Tom, Tom, Tom —

Tom hangs up.

By now every director wanted to work with her and the choice of roles became less divisive: good money and good material met in the middle, and Chekhov would no longer have to battle computer-generated dinosaurs in order to pay the bills. Collaborations followed with the Coen brothers in *The Big Lebowski* (1998), Neil Jordan in *The End of the Affair* (1999), Lasse Hallström in *The Shipping News* (2001) and Stephen Daldry in *The Hours* (2002), further establishing Moore's reputation as a bankable star with both talent and intelligence. In *Blindness* (2008) she plays a doctor's wife confronting the terror of a city where everyone has lost their sight:

            DOCTOR'S WIFE
    The only thing more terrifying than blindness
    is being the only one who can see.

The concept is deceptively simple and it reprises her role in *Safe* (1995) where a woman battles everything and nothing at the same time. In 2015, she won an Oscar for *Still Alice* (2014), a portrait of a college professor suffering from early-onset Alzheimer's disease. In all of these films her character's struggle is with herself, and they generate performances which have to be truthful because there is nothing extraneous to support them. Few actresses can conjure so much from so little, but Moore understands that in the right hands nothing is too simple to evoke the most powerful of emotions.

Often in life you cry when you're caught off-guard. That's where I need to be when I'm acting, too.

I like exposing my-self. There's not an awful lot that em-barrasses me

KATE WINSLET

Kate Elizabeth Winslet
5 October 1975–

Since I was thirteen or fourteen, I've always felt older than I actually am.

I was a wayward child, very passionate and very determined. If I made up my mind to do something, there was no stopping me.

I was suddenly really famous, and I didn't know how to cope. I didn't know myself well enough as a person, number one, and as an actor, number two. I wanted to escape.

My skin still crawls if you call me a movie star. I get embarrassed. I think, don't be ridiculous. Maybe it's because I'm British. To me, Julia Roberts, that's a movie star.

The experience of making a movie is far removed from watching the end result. It's exciting, but it still makes me squirm.

There are moments to indulge and enjoy, but I always know when it's time to go home and wash my knickers.

I love it when a character requires me to look less than my red-carpet best.

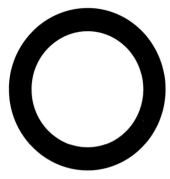nly in retrospect can the iconic status of a film seem inevitable; even James Cameron's *Titanic* (1997) was a huge risk and beset by mishaps and budget overruns. It could hardly be said to approach the real-life tragedy from an innovative angle as dozens of movies and television productions had told the story over the previous decades. *Titanic* (1953) had starred Barbara Stanwyck and *A Night to Remember* (1958) a young Honor Blackman, while Lew Grade's star-studded spin-off *Raise the Titanic* (1980) was so disastrously lavish that Grade lamented 'it would have been less costly to lower the ocean'. Cameron's twist – or, at least, his pitch to the studio – was effectively 'Romeo and Juliet get hit by an iceberg', and whether or not we consider his version to be a work of genius, we can at least be grateful it does not feature two of his original casting choices in the roles of Jack and Rose: Macaulay Culkin and Madonna.

After an impressively brief apprenticeship with small television roles, Kate Winslet made her big-screen debut in Peter Jackson's gruesome teen drama *Heavenly Creatures* (1994) and immediately attracted the attention of the press. *The Washington Post* wrote: '[she] is a bright-eyed ball of fire, lighting up every scene she's in', and the role earned her the London Film Critics' Circle Award for British Actress of the Year. Her next outing as Marianne Dashwood in *Sense and Sensibility* (1995) won her a BAFTA and nominations for both a Golden Globe and an Oscar; *Time* magazine declared '[she] is worthy of the camera's scrupulous adoration... She is perfect, a modernist ahead of her time.' She was still only twenty.

Winslet was now desperate to play the heroine in Cameron's epic, and wrote to him: 'You don't understand! I *am* Rose! ... I don't know why you're even seeing anyone else!' Her persistence won out, and audiences adored her as Rose DeWitt Bukater, a society girl engaged to be married to the rich but snobbish Cal Hockley (Billy Zane). As Rose is courted by the poor but charismatic artist Jack Dawson (DiCaprio), she realizes his love for her is more seductive than anything her fiancé can offer:

                    CAL
        Where are you going? To him? To be a whore to a
        gutter rat?

                    ROSE
        I'd rather be his whore than your wife.

One of the greatest hurdles Winslet faced was simply to survive the intensely physical shoot, which was extended from 138 to 160 days as the budget spiralled from $135m to $200m. Such was her commitment to authenticity that she refused to wear a wet suit beneath her costume and after one prolonged immersion fell sick with pneumonia, but mere physical endurance would not be the greatest of her challenges: the script itself is such a well-worn portrait of star-crossed and class-subverting love that its protagonists spend as much time dodging clichés as they do falling furniture.

```
        JACK
Promise me you'll survive. That you won't
give up, no matter what happens, no matter how
hopeless. Promise me now, Rose, and never let
go of that promise.

        ROSE
I promise.

        JACK
Never let go.

        ROSE
I'll never let go, Jack. I'll never let go.
```

Thankfully, Winslet succeeded in infusing her performance with a vivacity that matched her fresh-faced beauty, and she managed to make the inevitable ending both credible and poignant – no mean feat. The film won eleven Oscars, a total matched only by *Ben-Hur* (1959). The screenplay itself was not nominated, and neither Winslet nor DiCaprio carried home a statuette, despite appearing on the ballot form, but the picture still ranks as the fourth-highest-grossing production in cinema history. Winslet remains the youngest actress ever to have received six nominations, for *Sense and Sensibility* (1995), *Titanic* (1997), *Iris* (2002), *Eternal Sunshine of the Spotless Mind* (2004), *Little Children* (2006) and *The Reader* (2008) – the last of which finally yielded a win. Perhaps it is time to remind ourselves of her remark from many years earlier:

> *I'd rather do theatre and British films than move to L.A. in the hope of getting small roles in American films.*

I wouldn't dream of working on something that didn't make my gut rumble and my heart want to explode.

*I endeavour to find
the reason in the
unreasonable*

CATE
BLANCHETT

Catherine Élise Blanchett
14 May 1969–

If I had my way, if I was lucky enough, if I could be on the brink my entire life – that great sense of expectation and excitement without the disappointment – that would be the perfect state.

The more you do it, the more you learn to concentrate and then you sort of have to relax. I remember the first film I did, the lead actor would in between scenes be reading a newspaper or sleeping and I'd think, 'How can you do that?'

Men are boys for such a long time and really don't start getting the great roles until they're in their mid-thirties. Whereas for women, it's all about playing younger and younger and younger.

I'm one of those strange beasts who really likes a corset.

No one is ever who they purport to be. And I suppose I'm most interested in the gap between who we project socially and who we really are.

I can be a real pessimist. You know that when you win an Oscar and you walk offstage and your first thought is: 'Oh God, I've peaked'.

Sometimes a character is a crucial piece in a story's jigsaw, and sometimes she is the puzzle itself; Cate Blanchett seems to draw writers and directors who want her to inhabit the work entirely. She has appeared in seven films whose titles are simply the name of the woman she plays: *Oscar and Lucinda* (1997), *Thank God He Met Lizzie* (1997), *Elizabeth* (1998), *Charlotte Gray* (2001), *Veronica Guerin* (2003), *Elizabeth: The Golden Age* (2007) and *Blue Jasmine* (2013). A goth and then a punk as a teenager, Blanchett enjoyed taking part in school plays but only decided to study acting at the National Institute of Dramatic Art in Sydney after completing an undergraduate degree in economics. A successful run of stage productions led to leading roles in Australian films, but it was not until 1998 that – at the age of twenty-nine – she shot her first European production, Shekhar Kapur's *Elizabeth*.

Like the overture to an opera, the introductory scenes of the film paint a miniature of the story itself, which readies us for the full canvas waiting to unfold. The opening image of the young daughter of Henry VIII and Anne Boleyn, so different from the austere portraits in our history books, is radiant – unburdened by the challenges of the forty-five-year reign which lies ahead of her. We first see her as she dances in a meadow with a group of other young women, happy and carefree. When a handsome aristocrat arrives on horseback and the dancers flock to him, Elizabeth remains distant but courteous: she is herself, and no man's woman. A sudden cut later, and she is alone with Robert Dudley, the Earl of Leicester (Joseph Fiennes), melting into his arms and yielding utterly to sensuality. As they embrace, she is arrested by an emissary from her sister Queen Mary on charges of treason: Mary fears her half-sister Elizabeth, heir to the throne, will return her realm to Protestantism. In a heartbeat we have seen Blanchett express numberless emotions from guarded to carefree, ethereal to engaged, disbelieving to scornful, innocent to terrified. Another quick cut, and she enters the river gates of the Tower of London where she suffers the fury of her captors. Red-eyed, hoarse, child-like, horrified, indignant and unrepentant, she seems another woman entirely as each second passes. But as her interrogators return her to a bare cell in the Tower, one of them glimpses her humanity:

ARUNDEL
Madam, you are cold.

ELIZABETH
I do not need your pity.

ARUNDEL
Accept it, then, for my sake.

ELIZABETH
Thank you. I shall not forget this kindness.

Dignified and measured, her response is not mere courtesy but the absolute certainty that she will need to remember this man's gesture because she has no intention of allowing herself to be executed – and that these courtiers will depend on her mercy before long. Soon she is brought before Mary (Kathy Burke), who has been driven half insane as a result of illness and the political manoeuvrings of her advisers. Scornful, bitter, but afraid of her rival, Mary warns:

QUEEN MARY
They say [my] cancer will make you queen, but
they are wrong. Look there, it is your death
warrant. All I need do is sign it.

ELIZABETH
Mary, if you sign that paper you will be
murdering your own sister.

Mastering her own fear, Elizabeth opens her heart. Though they are virtual strangers, they are kin; a queen and an heir, alone, with the weight of their country's future in the balance. Scenes like this are clever fictions, compressing the turmoil of historic months and years into a single cinematic moment, and the pressure on Blanchett to evoke every facet of her character's predicament – and her feelings – is immense. But we see it all in her face, her eyes, her bearing and her gestures, and we hear it in her voice: pleading, soothing, seeking, and yet certain. Where Vivien Leigh charted the death and rebirth of a nation in *Gone with the Wind* (1939) across three-and-a-half hours, Blanchett distils the evolution of a monarch into fifteen minutes.

She delivered another regal performance as Galadriel in the *Lord of the Rings* trilogy (2001–2003), before teaming up again with Kapur for *Elizabeth: The Golden Age* (2007), but an Oscar for her turn as depressed divorcee Jasmine in Woody Allen's *Blue Jasmine* reminds us that she does not need a crown to reign as one of today's finest screen talents.

When you're a performer, of course you want an audience, but it's very, very different from courting fame.

The work gets more difficult as you get older

GWYNETH PALTROW

Gwyneth Kate Paltrow
27 September 1972–

Beauty, to me, is about being comfortable in your own skin. That, or a kick-ass red lipstick.

My dad always said he couldn't remember a time when I did not want to act.

I wasn't the high-school play queen or anything. And my parents would not let me act until I graduated from college.

I think part of the downside about being so successful and winning the Oscar at the age of twenty-six is that I sort of became insouciant about the things that I chose. I thought, 'Oh, I'll just try this, it'll be fun, or I'll do that for the money'. Things like that now I would absolutely never do.

I'm very happy here [in London] and I really like the way the film industry works, everybody cares. I like that it doesn't have this big capitalistic feeling.

If we were living in ancient Rome or Greece, I would be considered sickly and unattractive. The times dictate that thin is better for some strange reason, which I think is foolish.

Those who live by the column inch die by the column inch. Gwyneth Paltrow, daughter of actress Blythe Danner and producer/director Bruce Paltrow, was born and raised in Los Angeles, but until 2014 lived for many years in London with her former husband, Chris Martin of Coldplay, endearing herself to British audiences as a result of her mastery of the English accent. Alongside her film work she maintains a popular media presence through her website, Goop – 'where food, shopping, and mindfulness collide' – and her two million Twitter followers.

I understand that if you set out to be a celebrity, then you asked for it, but all I wanted to be was an actor.

Even so, several online magazines, including *Stylecaster*, have collected quotes suggesting she lives in a world mere mortals can barely imagine ('sometimes [producer] Harvey Weinstein will let me use the Miramax jet if I'm opening a supermarket for him'; 'I'd rather smoke crack than eat cheese from a tin'; 'I was starting to hike up the red rocks, and honestly, it was as if I heard the rock say: "You have the answers. You are your teacher"'), but an Oscar for her role as Viola de Lesseps in *Shakespeare in Love* (1998), along with a slew of other awards for a body of work spanning twenty-six years, serves to remind us how her power on screen remains indisputable.

After a brief stint studying anthropology at the University of California, Santa Barbara, she began to win roles in television and film, and by the age of twenty-three played Tracy, wife of detective David Mills (Brad Pitt) in *Se7en* (1995). Tracy fears the shadowy aggression of the unspecified city in which she lives, and her fragile, skittish performance brought Paltrow to wider attention. Turns in *Emma* (1996), *Sliding Doors* (1998) and *Great Expectations* (1998) confirmed her talent, but it was her witty, sexy appearance as Viola, inspiration and muse to Will Shakespeare (Joseph Fiennes), which won hearts worldwide.

```
                    VIOLA
        All the men at court are without poetry. If
        they see me, they see my father's fortune, I —
        will have poetry in my life. And adventure. And
        love. Love above all.
```

Janet Maslin wrote in *The New York Times* that 'Paltrow, in her first great, fully realized starring performance, makes a heroine so breathtaking that she seems utterly plausible as the playwright's guiding light':

                    VIOLA
    Master Shakespeare?

                 SHAKESPEARE
    The same, alas.

                    VIOLA
    Oh, but why 'alas'?

                 SHAKESPEARE
    A lowly player.

                    VIOLA
    Alas indeed, for I thought you the highest poet
    of my esteem and writer of plays that capture
    my heart.

                 SHAKESPEARE
    Oh — I am him too!

More intense roles followed with *The Talented Mr. Ripley* (1999), *Possession* (2002) and *Sylvia* (2003), but in 2001 Paltrow took on a very different kind of challenge as the severely overweight Rosemary Shanahan in the romantic comedy *Shallow Hal*: 'I put on the fat suit and went outside and walked around. I was really nervous about being found out, but nobody would even make eye contact with me. It really upset me.'

The experience inspired her to be more critical about the industry's demands on its female stars, and she also campaigns for Save the Children as an ambassador and works with the Robin Hood Foundation to alleviate poverty in New York City. Balancing creative work with charitable endeavours, she remains disarmingly realistic about what her life entails:

> I am who I am. I can't pretend to be somebody who makes $25,000 a year.

I'd rather not have a big house, a huge closet of clothes, diamonds and a private plane, and instead a body of work that I'm proud of.

Therapy? I don't need that. The roles that I choose are my therapy

ANGELINA JOLIE

Angelina Jolie Voight
4 June 1975–

If being sane is thinking there's something wrong with being different. . . I'd rather be completely fucking mental.

My role as goodwill ambassador has made my work as a film star relatively dull. I can't find anything that interests me enough to go back to work.

I'd like to play strong women who are also very feminine.

It may sound clichéd, but when you feel beautiful and strong on the inside, it shows on the outside.

I want to be part of the world in a positive way.

[on her earnings] Save one-third, live on one-third and give away one-third.

I always play women I would date.

What nourishes me also destroys me.

**S**tardom exists on its own terms; there may be many readers of the tabloids and of *Hello!* magazine who recognize Angelina Jolie as Hollywood royalty without ever having seen a film of hers – not *Mr. & Mrs. Smith* (2005), *Salt* (2010) or *Maleficent* (2014). Even ignoring the 'Brangelina' factor (media shorthand for her marriage to Brad Pitt and its attendant circus of glamour and gritty social campaigning), she has colonized our front pages and television screens – largely to the benefit of the humanitarian causes she supports. The official photographs of her first child with Pitt raised $4m in the US alone and all profits were donated to charity.

This identity, so different from the traditional glamour of a screen star, makes it hard for us to recall the excitement of her early performances: *Pushing Tin* (1999), *Gone in 60 Seconds* (2000) and *Lara Croft: Tomb Raider* (2001). The latter role casts her as as an über-Indiana Jones adventurer:

> CARLOS
> You are not human.
>
> LARA
> I'll take that as a compliment... Next time
> don't send boys to do a girl's work.

Her prominence as an actress (she has been Hollywood's highest-paid female star for three of the past five years) is further complicated by the fact that even her life as an activist has a movie-like quality. She has travelled for charities in over thirty countries, including Cambodia, Sierra Leone, Tanzania, Pakistan and Sudan, and often insists on sharing the living quarters and conditions of the aid workers in the front line. Photographs of her in combat trousers and dark T-shirt do little to dispel the memory of her first blockbuster role as Lara Croft, but her rise to fame remains an extraordinary tale in itself.

> *I don't think the money people in Hollywood have ever thought I was normal, but I am dedicated to my work and that's what counts.*

Remarkably for such a high-profile figure, Jolie employs neither an agent nor a PR team. Her interviews, which she arranges through her manager, are engagingly candid and show a rare self-awareness in a business fraught with spin. Daughter of Oscar-winning actor John Voight, she was raised largely by her mother Marcheline Bertrand, a former actor and subsequently a campaigner for the rights of Native Americans. Jolie said it was the experience of watching films with her mother that inspired her interest in performing. Aged twelve, she enrolled with the prestigious Lee Strasberg Theatre Institute, but two years later dropped out, subsequently telling *Rolling Stone* magazine that her ambition was to become a funeral director.

> *When other little girls wanted to be ballet dancers, I kind of wanted*
> *to be a vampire.*

Through her teens she supported herself as a model and enjoyed an unusual degree of liberty at home: 'I was either going to be reckless on the streets with my boyfriend or he was going to be with me in my bedroom with my mom in the next room. She made the choice, and because of it, I continued to go to school every morning and explored my first relationship in a safe way'. The statement is not quite as simple as it sounds: Jolie returned to full-time education at sixteen but found herself something of an outsider in a rich, middle-class world. Skinny and geeky, she identified increasingly as a punk and before long was experimenting with sexual knife-play, self-harm and 'just about every drug possible'.

> *You're young, you're drunk, you're in bed, you have knives; shit*
> *happens. . . Because I'm a 'bad girl', people always automatically*
> *think that I am a bad girl. . . I grew up in front of everybody, really.*
> *The big years of exploration. There was a certain madness I was going*
> *through. I learned a lot about myself.*

Despite episodes of depression during these early years, she remained focused on her beliefs and ambitions; she graduated and returned to theatre school. In 1993, aged eighteen, she began to win movie roles, including that of Legs Sadovsky in *Foxfire* (1996). The story tells of a group of young girls who revenge themselves on their sexually predatory high school teacher, but the production garnered press coverage largely as a result of Jolie's affair with co-star Jenny Shimizu. Quizzed by the press about her bisexuality, Jolie declared: 'If I fell in love with a woman tomorrow, would I feel that it's okay to want to kiss and touch her? Absolutely!' Her intense commitment to romantic statements had already been made clear: when she married actor Jonny Lee Miller that same year, she wore black rubber trousers and a white T-shirt emblazoned with her husband's name written in her blood. They divorced amicably in 1999, but when Jolie started dating another actor, Billy Bob Thornton, the couple displayed their mutual devotion by wearing vials of each other's blood around their necks.

By 1997 Jolie had won a Golden Globe for her role in the television film *George Wallace* (1997); the following year she played a self-destructive supermodel in *Gia* (1998).

> GIA
>
> Life and death, energy and peace. If I stopped today, it was still worth it. Even the terrible mistakes that I made and would have unmade if I could. The pains that have burned me and scarred my soul... it was worth it, for having been allowed to walk where I've walked, which was to hell on earth, heaven on earth, back again, into, under, far in between, through it, in it, and above.

Reel.com noted: 'Jolie is fierce in her portrayal, filling the part with nerve, charm and desperation, and her role in this film is quite possibly the most beautiful train wreck ever filmed'.

While still flamboyant in her private life, Jolie continued to nurture her career with a keen intuition, now seeking only the type of roles she could truly commit to. She had already withdrawn from acting twice, once after the spectacular flop of the straight-to-video *Cyborg 2* (1993) and then again, briefly, after *Gia* – feeling that she had 'nothing else to give' – but in 1999 *Girl, Interrupted* delivered the role that captured every aspect of her intensity and charisma. Jolie plays Lisa Rowe, a sociopath committed to a mental institution where the nature of her condition – and concomitant delight in provoking her fellow inmates simply because it amuses her – results in catastrophic damage to the recovery of the other patients. She causes one former colleague to commit suicide after delivering this searing attack:

> LISA
>
> They didn't release you 'cause you're better, Daisy, they just gave up. You call this a life, hmm? Taking Daddy's money, buying your dollies

and your knick-knacks... and eatin' his fuckin'
chicken, fattening up like a prize fuckin'
heifer? You changed the scenery, but not the
fucking situation — and the warden makes house
calls. And everybody knows. Everybody knows.
That he fucks you. What they don't know... is
that you like it. Hmm?
You like it.

Jolie avoided fraternizing with other cast members as she did not want any empathy to influence her performance opposite them, but when Lisa finally burns her fury out, she admits that she, too, needs help. Beneath the anger, her admission is terrifyingly poignant:

               LISA
You know, there's too many buttons in the
world. There's too many buttons and they're
just — they're just begging to be pressed, and
it makes me wonder, it really makes me fucking
wonder, why doesn't anyone ever press mine?
Why am I so neglected? Why doesn't anyone reach
in and rip out the truth and tell me that I'm
a fucking whore, or that my parents wish I
were dead?

Her performance is thrilling, visceral and ultimately heartbreaking. She inhabits her character through every millimetre of her physicality – her gaze is alternately scalpel-sharp and slyly seductive, her body poised like that of a sprinter, only to collapse into a boneless lassitude on the turn of a dime. Like a vagabond Hannibal Lecter on Valium, she compels as well as horrifies us. The part won her an Oscar for Best Supporting Actress, and even if that accolade is often overlooked in the light of her wider achievements, it remains a remarkably perceptive acknowledgement of the energy that drives her greatest appearances. As she later said, with her customary candour:

I am still at heart – and always will be – just a punk kid with tattoos.

If I make a fool of
myself, who cares?
I'm not frightened
by anyone's
perception of me.

I always got the job

CATHERINE ZETA-JONES

Catherine Zeta-Jones
25 September 1969–

I used to go around looking frumpy because it was inconceivable you could be attractive as well as be smart. It wasn't until I started being myself, the way I like to turn out to meet people, that I started to get any work.

In Wales it's brilliant. I go to the pub and everybody I went to school with goes 'So what you doing now?' And I go, 'Oh, I'm doing a film with Antonio Banderas and Anthony Hopkins'. And they go, 'Ooh, good'. And that's it.

I like to feel sexy. I know my husband thinks I'm sexy. But I don't go out half-naked with 'sex' written across my back.

For marriage to be a success, every woman and every man should have her and his own bathroom. The end.

Everyone knows we get paid a lot of money, so why pretend otherwise?

There are people who expect me to look the way I do on screen, where I have a great director of photography and fantastic lighting. I'm sorry to disappoint people, but I don't look like that all the time – no actress does.

For every thousand actresses who pay their dues with gruelling years of repertory theatre and bit parts in small movies, there is one who is spotted by a talent agent sitting at the counter of a diner. There may not have been many soda stands around Mumbles in the Gower Peninsula when Catherine Zeta-Jones grew up there (and where she and her husband Michael Douglas still have a home), but her start in show business still reprises one of the great movie legends.

> *I was a chorus girl. That's all I ever wanted – to be onstage. I would queue up for auditions and then change my costume or put on a different leotard and audition again. It might take me two tries, but I always got the job. I figured out what they wanted.*

Her teenage years brought roles in such classics as *Annie* and *Bugsy Malone*, but in 1987 she had a stroke of luck almost too poetically just to believe. Both the lead actress and her understudy in a West End production of *42nd Street* were taken ill and Zeta-Jones was cast at short notice to replace them. The play, based on Lloyd Bacon's 1933 hit film of the same name, recounts exactly this story: a chorus girl gets her first break (pun intended) when the star of a Broadway musical hurts her ankle, and her role is taken by the talented ingénue who proves an even greater star. The speech by the producer Julian Marsh (Warner Baxter) ends with a classic Hollywood cheer:

```
MARSH
You're going out a youngster but you've got to
come back a star!
```

And so she did. On the strength of it she was cast as Mariette Larkin in *The Darling Buds of May*, the British TV series based on H. E. Bates's novel, which proved an instant success:

> *Literally, with one hour of television my life completely changed. I couldn't go anywhere.*

After being recommended by Steven Spielberg for the lead in *The Mask of Zorro* (1998), Hollywood began to take notice, but it was Steven Soderbergh who gave her the role that first revealed her wider talents. *Traffic* (2000) is a multi-stranded narrative about the war on drugs; Zeta-Jones plays Helena Ayala, the conventional, well-to-do wife of a cocaine importer. When her husband Carlos

(Steven Bauer) is first arrested, she has no idea that her lavish lifestyle has been illegally funded. Before long, she realizes she has no choice but to step into his shoes or lose everything about the rich suburban lifestyle she enjoys. Still scheduling school runs and neighbourhood barbecues as she enters the world of international smuggling, she quickly shows herself to be more Machiavellian than any drug baron or bent cop:

```
            MARQUEZ
    That's good coke.


            HELENA
    It should be... It's yours. (Pause) I want
    our debt forgiven.  I want to be the exclusive
    distributor of Obregon brothers cocaine for
    the United States.  And I want the principal
    witness against my husband, Eduardo Ruiz,
    killed.
```

It is as if a svelte Lady Macbeth had begun her journey as a guileless virgin, and her transformation is more shocking than anything else in a film described by one reviewer as 'a beautiful and brutal work'.

Although Zeta-Jones was not nominated for her performance at the Academy Awards, she did not have to wait long for her due acclaim. Rob Marshall's 2002 adaptation of Bob Fosse's *Chicago* offered the perfect opportunity for her skills both musical and dramatic, and she delivers a blistering and darkly humorous performance as husband-killer Velma Kelly. Marshall had originally wanted her to keep her hair long, but she insisted on cutting it into a shorter bob so the audience would see her face at all times – proving that she never used a double for any of the elaborately choreographed routines. *The New York Times* wrote that '[she] makes a wonderfully statuesque and bitchy saloon goddess. . . she pumps her majestic, long legs like the cylinders of a Corvette about to redline, but always [knows] exactly when to stop short of throwing a piston'. Zeta-Jones herself admitted the dance work was 'almost as painful as giving birth to [my] son', but reward was swift to follow in the form of an Oscar for Best Supporting Actress. Mae West herself would have been proud to have as her epitaph the reviewer's parting words on Velma's turn: 'a famous smoulderer, a one-woman heat source'.

I'm more insecure than I ever let anyone know. . . sometimes you protect yourself with this kind of armour that people see more than they see you.

By some beautiful twist of fate I've landed in this vocation that demands that I feel, and helps me to learn

JENNIFER CONNELLY

Jennifer Lynn Connelly
12 December 1970–

You don't want to get rid of your experiences, because they're your experiences – good or bad – and you need them, but it would be great if they weren't on the video shelf.

I try to stay focused on my life and do try not to be brought into the Hollywood fantasy.

I always looked up to Meryl Streep when I was a kid. I think she's just a phenomenal actress. From time to time when I'm working I think, 'What would Meryl do?' and I've let that guide me.

Each film is a chapter in my life wherein I learn so much more about myself.

I so much enjoy being able to completely allow myself to be consumed by a role, once you've done that, it's hard to go back to working on things you don't care about.

Stars are often keen to remind us how their success came only as a result of blood, sweat and tears, but Jennifer Connelly enjoyed a contented, normal childhood, growing up in Brooklyn Heights, New York, and remained happily absorbed in her studies at Yale and Stanford until the momentum of her screen career became too tempting to resist.

> *I had no aspirations, I had no movie posters in my room, I wasn't a movie buff; I liked Evel Knievel and animals.*

She had been acting since she was a child but had never let the lure of Hollywood distract her. As a teenager she had played small parts in *Once Upon a Time in America* (1984) and *Labyrinth* (1986), and while still at college she narrowly missed out on the role of Vivian in *Pretty Woman* (1990), but the rest of the decade brought only modest notices. One review of Disney's retro adventure *The Rocketeer* (1991) in *New York* magazine went so far as to single her out with the faintest of praise: 'Connelly is properly cast; she has the moist, full-to-the-cheek bones sensuality of the Hollywood starlets of that period, but she's a little straight.' So far, it seemed no producer or director had seen past her cool beauty to notice the particular paradox of fire and vulnerability that would become her most remarkable characteristic.

As she was turning thirty, Darren Aronofsky offered her the role of Marion Silver in *Requiem for a Dream* (2000). Based on the controversial 1978 novel by Hubert Selby, Jr, the film portrays four key figures whose addictions of various kinds cause their lives to slide terrifyingly out of control. Marion is an aspiring young clothes designer who, in a painful and poignant co-dependent partnership with her boyfriend Harry (Jared Leto), becomes hooked on cocaine and heroin. As the story opens, she just seems like a good kid with a mischievous streak – a middle-class rebel with a clear-eyed, trusting gaze that transfixes the camera. By the middle of the film, as reliance on the drugs kicks in, her beauty and grace begin to be eroded by outbursts that add a disturbing angularity to her movements and to her looks. But she and Harry still want to believe they can go clean any time they choose:

<pre>
                    MARION
        Harry, it's stupid to panic and think the
        world's coming to an end just 'cause we can't
        score any solid weight.
</pre>

                    HARRY
    OK, fine.

But they reach for their stash. Flick, sizzle, snap,
suck, slap, rush, sigh...

By the end, her dependence and desperation have completely destroyed her. Aronofsky's handling of her performance leaves no room for ambiguity: 'I like to stick the camera into an actor's face and bring the eyes to the audience.' We track her evolution in wide-angle compositions that emphasize her fragility and in ultra-close-ups of her pupils as she shoots up, tracking her highs – and lows – with graphic intensity. Connelly has nowhere to hide, and we cannot avert our gaze. She immersed herself in the part, even moving into the building where her character lived and pursuing her interests as she worked with Aronofsky on what her role was – at its heart – to represent: 'The most helpful part of our time together was talking about the place the addiction comes from, more than the technical happenings of a particular drug. I just thought that was more of an important part of what Darren was talking about anyway. . . So we spent a lot of time trying to figure out what that could be in her, and what that would be in me. It was kind of like a really intensive therapy session'.

There is no moralizing to the story, nor any Method-acting rhetoric. At the end of the film, the other three characters have been variously imprisoned, maimed by gangrene and committed to an asylum. Marion remains physically free and unharmed, but she has already begun to prostitute herself to a dealer to support her habit. The final image of her, returning from a party at which she has been forced to perform for a crowd of drunken, rich voyeurs, shows her curled in a foetal position, cradling her hard-earned fix. Long after the final frame fades to black, the tragedy of her descent – to which she herself is oblivious – chills our veins.

The following year, Connelly won an Oscar as Alicia Nash in *A Beautiful Mind* (2001), and capitalized on that success with memorable roles in *Dark Water* (2005), *Blood Diamond* (2006), *Reservation Road* (2007) and *Noah* (2014). She continues to throw herself into her work with an admirably open mind:

> *If you get too attached to how you want it to come out the other side,*
> *you freeze. I try to trust that it will work out in the end.*

I don't always like my own behaviour. I haven't known anyone who is perfect all the time.

Acting, at its heart, is the ability to manipulate your own emotions

SCARLETT JOHANSSON

Scarlett Johansson
22 November 1984–

I have an obsessive character. I manicure my nails at three in the morning because nobody else can do it the right way. Maybe that's the secret to my success.

It's a great thing to get older and learn. I don't feel bound in any way by how many years I've lived. I identify just as much with my eighty-six-year-old grandmother as I do with my sister.

I don't need to be skinny to be sexy.

I don't think there's any kind of preparation for sudden celebrity. I think you almost have this slight nervous breakdown when that kind of media attention happens.

Los Angeles is a very hard place to be unless you have people there that love you. It can be very, very lonely, and it can eat you up if you don't take care of yourself.

I think it's hard for actors to date each other because they are so damn moody. You are away from people constantly and having a relationship that is strictly by phone – it's miserable.

ohansson, born in New York City to an architect father and film producer mother, had been encouraged by her parents to audition from an early age but recognized that her talents might be a little precocious:

> *I was always terrible at commercials because my voice was so deep. At the age of nine, I sounded like a whiskey-drinking, chain-smoking fool.*

She studied at the Professional Children's School in Manhattan and appeared in a handful of movies through her teens, most notably *Home Alone 3* (1997) and *The Horse Whisperer* (1998); *Manny & Lo* (1996) prompted one thoughtful review which suggested that 'if she can get through puberty with [her peaceful] aura undisturbed, she could become an important actress', while *Ghost World* (2001) elicited praise for a 'sensitivity and talent [that] belie her age'. Still, it seemed, she was waiting for a script which would allow her to capitalize on these notices.

Sofia Coppola, daughter of Francis Ford Coppola, had recently made a successful adaptation of *The Virgin Suicides* (1999) and was working on a loose set of ideas for a story set in Tokyo.

> *I remember having these weeks there that were sort of enchanting and weird. . . [The city] is so disorienting, and there's a loneliness and isolation. Everything is so crazy, and the jet lag is torture. I liked the idea of juxtaposing a midlife crisis with that time in your early 20s when you're, like, 'what should I do with my life?'*

Lost in Translation (2003) relates a series of encounters between ageing actor Bob Harris (Bill Murray) and Charlotte (Johansson), a young woman accompanying her celebrity photographer husband John (Giovanni Ribisi) on an assignment. She first meets Bob in the bar of their hotel as they wrestle with sleeplessness:

```
                    CHARLOTTE
          So, what are you doing here?

                       BOB
          Uh, a couple of things. Taking a break from my
          wife, forgetting my son's birthday. And, uh,
          getting paid two million dollars to endorse a
          whiskey when I could be doing a play somewhere.
```

                    CHARLOTTE
Oh.

                    BOB
But the good news is, the whiskey works.

Coppola later recalled the process of casting her two leads: 'I just liked [Johansson] from that movie *Manny & Lo*, and she was seventeen, but I had this idea of her being this young Lauren Bacall-type girl. I loved her low voice. You can't really gauge the chemistry unless you do tests before you start shooting, and I don't think they even met before we did, so I just picked someone I liked and hoped that it worked.' It certainly did: the film won Coppola an Oscar for Best Screenplay, returned a profit of $120m on a budget of $4m and remains an iconic example of millennial cinema.

The film's title has attracted attention from journals as obscure as *Linguistica Antverpiensia, New Series – Themes in Translation Studies*, but essentially it hints at a sense of dislocation. Charlotte and Bob are drifting in their own lives, in a strange city, and even within the tender, fleeting connection they forge. But dislocation is a hard quality to render in words, and film is a medium that resists soliloquy. Charlotte lives surrounded by her thoughts but – apart from Bob – she finds it almost impossible to express them to anybody. Early in the story, she tries:

Charlotte sits by a huge window high above Tokyo.
She waits on the phone. Lauren answers.

                    LAUREN
Charlotte, hey! Oh my God, how's Tokyo?

                    CHARLOTTE
It's great here, it's really great... I don't
know, I went to this shrine today and there
were these monks and they were chanting, and
I didn't feel anything, you know? And, I don't
know... I even tried ikebana, and John's using
these hair products... I don't know who I
married, and —

> LAUREN
> Can you... wait a second? Just — hold on, I'll
> be right back.

> CHARLOTTE
> OK, sure —

> LAUREN
> Sorry, what were you saying?

> CHARLOTTE
> Nothing — it's OK, I'll call you later.

And she is crying.

Somehow Johansson manages to turn the moment into a question that drives the entire film: what does she want – and how can she even know what she wants? Rarely can a performance based on such an elusive premise have resulted in such a precise energy, and one of Johansson's great achievements is that she never breaks the spell she weaves at the start.

In one scene Charlotte walks through the lobby with John and they run into a rising film star he has recently worked with. John and the star seem surprised to see each other but we sense there is an unspoken connection between them; as they chat excitedly, John forgets to introduce her to Charlotte. We expect Charlotte to feel snubbed, jealous or indignant at the lack of courtesy from either of them but we see only – in a series of wordless flashes – puzzlement, delight, amusement, bemusement, evaluation, re-evaluation, indifference, astonishment, resignation, disdain, fortitude. Coppola rightly frames Johansson at the centre of the exchange, letting us watch her as the others trade meaningless small talk, and it is like watching two movies running at the same time. In any other film it would be either a throw-away moment or a crucial plot twist, but here it is a small triumph of Coppola's style and a perfect encapsulation of what makes Johansson unique.

Johansson has subsequently become an A-list star, with hits including *Girl with a Pearl Earring* (2003), *Match Point* (2005), *Vicky Cristina Barcelona* (2008) and *Lucy* (2014), but the film that best reprises the startling assuredness of *Lost in*

Translation is Jonathan Glazer's *Under the Skin* (2013), loosely adapted from the 2000 novel by Michel Faber. Johansson plays an unnamed woman who flirts with random strangers in order to lure them back to a derelict house; there they follow her into a vast empty black space only to find themselves being absorbed into a womb-like ocean where their bodies dissolve. Nothing is overtly explained, but it seems the woman is an alien who draws her energy from the life force of her victims. The opening of the story, in an oblique manner reminiscent of Stanley Kubrick's *2001: A Space Odyssey* (1968), lets us overhear her extraterrestrial voice practising earthly speech:

```
          WOMAN
B-B-Buh- B-B-Buh, B-B-Beh, B-B-Beh, Bah, N-N-
Nuh- N-N-Nuh, N-N-Nuh- No. N-N-Nuh, F- Feel-
Field, Fill- Filled- Filts, Foil- Failed- Fell,
Felds- Pill- Pills, Pall- Nall.
```

The woman has no idea why her sexual attractiveness is such a powerful tool any more than a butterfly understands why the pattern on its wings draws mates, but she becomes curious to explore what it is that she represents to her prey – and what her incarnation as a human means for her, too. She seduces one victim with the tenderly awkward question:

```
          WOMAN
When is the last time you touched someone?
```

Reviewer Matt Zoller Seitz of *New York* magazine described the film as 'hideously beautiful. Its life force is overwhelming' – and if it were not such a bizarre compliment it might equally serve as a tribute to Johansson herself.

It would be such a waste to just continue to do the same thing. I don't have anything to lose really. Even if it doesn't work out, the gain if it does is so much greater.

*I'd rather be smart
than a movie star*

NATALIE
PORTMAN

Neta-Lee Hershlag
9 June 1981–

I didn't have this undying need to be an actress. I didn't have that fire in me ever – at any point. And still, I don't think I have that within me.

It's horrible to be a sex object at any age, but at least when you're an adult you can make the decision if you want to degrade yourself.

There are movies where we are interested in seeing people's lives without agreeing with what they're doing.

I wanted to be able to form my own sexual identity. If other people have you in their mind as some sort of sex object, you have two choices: either live up to it and become super-sexual or rebel against it and be super-asexual.

But we have to remember that almost all films are written and directed by men. Female characters are women imagined by men, so it's always this classic figure of a sexy woman with a childish innocence.

Elizabeth Taylor was twelve when she made *National Velvet* (1944), Jodie Foster was fourteen in *Taxi Driver* (1976), and Drew Barrymore seven in *E.T. the Extra-Terrestrial* (1982); they started big, and just got bigger. Mary Badham was ten when she played Scout in *To Kill a Mockingbird* (1962), Tatum O'Neal also ten in *Paper Moon* (1973) and Anna Paquin eleven in *The Piano* (1993): all great performances, but... it's a tough game. Not just tough because the industry is fickle and the public more so, but because shooting a movie can take a year of your life and you only have so many of those when you grow up: Shirley Temple made forty-four pictures between the age of four and twenty-one. To say that child stardom warps your view of the world is a tactful understatement, as Temple herself realized: 'I stopped believing in Santa Claus when I was six. Mother took me to see him in a department store and he asked for my autograph.'

Natalie Portman was born in Jerusalem, but her family soon moved to New York where she started dancing lessons at the age of four. She attended acting camps, but had an unusual degree of focus for one so young: when she was ten, Revlon asked her to model for them but she turned them down to concentrate on drama. By the time she was thirteen she had won her first screen role as Mathilda, the protégé of a hit man, in *Léon: The Professional* (1994). Her performance drew widespread attention and even her audition tape (since leaked on the internet) shows an unusual aplomb, uncannily evoking a young Ava Gardner. But the experience was not easy: 'In seventh grade, I cried every single day when I came back from shooting. My friends were not my friends. They were saying "she thinks she's so hot now".'

Portman realized that continuing to act would turn her life quite literally upside down: 'I wasn't really home when my friends were trying pot for the first time [but] I was always around adults who wouldn't curse or smoke or do anything like that around me.' She decided that however her career developed during her high school years, she would still go to college and, true to her word, refused to attend the premiere of *Star Wars: The Phantom Menace* (1999), in which she played Padmé Amidala, in order to study for her exams.

> *I don't care if [college] ruins my career. I'd rather be smart than a movie star.*

Four years later she graduated from Harvard and one of the first major roles she took on was as Alice in *Closer* (2004). Writer Patrick Marber and director Mike

Nichols are both noted for their uncompromising attention to character, and this project more than any other would show whether Portman had survived the challenges of childhood fame. The story is a complex portrait of tangled passion between its four protagonists and Portman's performance is as raw and fluid as it is intelligent. Tackling the highs and brutal lows of love, sex and betrayal head on, she is the only one who retains her integrity and independence: by the end, when all of the characters have lost so much, she somehow remains intact. Here, where Dan (Jude Law) tries to win her back one last time, she understands that while he is desperate to recreate their former passion, she can only exist in the present:

```
        DAN
I saw this face, this vision; the moment you
stepped into the road. It was the moment of my
life.

        ALICE
This is the moment of your life.

        DAN
You were perfect.

        ALICE
I still am.
```

The film is filled with coldly, unsettling scenes which might tempt any actress to overplay her hand, but Portman's instinct for the pitch of each encounter is uncanny; deservedly, the role won her an Academy Award nomination. A true star by now, she took roles in *V for Vendetta* (2006), *The Other Boleyn Girl* (2008) and *No Strings Attached* (2011). In *Black Swan* (2010), a dark psychological thriller directed by her husband Darren Aronofsky, she played ballet dancer Nina Sayers, later writing of the experience: 'There were some nights I thought I literally was going to die. It was the first time I understood how you could get so wrapped up in a role that it could sort of take you down.' Her performance won an Oscar, a BAFTA and a Golden Globe Award, but even as she relishes such challenging projects, she remains sceptical of glittering prizes:

I was reading the story of Abraham to my child and talking about not worshipping false idols. And [these awards are] literally like gold men.

I'm the anti-Method actor. As soon as we finish a scene, I need to go back to being myself, because it freaks me out.

*Perfect isn't nor-
mal, nor is
it interesting*

AMY
ADAMS

Amy Lou Adams
20 August 1974–

I grew up as a Mormon. . .
You can't really misbehave
without feeling badly about it.
At least, I can't.

I'm pretty Sicilian if I've been
crossed. I don't seek revenge,
but I never forget.

As an actress people always
tease me like: if there's
anything you can do to make
yourself unattractive you will
do it.

I have no features without
make-up. I am pale. I have
blond lashes. You could just
paint my face – it's like a
blank canvas. It can be great
for what I do.

I didn't get into acting to have
a moment, I got into it
because of people who've
inspired me, like Judi Dench,
Holly Hunter, and Jodie
Foster.

Being an actress hasn't made
me insecure. I was insecure
long before I declared I was
an actress.

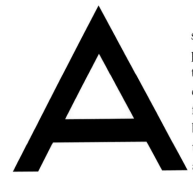**A**s comedian Steve Martin warns, 'some people have a way with words, and other people. . . oh, uh, not have way'. Many actors treat a screenplay like a bible, and trust it wholeheartedly: Mary Steenburgen (*Ragtime*, 1981, and *Nixon*, 1995) is convinced that 'there's a certain arrogance to an actor who will look at a script and feel like, because the words are simple, maybe they can paraphrase it and make it better'. On the other hand, who could argue with Roy Scheider, who improvised the classic line 'You're gonna need a bigger boat' on the spot in *Jaws* (1975)? Both approaches work, but Amy Adams prefers to be led by the screenplay:

I work from a very character-driven place. And I trust the writers.

Adams was born in Italy to a US army warrant officer father and a mother who would later become a semi-professional body-builder. The family settled in Colorado when she was eight, and her childhood – along with her six siblings – was filled with music and amateur stage productions. She had a sharp memory for dialogue and melodies, and quickly found work in dinner theatre before being cast in a number of small movies, but it would not be until she turned thirty that she would have her first proper hit.

Junebug (2005) takes place in a quiet North Carolina town as George Johnsten (Alessandro Nivola) returns to visit his provincial family for the first time since he married Madeleine (Embeth Davidtz), a smart Chicago art dealer. The respective in-laws do their best to welcome each other, but George's sister Ashley is expecting her first child and the events surrounding the birth bring about unexpected tensions. Adams plays Ashley, a preternaturally cheerful young woman who is desperate to be happy, to please others and to rekindle the love of her increasingly distanced husband. She is endlessly curious about the baby she carries:

                    ASHLEY
        I wonder what she looks like. I bet she's
        skinny. She probably is. She's skinnier'n me
        and prettier too. Now I'll hate her. Oh, I
        can't wait!

Words bubble out of her, not so much a stream of consciousness as the hum of a bee delirious with nectar – but beneath her effervescence lie the fears and uncertainties she shies from articulating. She depends on her chatter to soothe herself, to placate others and to fill the silences that lie heavy in this reserved community. Adams brings an explosive, irrepressible energy to the role: her eyes sparkle and dart, her pregnant body is weary yet restless, and her bright solicitousness makes us ache to care for her as she cares for others. Director Phil Morrison said of the script: 'Lots of people looked at Ashley and thought, "What's the sorrow she's masking?" To me, the fact that Amy didn't approach it from the angle of "What's she covering up?" was key.' Only once does Ashley have the courage to berate her husband for his anger, and she makes her platitude ring with sincerity:

> ASHLEY
> God loves you just the way you are, but he
> loves you too much to let you stay that way.

The performance won Adams an Academy Award nomination – the first of five across eight years, for films as diverse as *Doubt* (2008), *The Fighter* (2010) and *The Master* (2012).

In an early interview she admitted: 'I've always been attracted to characters who are positive and come from a very innocent place', but her turn as con-woman Sydney Prosser – 'the most miserable human being I've ever played' – in *American Hustle* (2013) proved she could embody darkness just as naturally as light. Chicago's *Newcity Film* singled Adams out as 'spectacular, febrile, dramatic, comic, sharp, sarcastic and magnificent to look upon', and her dialogue here is crisp and incisive, a world away from that of *Junebug*:

> SYDNEY
> You're nothing to me until you're everything.

The shoot was by all accounts tough, with one crew member revealing that director David O. Russell 'so abused Adams that Christian Bale got in his face and told him to stop acting like an asshole', but Adams – echoing Sydney – simply shrugged the experience off:

> *I've worked with some of the meanest people in the world. You can't do anything to intimidate me.*

I'd love to be a diva. But I'd then have to send so many apology notes for my abhorrent behaviour.

If I have a dark side, I haven't dis-covered it yet. How very boring of me

KEIRA KNIGHTLEY

Keira Christina Knightley
26 March 1985–

I'm dyslexic, and at six years old, they realized I couldn't read a word and had been fooling them. My mum said to me: 'If you come to me with a book in your hand and a smile on your face every day through the summer holiday, I'll get you an agent'.

[on making *Love Actually*] We had kind of done all our wedding and we felt like the stars of the show, then suddenly you've got all these other people with story lines and you think 'Excuse me, I know you're Alan Rickman, but get out of my film, please, thank you'.

In L.A., I'm twice the size – height and everything else – of most of the other actresses who are going for an audition.

There's always the moral question when you're playing real people. Is there any reason to do this, or are you simply exploiting somebody?

Every successful actress reaches a point in her career where talent and opportunity fall into step, often after years of thwarted ambitions and dogged efforts. But Keira Knightley's journey seemed destined from the womb:

> *I was a bet. My mum was desperate for another child, and my dad told her that the only way they could afford to have one was if she sold a play. So Mum wrote* When I Was a Girl, I Used to Scream and Shout.

The gamble paid off, and the production of actress Sharman Macdonald's first work won her an Evening Standard Award for Most Promising Playwright. Knightley's father Will was also an actor, and family life abounded with show-business friends and chatter. At the age of three, Keira asked if she could get an agent – she didn't know what the word meant, but she was jealous that her parents each had one – and by the age of six, she did. Precocious from the start, her reflections on her early projects are both revealing and charming. Her first major film role was as Sabé in *Star Wars Episode I: The Phantom Menace* (1999), but the experience proved less than thrilling since she was such a keen fan of the original movies: "The Force" wasn't there when we were filming it, and they didn't have real light sabres, which annoyed me'. Three years later, she appeared as the young footballer Jules in *Bend It Like Beckham* (2002). It was a huge hit in Britain, even if it lacked the budget of a George Lucas blockbuster: 'I thought there would be doubles – stunt doubles – and I would just run in for the close-ups, but unfortunately they didn't have the money for that'.

Her exuberance and charm on the pitch earned her a London Film Critics' Circle Award for Best Newcomer, and within a year she was cast as Elizabeth Swann in *Pirates of the Caribbean: The Curse of the Black Pearl* (2003) opposite Johnny Depp. The film took $654m [$853m] at the box office, and put its young star in a position of immense power; from the deluge of scripts which followed, Knightley made two smart choices: Richard Curtis's *Love Actually* (2003) and Joe Wright's *Pride & Prejudice* (2005). She adored Jane Austen's novel, and had used the first pay cheque she ever received to buy a doll's house of the hero's mansion; she embraced the part of Elizabeth Bennet with a winning naturalism as she pursues her eventual husband, Mr Darcy (Matthew Macfadyen):

```
                      ELIZABETH
        I wish you would not call me 'my dear'.
```

```
                MR DARCY
Why?


                ELIZABETH
Because it's what my father always calls my
mother when he's cross about something.


                MR DARCY
What endearments am I allowed?


                ELIZABETH
Well let me think... 'Lizzy' for every day,
'My Pearl' for Sundays, and... 'Goddess
Divine'... but only on very special
occasions.
```

Variety wrote: 'Looking every bit a star, Knightley, who's shown more spirit than acting smarts so far in her career, really steps up to the plate here... with a luminous strength that recalls a young Audrey Hepburn', and the turn won her nominations for both a Golden Globe and an Oscar.

She teamed up again with Wright in 2007 for his adaptation of Ian McEwan's novel *Atonement* (2001). Although the film is set during the 1940s, its boldness and sexual intrigue are completely modern. Peter Travers of *Rolling Stone* magazine insisted: 'Stuffy? Not a bit. This potently erotic spellbinder is not your father's period piece... Knightley's star has never shone this brightly.' She brought the same era to life again with her appearance as wartime code-breaker Joan Clarke in *The Imitation Game* (2014), which once more saw her nominated for an Academy Award. Despite the swarms of paparazzi who surround her whenever she steps onto the red carpet, she is cheerfully modest – 'A newspaper here voted me one of the scruffiest people in Britain. I'm quite proud of that. It's completely true' – and is proud to remain close to her bohemian roots:

> *To be honest, I'd sooner be with my mates having a pint.*

Every part I've ever got, I always thought it was completely ridiculous that I was up for it. With [*Pirates of the Caribbean: The Curse of the Black Pearl*] I only packed for a week because I was sure that I was going to get sacked.

I need to feel that for a director it's a matter of life and death; he needs to tell this story

MARION COTILLARD

Marion Cotillard
30 September 1975–

I didn't like anything about myself – my looks, my personality. I was very, very angry.

When I was a kid, I started to have a lot of questions about human beings, and I was a troubled child because of all of these questions. I guess that's why I became an actress.

I was raised with the idea of beauty in a different way. To me, it is something that really comes out of you and surrounds you.

It is much easier for me to understand something vast and complex than something light and uncomplicated. Perhaps that makes me very French.

I adore my own life, more and more I love being myself, but I love this work of totally changing personalities, of creating something radically different from myself. I want to go profoundly into my roles. If not, what's the point?

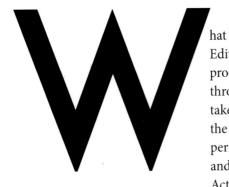

What producer or director could resist telling the story of legendary chanteuse Edith Piaf, featuring all of her greatest hits in a lavishly photographed period production? Her glorious successes and shocking setbacks made headlines throughout her career, but her memory is sacrosanct: what actress would dare take on such a challenge? Marion Cotillard, at the age of thirty-two (playing the character from a teenager until her death at forty-seven), did – and her performance in *La Vie en rose* (2007) won her a César, a BAFTA, a Golden Globe and an Oscar. Even the Oscar itself was unique, the first ever given for a Best Actress performance in French.

> *I find it easier to play someone who is so far from me because you create someone – you build this person based on the story and the script, with the director.*

As with many stars, Cotillard's overnight acclaim came after a prolonged period of paying her dues. Born in Paris to parents who were both actors and teachers, she first began performing as a child in one of her father's plays. Theatre engagements led to television appearances, and then to small parts in French movies. She made forty-two films over fourteen years, including *Taxi* (1998), for which she was nominated for a César for Most Promising Actress, but by the time she was twenty-seven she despaired of her progress: 'I told my agent I was stopping and going to work for Greenpeace. He said, "Please just have this one meeting". It was with Tim Burton, for *Big Fish* (2003), and I got the part.' Her turn in the film led swiftly to roles in Jean-Pierre Jeunet's *A Very Long Engagement* (2004), Abel Ferrara's *Mary* (2005) and Ridley Scott's *A Good Year* (2006) – but in 2007 she got the call that would change everything:

> *I remember when I read the script [for* La Vie en rose] *I asked my agent 'Which part am I going to do?' and he said '[The director] wants you to do the whole thing'. I said it wasn't possible. . . but I didn't say it too loud.*

Her turn as Piaf is astonishing, embracing every aspect of a life that seized triumph and glamour from poverty, fear, addiction and loneliness. These moments unfold in a series of vignettes interspersed with flashbacks, but Cotillard weaves them together in a tour de force of technical as well as emotional skills. Her portrayal of Piaf's frail twilight articulates the vulnerability and resentment of ageing with uncanny accuracy– a decline all the more poignant in the light of her former joy:

                    JOURNALIST
If you were to give advice to a woman, what
would it be?

                    PIAF
Love.

                    JOURNALIST
To a young girl?

                    PIAF
Love.

                    JOURNALIST
To a child?

                    PIAF
Love.

Cotillard's mercurial energy manifested itself in a string of further hits, including *Nine* (2009), *Inception* (2010) and *Midnight in Paris* (2011):

                    ADRIANA
That Paris exists and anyone could choose to
live anywhere else in the world will always be
a mystery to me.

Yet there remains something restless about her ambition which acting in movies cannot sate. She sings with various bands, including Franz Ferdinand, and has performed in Arthur Honegger's modern oratorio *Jeanne d'Arc au bûcher*, but perhaps her most unexpected turn was in 2013 when she shut herself in a cage outside the Louvre to wave a banner stating 'I am a climate defender' to protest the imprisonment of thirty Greenpeace volunteers in Russia. Whatever her next roles bring, she will no doubt surprise us:

> *I think that when you don't see the boundaries, you cross them without even knowing they exist in the first place.*

I do like extreme characters, but I think they are extreme because they are full of passion – they are rich inside.

I never play char-
acters that are like
me because I'm a
boring person

JENNIFER LAWRENCE

Jennifer Shrader Lawrence
15 August 1990–

[on sudden fame] I think about this all the time. But when you get a promotion at your job, you don't go 'That was too fast. Can I stay in the mailroom a while longer?' You take it.

I'm excited to be seen as sexy. But not slutty.

Where are the Robert Redfords and Paul Newmans of my age group? Where are the hunks who can act?

There's just no imagination in Hollywood. I wanted to show people *Winter's Bone* for the performance, but it ended up having the opposite effect. People were like, no, she's not feminine, she's not sexual.

I don't invest any of my real emotions. I don't take any of my characters' pain home with me. . . I just use my imagination. If it ever came down to the point where, to make a part better, I had to lose a little bit of my sanity, I wouldn't do it.

Maybe one day I'll turn into an asshole. But there are too many out there already.

For some stars, the mere facts suffice. Jennifer Lawrence was born in Louisville, Kentucky, to blue-collar parents, and by the age of fourteen had decided she wanted to be an actor; four years later she won the Los Angeles Film Festival Award for Outstanding Performance as Agnes in *The Poker House* (2008), and at the age of twenty was nominated for her first Oscar as Ree Dolly in *Winter's Bone* (2010). She won Best Actress for her turn as Tiffany Maxwell in *Silver Linings Playbook* (2012) and was nominated again as Rosalyn Rosenfeld in *American Hustle* (2013). She played Katniss Everdeen in *The Hunger Games* (2012), which set box-office records for its opening weekend, and *Rolling Stone* magazine called her 'the most talented young actress in America'. She is the highest-earning star in Hollywood, and she graduated two years early from high school with a grade point average of 3.9 out of 4 in order to pursue her ambitions on screen. At the time of writing, she is twenty-five.

Winter's Bone is a harrowing thriller whose protagonist, Ree Dolly, is a seventeen-year-old girl trying to support her family single-handedly in the backwaters of an Ozark community ravaged by poverty and crystal meth. The battles she fights – both emotional and physical – to save their home are primal, and thrown into sharp relief by her open, earnest youthfulness. Her friend Megan fears Ree is getting out of her depth:

> MEGAN
> What are we ever gonna do with you, baby girl?

> REE
> Kill me, I guess.

> MEGAN
> That idea's been said already. Got any others?

> REE
> Help me. Nobody's said that idea yet, have they?

Lawrence conveys a shattering sense of weariness – she is tired of fear, hunger, hard work and uncertainty, of the advances of predatory men and of dreams she knows will never be realized. It is a performance astonishing for its balance of passion and emotional reticence. Here, taking her depressed, mute mother for her daily walk, she cannot stay strong any longer:

                    REE
There's things happening and I don't know what
to do. Can you please help me this one time,
Momma?

Her mother does not react. Tears roll down Ree's
face, but her voice does not break.

                    REE
I don't know what to do.

Today, more than ever in this post-internet world, fame comes fast and it hits hard; nurturing a career – choosing roles, cultivating collaborators, establishing a public face – is done under instantaneous media scrutiny, amid a frenzy of speculation and gossip. Lawrence responded to the relentless press attention cautiously – 'I'm just a normal girl and a human being, and I haven't been in this long enough to feel like this is my new normal' – but it proved harder even than she had imagined: 'I'm from Kentucky. I used to be very personable and make eye contact and smile at people, and now all I do is look down. When I'm at dinner and one person after another keeps interrupting to take pictures, it's like "I can't live like this".'

Hardening her public face must feel doubly unwelcome, since she confesses an unusual technique for approaching a role; where many Method-schooled actors immerse themselves almost aggressively in their fictive world, she prefers kindness.

> *I have this feeling of protectiveness over characters I want to play. I worry about them – if someone else gets the part, I'm afraid they won't do it right; they'll make the character a victim or they'll make her a villain or they'll just get it wrong somehow.*

In a lesser actor this tenderness might prove a trap, since audiences are quick to see through a performance which plays to the gallery. But Lawrence is in no danger of losing her focus:

> *There are actresses who build themselves, and then there are actresses who are built by others. I want to build myself.*

I never felt like I completely, 100 per cent understood something so well as acting.

MARY PICKFORD

***Hearts Adrift* (1914)**
dir. Edwin S. Porter

Their First Misunderstanding
(1911)
Tess of the Storm Country
(1914)
Rags (1915)
The Poor Little Rich Girl (1917)
Stella Maris (1918)
Pollyanna (1920)
Suds (1920)
The Love Light (1921)
Rosita (1923)
Sparrows (1926)
My Best Girl (1927)

LILLIAN GISH

***The Birth of a Nation* (1915)**
dir. D. W. Griffith

An Unseen Enemy (1912)
Intolerance (1916)
Broken Blossoms (1919)
Way Down East (1920)
Orphans of the Storm (1921)
The Wind (1928)
Duel in the Sun (1946)
Portrait of Jennie (1948)
The Night of the Hunter (1955)
The Whales of August (1987)

CLARA BOW

***It* (1927)**
dir. Clarence G. Badger

Down to the Sea in Ships (1922)
Grit (1924)
The Adventurous Sex (1925)
Mantrap (1926)
Wings (1927)
Kick In (1931)
Hoop-La (1933)

GLORIA SWANSON

***Sadie Thompson* (1928)**
dir. Raoul Walsh

Don't Change Your Husband
(1919)
Male and Female (1919)
Why Change Your Wife? (1920)
The Affairs of Anatol (1921)
Beyond the Rocks (1922)
Stage Struck (1925)
Queen Kelly (1929)
The Trespasser (1929)
Music in the Air (1934)
Sunset Boulevard (1950)

BARBARA STANWYCK

***Ladies of Leisure* (1930)**
dir. Frank Capra

Baby Face (1933)
Stella Dallas (1937)
Golden Boy (1939)
Remember the Night (1940)
Ball of Fire (1941)
The Lady Eve (1941)
Double Indemnity (1944)
Sorry, Wrong Number (1948)
Titanic (1953)
Forty Guns (1957)

JEAN HARLOW

***Hell's Angels* (1930)**
dir. Howard Hughes

Double Whoopee (1929)
The Secret Six (1931)
The Public Enemy (1931)
Platinum Blonde (1931)
Red Dust (1932)
Dinner at Eight (1933)
Bombshell (1933)
Libeled Lady (1936)
Wife vs. Secretary (1936)
Saratoga (1937)

MARLENE DIETRICH

***Morocco* (1930)**
dir. Josef von Sternberg

The Blue Angel (1930)
Dishonored (1931)
Blonde Venus (1932)
Shanghai Express (1932)
The Scarlet Empress (1934)
The Devil is a Woman (1935)
A Foreign Affair (1948)
Witness for the Prosecution
(1957)
Touch of Evil (1958)
Judgment at Nuremberg (1961)

GRETA GARBO

***Mata Hari* (1931)**
dir. George Fitzmaurice

The Temptress (1926)
Flesh and the Devil (1926)
Love (1927)
The Kiss (1929)
Anna Christie (1930)
Grand Hotel (1932)
Queen Christina (1933)
Anna Karenina (1935)
Camille (1936)
Ninotchka (1939)

NOTABLE
FILMS

HEDY
LAMARR

Ecstasy (1933)
dir. Gustav Machatý

Algiers (1938)
Ziegfeld Girl (1941)
Tortilla Flat (1942)
Samson and Delilah (1949)
My Favorite Spy (1951)
The Female Animal (1958)

GINGER
ROGERS

Flying Down to Rio (1933)
dir. Thornton Freeland

42nd Street (1933)
Gold Diggers of 1933 (1933)
The Gay Divorcee (1934)
Top Hat (1935)
Roberta (1935)
Follow the Fleet (1936)
Swing Time (1936)
Shall We Dance (1936)
Stage Door (1937)
Kitty Foyle (1940)
The Major and the Minor
(1942)
The Barkleys of Broadway
(1949)
Monkey Business (1952)

MAE
WEST

I'm No Angel (1933)
dir. Wesley Ruggles

Night After Night (1932)
She Done Him Wrong (1933)
Klondike Annie (1936)
Go West, Young Man (1936)
My Little Chickadee (1940)
Myra Breckinridge (1970)

BETTE
DAVIS

Of Human Bondage (1934)
dir. John Cromwell

Dangerous (1935)
Jezebel (1938)
Dark Victory (1939)
*The Private Lives of Elizabeth
and Essex* (1939)
The Little Foxes (1941)
Now, Voyager (1942)
All About Eve (1950)
The Virgin Queen (1955)
*What Ever Happened to Baby
Jane?* (1962)
The Nanny (1965)
The Anniversary (1968)

CLAUDETTE
COLBERT

It Happened One Night (1934)
dir. Frank Capra

For the Love of Mike (1927)
The Lady Lies (1929)
Three-Cornered Moon (1933)
Cleopatra (1934)
Imitation of Life (1934)
The Gilded Lily (1935)
I Met Him in Paris (1937)
Tovarich (1937)
Bluebeard's Eighth Wife (1938)
Midnight (1939)
The Palm Beach Story (1942)
Three Came Home (1950)

CAROLE
LOMBARD

Twentieth Century (1934)
dir. Howard Hawks

Marriage in Transit (1925)
My Best Girl (1927)
Virtue (1932)
Hands Across the Table (1935)
My Man Godfrey (1936)
True Confession (1937)
Nothing Sacred (1937)
In Name Only (1939)
To Be or Not to Be (1942)

VIVIEN
LEIGH

Gone with the Wind (1939)
dir. Victor Fleming

The Village Squire (1935)
Fire Over England (1937)
A Yank at Oxford (1938)
That Hamilton Woman (1941)
Caesar and Cleopatra (1945)
Anna Karenina (1948)
A Streetcar Named Desire
(1951)
The Deep Blue Sea (1955)
*The Roman Spring of Mrs.
Stone* (1961)

INGRID BERGMAN

Intermezzo: A Love Story (1939)
dir. Gregory Ratoff

Casablanca (1942)
For Whom the Bell Tolls (1943)
Gaslight (1944)
Spellbound (1945)
The Bells of St. Mary's (1945)
Notorious (1946)
Joan of Arc (1948)
Stromboli (1950)
Anastasia (1956)
The Visit (1964)
Murder on the Orient Express (1974)
Autumn Sonata (1978)

RITA HAYWORTH

Only Angels Have Wings (1939)
dir. Howard Hawks

Charlie Chan in Egypt (1935)
Hit the Saddle (1937)
Blood and Sand (1941)
The Strawberry Blonde (1941)
Tales of Manhattan (1942)
You Were Never Lovelier (1942)
Cover Girl (1944)
Gilda (1946)
The Lady from Shanghai (1947)
Pal Joey (1957)
Separate Tables (1958)

KATHARINE HEPBURN

The Philadelphia Story (1940)
dir. George Cukor

A Bill of Divorcement (1932)
Little Women (1933)
Morning Glory (1933)
Bringing Up Baby (1938)
Holiday (1938)
Stage Door (1937)
Adam's Rib (1949)
The African Queen (1951)
Guess Who's Coming to Dinner (1967)
The Lion in Winter (1968)
On Golden Pond (1981)

JANE RUSSELL

The Outlaw (1943)
dir. Howard Hughes

Young Widow (1946)
The Paleface (1948)
Double Dynamite (1951)
His Kind of Woman (1951)
Son of Paleface (1952)
Gentlemen Prefer Blondes (1953)
The French Line (1954)
Underwater! (1955)
The Fuzzy Pink Nightgown (1957)
Johnny Reno (1966)
Born Losers (1967)

LAUREN BACALL

To Have and Have Not (1944)
dir. Howard Hawks

The Big Sleep (1946)
Key Largo (1948)
How to Marry a Millionaire (1953)
Blood Alley (1955)
Written on the Wind (1956)
Harper (1966)
The Shootist (1976)
The Fan (1981)
The Mirror Has Two Faces (1996)
Dogville (2003)
Birth (2004)

TALLULAH BANKHEAD

Lifeboat (1944)
dir. Alfred Hitchcock

Tarnished Lady (1931)
Thunder Below (1932)
Make Me a Star (1932)
Devil and the Deep (1932)
Faithless (1932)
Lifeboat (1944)
A Royal Scandal (1945)
Fanatic (1965)

JOAN CRAWFORD

Mildred Pierce (1945)
dir. Michael Curtiz

Our Dancing Daughters (1928)
Our Blushing Brides (1930)
Paid (1930)
This Modern Age (1931)
Possessed (1931)
Grand Hotel (1932)
The Women (1939)
Humoresque (1946)
Flamingo Road (1949)
Sudden Fear (1952)
Johnny Guitar (1954)
Whatever Happened to Baby Jane? (1962)

AVA GARDNER

The Killers (1946)
dir. Robert Siodmak

The Bribe (1949)
Show Boat (1951)
Mogambo (1953)
The Barefoot Contessa (1954)
Bhowani Junction (1956)
The Sun Also Rises (1957)
On the Beach (1959)
Seven Days in May (1964)
The Night of the Iguana (1964)
The Life and Times of Judge Roy Bean (1972)

NOTABLE FILMS

LANA TURNER

The Postman Always Rings Twice (1946)
dir. Tay Garnett

Topper (1937)
Love Finds Andy Hardy (1938)
Dr. Jekyll and Mr. Hyde (1941)
Ziegfeld Girl (1941)
Johnny Eager (1941)
The Three Musketeers (1948)
The Bad and the Beautiful (1952)
Peyton Place (1957)
Imitation of Life (1959)
Madame X (1966)

DEBORAH KERR

Black Narcissus (1947)
dir. Michael Powell and Emeric Pressburger

Contraband (1940)
The Life and Death of Colonel Blimp (1943)
I See a Dark Stranger (1946)
Edward, My Son (1949)
King Solomon's Mines (1950)
Quo Vadis (1951)
From Here to Eternity (1953)
The End of the Affair (1955)
The King and I (1956)
Bonjour Tristesse (1958)
The Innocents (1961)
Casino Royale (1967)

ELIZABETH TAYLOR

A Place in the Sun (1951)
dir. George Stevens

Lassie Come Home (1943)
National Velvet (1944)
Little Women (1949)
Giant (1956)
Cat on a Hot Tin Roof (1958)
Suddenly, Last Summer (1959)
BUtterfield 8 (1960)
Cleopatra (1963)
Who's Afraid of Virginia Woolf? (1966)
The Taming of the Shrew (1967)
Reflections in a Golden Eye (1967)
The Flintstones (1994)

GRACE KELLY

High Noon (1952)
dir. Fred Zinnemann

Dial M for Murder (1954)
Rear Window (1954)
The Country Girl (1954)
To Catch a Thief (1955)
High Society (1956)

AUDREY HEPBURN

Roman Holiday (1953)
dir. William Wyler

Sabrina (1954)
Funny Face (1957)
Breakfast at Tiffany's (1961)
Charade (1963)
My Fair Lady (1964)
How to Steal a Million (1966)
Wait Until Dark (1967)
Robin and Marian (1976)

JUDY GARLAND

A Star is Born (1954)
dir. George Cukor

Love Finds Andy Hardy (1938)
The Wizard of Oz (1939)
Strike Up the Band (1940)
Ziegfeld Girl (1941)
Girl Crazy (1943)
Meet Me in St. Louis (1944)
The Clock (1945)
Easter Parade (1948)
Summer Stock (1950)
Judgment at Nuremberg (1961)

KIM NOVAK

Picnic (1955)
dir. Joshua Logan

Pushover (1954)
Phffft (1954)
The Man with the Golden Arm (1955)
Pal Joey (1957)
Vertigo (1958)
Bell Book and Candle (1958)
Middle of the Night (1959)
Strangers When We Meet (1960)
Of Human Bondage (1964)
Kiss Me, Stupid (1964)
The Great Bank Robbery (1969)

BRIGITTE BARDOT

***And God Created Woman
(Et Dieu . . . créa la femme)
(1956)*** dir. Roger Vadim

*Crazy for Love (1952)
Doctor at Sea (1955)
Helen of Troy (1956)
Naughty Girl (1956)
Nero's Mistress (1956)
Love is my Profession (1958)
The Truth (1960)
A Very Private Affair (1962)
Contempt (1963)
Viva Maria! (1965)
Les Novices (1970)
Don Juan (or If Don Juan Were
a Woman) (1973)*

JEANNE MOREAU

***The Lovers (Les Amants)
(1958)*** dir. Louis Malle

*Elevator to the Gallows (1958)
The Four Hundred Blows
(1959)
La Notte (1961)
The Trial (1962)
Jules et Jim (1962)
The Fire Within (1963)
Bay of Angels (1963)
Diary of a Chambermaid
(1964)
Chimes at Midnight (1965)
Monte Walsh (1970)
Mr. Klein (1976)*

MARILYN MONROE

Some Like it Hot (1959)
dir. Billy Wilder

*Ladies of the Chorus (1948)
The Asphalt Jungle (1950)
All About Eve (1950)
Don't Bother to Knock (1952)
Niagara (1953)
Gentlemen Prefer Blondes
(1953)
How to Marry a Millionaire
(1953)
The Seven Year Itch (1955)
Bus Stop (1956)
The Prince and the Showgirl
(1957)
The Misfits (1961)*

ANITA EKBERG

La Dolce Vita (1960)
dir. Federico Fellini

*Abbott and Costello Go to Mars
(1953)
The Golden Blade (1953)
War and Peace (1956)
Hollywood or Bust (1956)
Screaming Mimi (1958)
Boccaccio '70 (1962)
Call Me Bwana (1963)
How I Learned to Love Women
(1966)
Way . . . Way Out (1966)
Fangs of the Living Dead (1969)
Death Knocks Twice (1969)
Killer Nun (1978)*

SOPHIA LOREN

Two Women (1960)
dir. Vittorio De Sica

*The Gold of Naples (1954)
Houseboat (1958)
The Black Orchid (1958)
El Cid (1961)
Boccaccio '70 (1962)
Yesterday, Today and
Tomorrow (1963)
Marriage Italian-Style (1964)
The Fall of the Roman Empire
(1964)
Sunflower (1970)
A Special Day (1977)
Nine (2009)*

URSULA ANDRESS

Dr. No (1962)
dir. Terence Young

*The 10th Victim (1965)
What's New Pussycat (1965)
The Blue Max (1966)
Casino Royale (1967)
Clash of the Titans (1981)*

JULIE CHRISTIE

Billy Liar (1963)
dir. John Schlesinger

*Darling (1965)
Doctor Zhivago (1965)
Far from the Madding Crowd
(1967)
Petulia (1968)
The Go-Between (1970)
McCabe & Mrs. Miller (1971)
Don't Look Now (1973)
Shampoo (1975)
Nashville (1975)
Heaven Can Wait (1978)
Heat and Dust (1983)
Hamlet (1996)
Away from Her (2006)*

JULIE ANDREWS

Mary Poppins (1964)
dir. Robert Stevenson

*The Sound of Music (1965)
Torn Curtain (1966)
Hawaii (1966)
Thoroughly Modern Millie
(1967)
Star! (1968)
Darling Lili (1970)
10 (1979)
S.O.B. (1981)
Victor Victoria (1982)
The Princess Diaries (2001)*

NOTABLE
FILMS

CATHERINE DENEUVE

***The Umbrellas of
Cherbourg* (1964)**
dir. Jacques Demy

Repulsion (1965)
Belle de jour (1967)
Mississippi Mermaid (1969)
Tristana (1970)
The Last Metro (1980)
The Hunger (1983)
Indochine (1992)
My Favorite Season (1993)
Dancer in the Dark (2000)
8 Women (2002)
Potiche (2010)

ANOUK AIMÉE

***A Man and a Woman
(Un Homme et une femme)*
(1966)** dir. Claude Lelouch

La Fleur de l'âge (1947)
*Modigliani of Montparnasse
(Montparnasse 19)*(1958)
La Dolce Vita (1960)
Lola (1961)
8½ (1963)
Justine (1969)
Tragedy of a Ridiculous Man
(1981)
Success is the Best Revenge
(1984)

LIV ULLMANN

***Persona* (1966)**
dir. Ingmar Bergman

Shame (1968)
Hour of the Wolf (1968)
The Emigrants (1971)
Cries and Whispers (1972)
Scenes from a Marriage (1973)
Face to Face (1976)
A Bridge Too Far (1977)
Autumn Sonata (1978)
The Rose Garden (1989)

VANESSA REDGRAVE

***Morgan: A Suitable Case
for Treatment* (1966)**
dir. Karel Reisz

A Man For All Seasons (1966)
Blow-Up (1966)
Camelot (1967)
Oh! What a Lovely War (1969)
Mary, Queen of Scots (1971)
The Devils (1971)
Julia (1977)
Yanks (1979)
Prick Up Your Ears (1987)
Howards End (1992)
Mission: Impossible (1996)
Girl, Interrupted (1999)
Atonement (2007)

FAYE DUNAWAY

***Bonnie and Clyde* (1967)**
dir. Arthur Penn

The Thomas Crown Affair
(1968)
Little Big Man (1970)
Puzzle of a Downfall Child
(1970)
Chinatown (1974)
The Towering Inferno (1974)
Three Days of the Condor
(1975)
Network (1976)
Eyes of Laura Mars (1978)
Mommie Dearest (1981)
Barfly (1987)

BARBRA STREISAND

***Funny Girl* (1968)**
dir. William Wyler

Hello, Dolly! (1969)
The Owl and the Pussycat
(1970)
What's Up, Doc? (1972)
The Way We Were (1973)
Funny Lady (1975)
A Star is Born (1976)
Yentl (1983)
Nuts (1987)
The Prince of Tides (1991)
The Mirror Has Two Faces
(1996)
Meet the Fockers (2004)

LIZA MINNELLI

***The Sterile Cuckoo* (1969)**
dir. Alan J. Pakula

Charlie Bubbles (1967)
*Tell Me That You Love Me,
Junie Moon* (1970)
Cabaret (1972)
Journey Back to Oz (1974)
Lucky Lady (1975)
A Matter of Time (1976)
New York, New York (1977)
Arthur (1981)
Rent-a-Cop (1987)

JANE FONDA	CHARLOTTE RAMPLING	SISSY SPACEK	DIANE KEATON
Klute (1971) dir. Alan J. Pakula	*The Night Porter* (1974) dir. Liliani Cavani	*Carrie* (1976) dir. Brian De Palma	*Looking for Mr. Goodbar* (1977) dir. Richard Brooks

Period of Adjustment (1962)
Sunday in New York (1963)
Cat Ballou (1965)
Barefoot in the Park (1967)
Barbarella (1968)
They Shoot Horses, Don't They? (1969)
Fun with Dick and Jane (1977)
Julia (1977)
Coming Home (1978)
The China Syndrome (1979)
Nine to Five (1980)
On Golden Pond (1981)
Monster-in-Law (2005)

Georgy Girl (1966)
The Damned (1969)
Vanishing Point (1971)
Farewell, My Lovely (1975)
Stardust Memories (1980)
The Verdict (1982)
Angel Heart (1987)
The Wings of the Dove (1997)
Spy Game (2001)
Swimming Pool (2003)
The Duchess (2008)
Melancholia (2011)

Badlands (1973)
Coal Miner's Daughter (1980)
Raggedy Man (1981)
Missing (1982)
Crimes of the Heart (1986)
JFK (1991)
The Grass Harp (1995)
The Straight Story (1999)
Affliction (1997)

The Godfather (1972)
Play it Again, Sam (1972)
The Godfather: Part II (1974)
Annie Hall (1977)
Manhattan (1979)
Reds (1981)
Shoot the Moon (1982)
The Godfather: Part III (1990)
Manhattan Murder Mystery (1993)
The First Wives Club (1996)
Marvin's Room (1996)
Something's Gotta Give (2003)
The Family Stone (2005)

HELEN MIRREN	MERYL STREEP	MICHELLE PFEIFFER	DEMI MOORE
The Long Good Friday (1980) dir. John Mackenzie	*Sophie's Choice* (1982) dir. Alan J. Pakula	*Scarface* (1983) dir. Brian De Palma	*About Last Night. . .* (1986) dir. Edward Zwick

A Midsummer Night's Dream (1968)
O Lucky Man! (1973)
Excalibur (1981)
The Cook, the Thief, his Wife and her Lover (1989)
The Madness of King George (1994)
Gosford Park (2001)
Calendar Girls (2003)
The Queen (2006)
The Last Station (2009)
RED (2010)
Hitchcock (2012)

The Deer Hunter (1978)
Kramer vs. Kramer (1979)
Manhattan (1979)
The French Lieutenant's Woman (1981)
Silkwood (1983)
Out of Africa (1985)
The Bridges of Madison County (1995)
Adaptation (2002)
The Manchurian Candidate (2004)
The Devil Wears Prada (2006)
The Iron Lady (2011)

Grease 2 (1982)
Ladyhawke (1985)
The Witches of Eastwick (1987)
Dangerous Liaisons (1988)
Married to the Mob (1988)
The Fabulous Baker Boys (1989)
The Russia House (1990)
Batman Returns (1992)
The Age of Innocence (1993)
Wolf (1994)
What Lies Beneath (2000)
Hairspray (2007)

St. Elmo's Fire (1985)
Ghost (1990)
A Few Good Men (1992)
Indecent Proposal (1993)
Disclosure (1994)
Striptease (1996)
Deconstructing Harry (1997)
G.I. Jane (1997)
Bobby (2006)
Flawless (2007)
Mr. Brooks (2007)
Margin Call (2011)

UMA THURMAN

***Dangerous Liaisons* (1988)**
dir. Stephen Frears

The Adventures of Baron Munchausen (1988)
Henry and June (1990)
Pulp Fiction (1994)
Batman & Robin (1997)
Gattaca (1997)
The Avengers (1998)
Sweet and Lowdown (1999)
Kill Bill: Vol. 1 (2003)
Kill Bill: Vol. 2 (2004)
The Producers (2005)
Bel Ami (2012)

JULIETTE BINOCHE

***The Unbearable Lightness of Being* (1988)**
dir. Philip Kaufman

Rendez-vous (1985)
Hail Mary (1985)
Les Amants du Pont-Neuf (1991)
Damage (1992)
Wuthering Heights (1992)
Three Colours: Blue (1993)
The English Patient (1996)
Chocolat (2000)
Mary (2005)
Certified Copy (2010)
Camille Claudel 1915 (2013)
Godzilla (2014)
Clouds of Sils Maria (2014)

NICOLE KIDMAN

***Dead Calm* (1989)**
dir. Philip Noyce

To Die For (1995)
The Portrait of a Lady (1996)
Eyes Wide Shut (1999)
Moulin Rouge! (2001)
The Others (2001)
The Hours (2002)
Cold Mountain (2003)
Dogville (2003)
Birth (2004)
The Interpreter (2005)
The Golden Compass (2007)
Australia (2008)
Nine (2009)
Rabbit Hole (2010)

JULIA ROBERTS

***Pretty Woman* (1990)**
dir. Garry Marshall

Mystic Pizza (1988)
Steel Magnolias (1989)
Hook (1991)
Mary Reilly (1996)
My Best Friend's Wedding (1997)
Notting Hill (1999)
Runaway Bride (1999)
Erin Brockovich (2000)
Ocean's Eleven (2001)
Closer (2004)
Duplicity (2009)
Eat Pray Love (2010)
August: Osage County (2013)

JODIE FOSTER

***The Silence of the Lambs* (1991)**
dir. Jonathan Demme

Taxi Driver (1976)
Bugsy Malone (1976)
Freaky Friday (1976)
The Accused (1988)
Maverick (1994)
Nell (1995)
Contact (1997)
Panic Room (2002)
Flight Plan (2005)
Inside Man (2006)
Carnage (2011)

PENÉLOPE CRUZ

***Jamón Jamón* (1992)**
dir. Bigas Luna

Live Flesh (1997)
Open Your Eyes (1997)
The Hi-Lo Country (1998)
All About My Mother (1999)
All the Pretty Horses (2000)
Blow (2001)
Captain Corelli's Mandolin (2001)
Vanilla Sky (2001)
Sahara (2005)
Volver (2006)
Vicky Cristina Barcelona (2008)
Nine (2009)

EMMA THOMPSON

***Howards End* (1992)**
dir. James Ivory

Henry V (1989)
Dead Again (1991)
The Remains of the Day (1993)
Carrington (1995)
Sense and Sensibility (1995)
The Winter Guest (1997)
Primary Colors (1998)
Love Actually (2003)
Harry Potter and the Prisoner of Azkaban (2004)
Nanny McPhee (2005)
Brideshead Revisited (2008)
An Education (2009)
Saving Mr. Banks (2013)

TILDA SWINTON	SANDRA BULLOCK	JULIANNE MOORE	KATE WINSLET
***Orlando* (1992)**	***Speed* (1994)**	***Boogie Nights* (1997)**	***Titanic* (1997)**
dir. Sally Potter	dir. Jan de Bont	dir. Paul Thomas Anderson	dir. James Cameron

Caravaggio (1986)	*Demolition Man* (1993)	*Short Cuts* (1993)	*Heavenly Creatures* (1994)
Love is the Devil (1998)	*A Time to Kill* (1996)	*The Fugitive* (1993)	*Sense and Sensibility* (1995)
The Beach (2000)	*Miss Congeniality* (2000)	*Vanya on 42nd Street* (1994)	*Jude* (1996)
Possible Worlds (2000)	*28 Days* (2000)	*Safe* (1995)	*Quills* (2000)
Adaptation (2002)	*Crash* (2004)	*The Lost World: Jurassic Park*	*Iris* (2001)
The Chronicles of Narnia:	*Infamous* (2006)	(1997)	*The Life of David Gale* (2003)
The Lion, the Witch and the	*The Lake House* (2006)	*The Big Lebowski* (1998)	*Finding Neverland* (2004)
Wardrobe (2005)	*The Blind Side* (2009)	*The End of the Affair* (1999)	*Eternal Sunshine of the*
Michael Clayton (2007)	*The Proposal* (2009)	*Far from Heaven* (2002)	*Spotless Mind* (2004)
I Am Love (2009)	*Extremely Loud & Incredibly*	*The Hours* (2002)	*Little Children* (2006)
We Need to Talk About Kevin	*Close* (2011)	*Children of Men* (2006)	*Revolutionary Road* (2008)
(2011)	*Gravity* (2013)	*Blindness* (2008)	*The Reader* (2008)
Only Lovers Left Alive (2013)		*The Kids Are All Right* (2010)	*Carnage* (2011)
The Grand Budapest Hotel		*Still Alice* (2014)	*Insurgent* (2015)
(2014)			

CATE BLANCHETT	GWYNETH PALTROW	ANGELINA JOLIE	CATHERINE ZETA-JONES
***Elizabeth* (1998)**	***Shakespeare in Love* (1998)**	***Girl, Interrupted* (1999)**	***Traffic* (2000)**
dir. Shekhar Kapur	dir. John Madden	dir. James Mangold	dir. Steven Soderbergh

Paradise Road (1997)	*Se7en* (1995)	*Hackers* (1995)	*Les 1001 Nuits* (1990)
Oscar and Lucinda (1997)	*Emma* (1996)	*Gia* (1998)	*Splitting Heirs* (1993)
Pushing Tin (1999)	*Sliding Doors* (1998)	*Playing by Heart* (1998)	*The Mask of Zorro* (1998)
The Talented Mr. Ripley (1999)	*The Talented Mr. Ripley* (1999)	*Pushing Tin* (1999)	*Entrapment* (1999)
Charlotte Gray (2001)	*Shallow Hal* (2001)	*The Bone Collector* (1999)	*Chicago* (2002)
The Lord of the Rings: The	*Possession* (2002)	*Gone in 60 Seconds* (2000)	*High Fidelity* (2000)
Fellowship of the Ring (2001)	*Sylvia* (2003)	*Lara Croft: Tomb Raider* (2001)	*Intolerable Cruelty* (2003)
Veronica Guerin (2003)	*View from the Top* (2003)	*Mr. & Mrs. Smith* (2005)	*Ocean's Twelve* (2004)
Notes on a Scandal (2006)	*Proof* (2005)	*The Good Shepherd* (2006)	*The Legend of Zorro* (2005)
The Curious Case of	*Infamous* (2006)	*Wanted* (2008)	*Death Defying Acts* (2007)
Benjamin Button (2008)	*Iron Man* (2008)	*Salt* (2010)	*Lay the Favourite* (2012)
Robin Hood (2010)	*The Avengers* (2012)	*The Tourist* (2010)	
Hanna (2011)		*Maleficent* (2014)	
Blue Jasmine (2013)			

JENNIFER
CONNELLY

***Requiem for a Dream* (2000)**
dir. Darren Aronofsky

Once Upon a Time in America
(1984)
Labyrinth (1986)
The Rocketeer (1991)
Mulholland Falls (1995)
Dark City (1998)
A Beautiful Mind (2001)
Hulk (2003)
Dark Water (2005)
Blood Diamond (2006)
Reservation Road (2007)
Creation (2009)
He's Just Not That Into You
(2009)
Noah (2014)

SCARLETT
JOHANSSON

***Lost in Translation* (2003)**
dir. Sofia Coppola

Manny & Lo (1996)
The Horse Whisperer (1998)
Ghost World (2001)
Girl with a Pearl Earring (2003)
The Island (2005)
The Prestige (2006)
The Nanny Diaries (2007)
The Other Boleyn Girl (2008)
Vicky Cristina Barcelona (2008)
Iron Man 2 (2010)
Under the Skin (2013)
Lucy (2014)

NATALIE
PORTMAN

***Closer* (2004)**
dir. Mike Nichols

Léon: The Professional (1994)
Everyone Says I Love You
(1996)
Mars Attacks! (1996)
Star Wars Episode 1: The Phan-
tom Menace (1999)
Cold Mountain (2003)
Garden State (2004)
V for Vendetta (2006)
The Other Boleyn Girl (2008)
Black Swan (2010)
No Strings Attached (2011)
Thor (2011)

AMY
ADAMS

***Junebug* (2005)**
dir. Phil Morrison

Catch Me If You Can (2002)
Charlie Wilson's War (2007)
Enchanted (2007)
Doubt (2008)
Miss Pettigrew Lives for a Day
(2008)
Julie & Julia (2009)
The Fighter (2010)
The Master (2012)
American Hustle (2013)
Her (2013)
Man of Steel (2013)
Big Eyes (2014)

KEIRA
KNIGHTLEY

***Pride & Prejudice* (2005)**
dir. Joe Wright

Star Wars Episode 1: The Phan-
tom Menace (1999)
Bend It Like Beckham (2002)
Love Actually (2003)
Pirates of the Caribbean: The
Curse of the Black Pearl (2003)
Domino (2005)
Atonement (2007)
The Duchess (2008)
Never Let Me Go (2010)
A Dangerous Method (2011)
Anna Karenina (2012)
The Imitation Game (2014)

MARION
COTILLARD

***La Vie en rose* (2007)**
dir. Olivier Dahan

Taxi (1998)
Love Me if You Dare (2003)
Big Fish (2003)
A Very Long Engagement
(2004)
Mary (2005)
A Good Year (2006)
Nine (2009)
Inception (2010)
Midnight in Paris (2011)
Rust and Bone (2012)
The Dark Knight Rises (2012)
Two Days, One Night (2014)

JENNIFER
LAWRENCE

***Winter's Bone* (2010)**
dir. Debra Glanik

The Poker House (2008)
X-Men: First Class (2011)
The Hunger Games (2012)
Silver Linings Playbook (2012)
American Hustle (2013)
Serena (2014)

INDEX

Page references in **bold** denote a chapter devoted to the subject

A

About Last Night.... 289
Academy Awards 274
Accused, The 316
Adams, Amy **378–81**, 403
Adventures of Baron Munchausen, The 293
Algonquin Round Table 130
Allen, Woody 268, 269–70
Almodóvar, Pedro 323
Altman, Robert 338
Amants, Les (The Lovers) 186–7
American Hustle 381
Amiée, Anouk **222–5**, 399
....And God Created Woman 180–2, 203
Andress, Ursula **204–9**, 398
Andrews, Julie **214–17**, 398
Anna Christie 58
Annie Hall 268–70
Antheil, George 66
Anthony and Cleopatra 132
Aronofsky, Darren 366, 367
Astaire, Fred 70, 169
Atonement 385

B

Bacall, Lauren **124–7**, 298, 396
Badlands 264
Bale, Christian 327, 381
Bankhead, Tallulah **128–33**, 396
Barbarella 257
Bardot, Brigitte 178–83, 203, 398
Barry, Philip 118
Baxter, Beverley 150

Bayonas, Katrina 320
Beatty, Warren 212–13, 236–7, 239
Beery, Wallace 34
Belle de jour 221
Bend It Like Beckham 384
Bergman, Ingmar 228
Bergman, Ingrid 66, **100–3**, 396
Berkeley, Busby 168
Berry, Halle 274
Bill of Divorcement, A 116
Billy Liar 212
Binoche, Juliette **296–9**, 401
Birth of a Nation, The 24
Black Narcissus 150–1, 335
Black Swan 377
Blanchett, Cate **346–9**, 402
Blindness 341
Blue Angel, The 52
Blue Jasmine 349
Boccacci '70 198
Bogarde, Dirk 225, 260
Bogart, Humphrey 104, 126, 127, 143
Bond girl 206
Bonnie and Clyde 236–8
Boogie Nights 339–41
Born Yesterday 37
Bosley, Crowther 180
Bow, Clara **26–31**, 394
Branagh, Kenneth 326
Brando, Marlon 133, 206, 232
Brandt, Harry 117–18
Brantley, Ben 251
Breakfast at Tiffany's 165, 203
Breen, Joseph 65, 122
Brice, Fanny 242–3
Broccoli, Cubby 212
Brody, Richard 127
Bullock, Sandra 332–5, 402
Burlesque 40
Burton, Richard 155

Bus Stop 191
Butterfield 8 154

C

Cabaret 250–1
Call Me Bwana 198–9
Cameron, James 274, 344
Capra, Frank 40, 41, 48, 86, 87, 88, 89
Carrie 264–5
Casablanca 66, 104, 105
Casino Royale 209
Cavanagh, Dean 274
Chaplin, Charlie 21, 34, 35, 35, 155
Chevalier, Maurice 54
Chicago 363
Chinatown 238, 239
Christie, Julie **210–13**, 398
Cleopatra 86–7
Closer 376–7
Cohen, Hubert 228
Cohn, Harry 108–9, 174
Colbert, Claudette 82, **84–9**, 395
Columbia Pictures 108, 174
Conchita 130
Connelly, Jennifer **364–7**, 403
Cooper, Gary 131
Coppola, Sofia 370, 371, 372
Cotillard, Marion **386–9**, 403
Coward, Noël 86
Crane, Cheryl 147
Crawford, Joan 83, **134–9**, 396
Cruz, Penélope **318–23**, 401
Cukor, George 36, 116, 118
Curtis, Tony 191
Curtiz, Michael 104

D

Damned, The 260

Dangerous Liaisons 293–5
Darling Lili 217
Davis, Bette 25, **78–83**, 298, 395
Davis, Geena 284
de Beauvoir, Simone 182–3
de Gaulle, Charles 180
de Havilland, Olivia 97
De Laurentiis, Dino 280, 317
De Palma, Brian 284–5
De Sica, Vittorio 202–3
Dead Calm 302–3
Dean, James 206
DeMille, Cecil B. 34, 35, 66, 86
Deneuve, Catherine **218–21**, 399
Depardieu, Gérard 299
Derek, John 206
Dietrich, Marlene **50–5**, 61, 394
Doctor Zhivago 212, 213
Dolce Vita, La 196, 197–8, 199, 203, 224
Don't Look Now 213
Double Indemnity 42–3, 146
Double Whoopee 46
Dr. No 206–8, 209, 212
Drag, The 74
Dunaway, Faye **234–9**, 399

E

Easter Parade 169
Ebert, Roger 244, 280, 302
Ecstasy 64–5
Edwards, Blake 217
Ekberg, Anita **194–9**, 202, 203, 398
Elizabeth 348–9
English Patient, The 299
Eyes of Laura Mars 238

F

Fairbanks, Douglas 21, 35
Fairbanks Jr, Douglas 137

Fellini, Federico 196, 197, 198
Fitzgerald, Geraldine 104
Fleming, Victor 30, 97–8
Flying Down to Rio 70
Fonda, Jane 232, **252–7**, 400
For the Love of Mike 86, 88
Fosse, Bob 251
Foster, Jodie 312–17, 401
Foxfire 357
From Here to Eternity 150, 151
Funny Girl 242–5

G
Gable, Clark 49, 54, 87, 93
Garbo, Greta 25, 53, **56–61**, 103, 394
Gardner, Ava **140–3**, 396
Garland, Judy **166–71**, 248, 249, 284, 397
Gentlemen Prefer Blondes 123
Gere, Richard 308
Gia 358
Gilda 110–11
Girl Crazy 70
Girl, Interrupted 358–9
Gish, Lilian **22–5**, 394
Glyn, Elinor 30
Godfather trilogy 268
Gone with the Wind 96–9, 117, 130, 298
Grade, Lew 344
Grant, Cary 108, 171
Gravity 335
Grease 2 284
Gregory, Andre 338
Griffith, D.W. 20, 21, 24, 25, 35
Grit 29

H
Hannibal 317
Harlow, Jean **44–9**, 394

Hawks, Howard 108, 126, 127
Hawks, Nancy 126
Hays Code (Motion Picture Production Code) 55, 87, 102, 122, 146, 187
Hayworth, Rita **106–11**, 396
Hearts Adrift 20
Heavenly Creatures 344
Hell's Angels 47–8
Hemingway, Ernest 55
Hepburn, Audrey 162–5, 182, 202, 203, 397
Hepburn, Katharine **114–19**, 396
High Noon 158
Hill, Jonah 338
Hitchcock, Alfred 24, 105, 133, 158–9, 161, 176, 326
Holliday, Judy 37
Hollywood 142, 284
Homme et une femme, Un (A Man and a Woman) 224–5
Hope, Bob 198–9
Hopkins, Arthur 40
Hoskins, Bob 276
Howard, Gertrude 77
Howard, Leslie 81, 82, 83, 97, 103
Howards End 326–7
Hughes, Howard 46–7, 48, 118, 122, 123, 155, 196
Human Figure in Motion, The 288
Hunger Games, The 392
Hurry Sundown 236

I
I'm No Angel 75–7
Imitation Game, The 385
Imitation of Life 147
Intermezzo: A Love Story 102, 103–4

Iron Lady, The 281
It 30–1
It Happened One Night 82, 87–9

J
Jacobellis, Nico 186–7
Jamón Jamón 320–2
Jazz Singer, The 58
Johansson, Scarlett **368–73**, 403
Jolie, Angelina 232, **354–9**, 402
Jules et Jim 187
Julia 232
Junebug 380–1
Jurassic Park: The Lost World 339

K
Kael, Pauline 42, 221, 224, 285
Kaufman, Philip 298
Keaton, Diane **266–71**, 406
Kelly, Grace **156–61**, 182, 397
Kerr, Deborah **148–51**, 335, 397
Kidman, Nicole **300–3**, 326, 401
Killers, The 143
Kitty Foyle 70–1
Klute 255, 256–7
Knightley, Keira **382–5**, 403
Koch, Howard 105
Koenig, Rhoda 92

L
Ladies of Leisure 40–2
Lake, The 117
Lamarr, Hedy **62–7**, 395
Lara Croft: Tomb Raider 356
Lawrence, Jennifer **390–3**, 403

Iron Lady, The 281
Leigh, Vivien **94–9**, 182, 298, 395
Lelouch, Claude 224, 225
Léon: The Professional 376
Lifeboat 132–3
Lion in Winter, The 116
Littlefeather, Sacheen 232
Loaded Guns 208–9
Logan, Joshua 175
Lohan, Lindsay 338
Lombard, Carole **90–3**, 395
Long Good Friday, The 275–6
Looking for Mr. Goodbar 270–1
Loren, Sophia **200–3**, 398
Lost in Translation 370–2
Lubitsch, Ernst 86

M
Maas, Frederica Sagor 136
Macbeth 275
McCabe & Mrs. Miller 212
Machatý, Gustave 64, 65
Make Me a Star 131
Mamoulian, Rouben 59, 110
Man with the Golden Arm, The 174
Man Who Played God, The 80
Mandl, Friedrich 65
Mantrap 30
Marber, Patrick 376–7
Marshall, Garry 308
Mary Poppins 216
Mask of Virtue, The 96
Mata Hari 59–61
Mayer, Louis B. 65, 142, 146, 154, 168, 169
Method school 104, 191, 393
MGM 25, 58, 65, 137, 142, 143, 146, 168–9
Michael Clayton 331
Mildred Pierce 138–9

Minnelli, Liza **246–51**, 399
Minnelli, Vincente 248
Mirren, Helen 272–7, 400
Mitchum, David 326
Monroe, Marilyn 31,
    188–91, 398
Monster's Ball 274
Moore, Demi **286–9**, 400
Moore, Julianne **336–41**,
    402
Moreau, Jeanne **184–7**, 398
*Morgan: A Suitable Case for
    Treatment* 233
Morocco 53–4, 55
Moser, Stephen MacMillan
    147
Motion Picture Producers
    and Distributors of
    America (MPPDA) 65,
    122
Motion Picture Production
    Code *see* Hays Code
Müller, Jürgen 224
Mulvey, Laura 196
Myers, Mike 284

N

National Legion of Decency
    181
Network 238
Nichols, Mike 377
Night After Night 74–5
Night Porter, The 260–1
Nine 323
Nine to Five 255
Noose, The 40
Norman, Barry 261
Notting Hill 310–11
Novak, Kim 172–7, 397

O

Of Human Bondage 80–3,
    298
Olivier, Laurence 96, 97,
    191

Only Angels Have Wings
    109–10, 198
Orlando 330
Our Dancing Daughters 137
Out of Africa 280
Outlaw, The 47, 122–3

P

Pacino, Al 213, 285
Pagano, Alfred 49
Paglia, Camille 159
Pakula, Alan J. 249
Paltrow, Gwyneth **350–3**,
    402
Paramount 34, 35, 53, 74,
    86
Parker, Dorothy 117
Pearce, Guy 327
Peck, Gregory 164
Persona 228–9, 298
Pfeiffer, Michelle **282–5**, 400
Philadelphia Story, The
    118–19
Pickford, Mary **18–21**, 35,
    80, 394
Picnic 175–6, 177
*Pirates of the Caribbean:
    The Curse of the Black
    Pearl* 384
Pitt, Brad 356
Place in the Sun, A 154–5
Platinum Blonde 48
Plummer, Christopher 216
Polanski, Roman 239
politics, mixing with show
    business 232, 254–5
Ponti, Carlo 203
Portman, Natalie **374–7**,
    403
Possible Worlds 331
*Postman Always Rings
    Twice, The* 146–7
Powell, Michael 150, 151
Preminger, Otto 236
Pretty Woman 308–10

Pride & Prejudice 384–5
Pulp Fiction 292

Q

Queen Christina 59
Queen, The 277

R

Raft, George 74
Rampling, Charlotte
    258–61, 400
Reader, The 345
Rear Window 159–61
Réard, Louis 208
RED 276–7
Redgrave, Vanessa **230–3**,
    399
Reed, Oliver 229
Remarque, Erich Maria 52
Requiem for a Dream 366–7
Riskin, Robert 87
RKO 116, 118, 196
Roberts, Julia **306–11**, 401
Rocketeer, The 366
Roeg, Nic 213
Rogers, Ginger **68–71**, 395
Roman Holiday 164–5
Rooney, Mickey 142–3
Rosselini, Isabella 104
Routh, Brandon 284
Russell, David O. 381
Russell, Jane 47, **120–3**, 396
Russell, Rosalind 175

S

Sadie Thompson 35–6
Safe 339, 341
Samson and Delilah 66
Saratoga 49
Scarface 284–5
Scheider, Roy 380
Schlesinger, John 212, 213
Scorsese, Martin 151, 176
Screaming Mimi 197
Se7en 352

Selznick, David O. 96–7,
    102, 117, 130
Selznick, Myron 96
Sense and Sensibility 327,
    344, 345
Sex 74
Shakespeare in Love 352–3
Shallow Hal 353
Shampoo 213
Short Cuts 338–9
Sieber, Rudolf 54
Silence of the Lambs, The
    265, 316–17
Sinatra, Frank 143, 248–9
Smiling Lieutenant, The 86
S.O.B. 217
Soderbergh, Steven 362–3
Some Like It Hot 191
Sophie's Choice 208, 280–1
Sound of Music, The 216
Spacek, Sissy **262–5**, 400
Speed 334–5
Stampanato, Johnny 147
Stanwyck, Barbara **38–43**,
    394
Star is Born, A 170–1
Stark, Ray 243, 245
Steel Magnolias 308
Steenburgen, Mary 380
Sterile Cuckoo, The 249–50
Sternberg, Josef von 52–3,
    54
Stevens, George 154
Still Alice 341
Stiller, Mauritz 58, 61
Stradling, Harry 102
Strasberg, Lee 254
Strasberg, Paula 191
Streep, Meryl 208, 274,
    278–81, 400
Streisand, Barbra **240–5**,
    250, 399
Stroheim, Erich von 36
Styron, William 208
Sunset Boulevard 34, 36–7

Swanson, Gloria 32–7, 394
Sweet and Lowdown 292
Swerling, Jo 40–1
Swinton, Tilda **328–31**, 402

T

Tabery, Karel 225
Taxi Driver 314–15
Taylor, Elizabeth **152–5**, 232, 397
Tea and Sympathy 151
Teller, Jürgen 261
Temple, Shirley 376
Tess of the Storm Country 20
Thalberg, Irving 131
Their First Misunderstanding 20
Thomas Crown Affair, The 238
Thompson, Emma **324–7**, 401
Thomson, David 41, 176, 339
Thurman, Uma **290–5**
Titanic 274, 344–5
To Have and Have Not 126–7, 298
Toland, Gregg 102, 104
Tracy, Spencer 117
Traffic 363
Travers, Peter 385
Truffaut, François 187
Turner, Lana **144–7**, 397
Twentieth Century 92, 93
Two Women 202–3
Tynan, Kenneth 54

U

Ullmann, Liv **226–9**, 298, 399
Umbrellas of Cherbourg, The 220–1
Unbearable Lightness of Being, The 298–9

Under the Skin 373
United Artists 21, 34, 35
Universal Studios 80, 196
Unseen Enemy, The 24

V

Vadim, Roger 180
Vanilla Sky 320
Vertigo 176–7
Vicky Cristina Barcelona 323
Vie en rose, La 388–9
Volver 323

W

Walters, Charles 169
Warner Brothers 138
Way Down East 25
Wayne, John 55
Welch, Raquel 108
Welles, Orson 93, 110, 187
West, Mae **72–7**, 395
Whale, James 47
Whales of August, The 25
Who's Afraid of Virginia Woolf? 155
Wilder, Billy 34, 42, 191
Winders, Wim 221
Winslet, Kate **342–5**, 402
Winter's Bone 392–3
Wizard of Oz, The 168, 248
Wyler, William 80, 164, 165, 242, 243

Z

Zeta-Jones, Catherine **360–3**, 402
Zinnemann, Fred 158
Zsigmond, Vilmos 242
Zukor, Adolf 20

PICTURE CAPTIONS AND CREDITS

All the images in this book are from the archives of The Kobal Collection which owes its existence to the vision, talent and energy of the men and women who created the movie industry and whose legacies live on through the films they made, the studios they built, and the publicity photographs they took. Kobal collects, preserves, organizes and makes these images available to enhance our understanding of this cinematic art.

The publisher wishes to thank all of the photographers (known and unknown) and the film production and distribution companies whose publicity images appear in this book. We apologize in advance for any omissions, or neglect, and will be pleased to make any corrections in future editions.

Cover artwork based on a photograph of Audrey Hepburn by Richard Avedon; 2 and 106 Rita Hayworth in *Gilda*; Columbia/Bob Coburn; 8 Audrey Hepburn in *Breakfast at Tiffany's*; Paramount/Howell Conant; 14 Uma Thurman in *Kill Bill: Volume 2*; A Band Apart/Miramax; 18 Mary Pickford in *Daddy Long Legs*; Mary Pickford Company; 22 Lillian Gish; D.W. Griffith Productions; 26 Clara Bow in *It*; Paramount; 32 Gloria Swanson in *Sadie Thompson*; United Artists; 38 Barbara Stanwyck; Warner Bros.; 44 Jean Harlow; MGM; 50 Marlene Dietrich in *Morocco*; Paramount/E.R. Richee; 56 Greta Garbo in *Mata Hari*; MGM/Clarence Sinclair Bull; 62 Hedy Lamarr in *Ecstasy*; Elekta; 68 Ginger Rogers in *Roberta*; RKO; 72 Mae West in *I'm No Angel*; Paramount; 78 Bette Davis in *Of Human Bondage*; RKO; 84 Claudette Colbert in *It Happened One Night*; Columbia/Irving Lippman; 90 Carole Lombard in *Twentieth Century*; Columbia; 94 Vivien Leigh in *Gone with the Wind*; Selznick/MGM; 100 Ingrid Bergman in *Intermezzo*; Selznick/United Artists; 114 Katharine Hepburn; RKO/Ernest Bachrach; 120 Jane Russell in *The Outlaw*; RKO/George Hurrell; 124 Lauren Bacall; Warner Bros./Scotty Welbourne; 128 Tallulah Bankhead in *Lifeboat*; 20th Century Fox; 134 Joan Crawford; Warner Bros./Bert Six; 140 Ava Gardner in *The Killers*; Universal/Ray Jones; 144 Lana Turner in *The Postman Always Rings Twice*; MGM; 148 Deborah Kerr in *Hatter's Castle*; Paramount; 152 Elizabeth Taylor; Paramount/Bud Fraker; 156 Grace Kelly; MGM/Virgil Apger; 162 Audrey Hepburn in *Breakfast at Tiffany's*; Paramount/Howell Conant; 166 Judy Garland in *A Star is Born*; Warner Bros.; 172 Kim Novak; Columbia; 178 Brigitte Bardot in *En Cas de Malheur*; UCIL/Iena/Incom/Limot; 184 Jeanne Moreau in *Eve*; Paris Film/Interopa; 188 Marilyn Monroe; 20th Century Fox/Frank Powolny; 194 Anita Ekberg in *La Dolce Vita*; Riama-Pathé; 200 Sophia Loren in *Two Women*; Embassy; 204 Ursula Andress in *Dr. No*; Danjaq/Eon/UA; 210 Julie Christie in *Billy Liar*; Vic/Waterhall; 214 Julie Andrews in *The Sound of Music*; 20th Century Fox; 218 Catherine Deneuve in *Belle de jour*; Paris Film/Five Film; 222 Anouk Aimée *La Dolce Vita*; Riama-Pathé; 226 Liv Ullmann in *Richard's Things*; Southern Pictures; 230 Vanessa Redgrave in *Morgan: A Suitable Case for Treatment*; British Lion/Aubrey Dewar; 234 Faye Dunaway in *Bonnie and Clyde*; Warner Bros./Seven Arts/Tatira-Hiller Productions; 240 Barbra Streisand in *Funny Girl*; Columbia; 246 Liza Minnelli in *Cabaret*; ABC/Allied Artists; 252 Jane Fonda in *Barbarella*; Paramount; 258 Charlotte Rampling in *The Night Porter*; Italonegglio/Lotar Film; 262 Sissy Spacek in *Carrie*; United Artists; 266 Diane Keaton in *Annie Hall*; Rollins-Joffe/United Artists; 272 Helen Mirren in *The Cook, the Thief, his Wife and her Lover*; Allarts/Erato; 278 Meryl Streep in *The Deer Hunter*; EMI/Columbia/Universal; 282 Michelle Pfeiffer in *Scarface*; Universal; 286 Demi Moore in *About Last Night*; Tri-Star; 290 Uma Thurman in *Dangerous Liaisons*; Warners Bros.; 296 Juliette Binoche in *The Unbearable Lightness of Being*; Saul Zaentz Company; 300 Nicole Kidman in *Cold Mountain*; Miramax; 306 Julia Roberts in *Pretty Woman*; Touchstone Pictures; 312 Jodie Foster in *The Silence of the Lambs*; Orion Pictures; 318 Penélope Cruz in *Jamón, Jamón*; Lola Film; 324 Emma Thompson in *Howard's End*; Merchant Ivory; 328 Tilda Swinton in *Edward II*; Working Title/BBC/BR Screen; 332 Sandra Bullock in *Speed*; 20th Century Fox/Richard Foreman; 336 Julianne Moore in *Boogie Nights*; New Line; 342 Kate Winslet in *Titanic*; 20th Century Fox/Paramount/Merie W. Wallace; 346 Cate Blanchett in *Elizabeth*; Polygram/Alex Bailey; 350 Gwyneth Paltrow in *Shakespeare in Love*; Miramax Films/Universal/Laurie Sparham; 354 Angelina Jolie in *Girl, Interrupted*; Columbia Tristar/Suzanne Tenner; 360 Catherine Zeta-Jones in *Chicago*; Miramax/Producers Circle/Storyline Entertainment; 364 Jennifer Connelly in *Requiem for a Dream*; Artisan Pictures/John Baer; 368 Scarlett Johansson in *Lost in Translation*; Focus Features; 374 Natalie Portman in *Closer*; Columbia; 378 Amy Adams in *Trouble with the Curve*; Malpaso Productions; 382 Keira Knightley in *Pride and Prejudice*; Working Title; 386 Marion Cotillard in *La Vie en rose*; Legende/TFI International; 390 Jennifer Lawrence in *Winter's Bone*; Winter's Bone Productions

GEORGE TIFFIN
is a writer and film-maker who has travelled
from Siberia to the Seychelles shooting and
directing music videos and commercials. He
is the author of *All the Best Lines*, published by
Head of Zeus in 2013, and the thriller *Mercy
Alexander*.

First published in 2015 by Head of Zeus Ltd

Copyright © George Tiffin 2015

The moral right of George Tiffin to be identified as the
author of this work has been asserted in accordance
with the Copyright, Designs and Patents Act of 1988.

1 3 5 7 9 10 8 6 4 2

A catalogue record for this book is available from the
British Library.

ISBN (HB) 9781781859377
      (E) 9781781859360

Printed and bound in China by 1010 Printing
International Ltd

Design Nick Clark

Head of Zeus Ltd
Clerkenwell House
45–47 Clerkenwell Green
London EC1R 0HT

WWW.HEADOFZEUS.COM